WINNING YOUR PERSONAL INJURY SUIT

Also by the same author:

THE MALPRACTITIONERS
1978 Anchor Press

MORALISTS AND MANAGERS
1976 Anchor Press

John Guinther
WINNING YOUR PERSONAL INJURY SUIT

A Doubleday Anchor Original
ANCHOR PRESS/DOUBLEDAY
Garden City, New York, 1980

The case histories used throughout this book are intended for illustrative purposes only. All names are fictional and are not intended to describe any person, living or dead, or any existent company or institution.

ISBN: 0-385-15005-9
Library of Congress Catalog Card Number: 79–6575
Copyright © 1980 by John Guinther
All Rights Reserved
Printed in the United States of America
First Edition

ONCE AGAIN FOR CAROL

Introduction

The average citizen is more likely to have need for a lawyer than at any other time in the history of our country. With our progress in civil rights legislation, divorce reform laws, consumer education, intensified corporate competition, and the increased affluency of our society, we are in the midst of a litigation explosion, wherein thousands of untried cases crowd our court dockets.

One of the most common areas of litigation occurs when a person believes he or she has been the victim of an injury, negligently inflicted by another and wants to bring suit against the culpable party. The wide sphere of personal-injury litigation includes the fields of products' liability, workmen's compensation, medical malpractice and injuries sustained by the use of the automobile. The hordes of automobiles that began to clutter our highways following the end of the Second World War have inevitably led to ever increasing numbers of accidents caused by careless drivers of defectively designed automobiles. Medical malpractice actions alone have been increasing at a 15 percent rate each year since 1966.

The increased awareness by the public, as to their opportunities to gain financial redress for their injuries, is, unfortunately, offset by the mystery and concern that most people harbor relative to the actual process of litigation. This problem is aggravated by the suspicions that many people have toward lawyers and the legal process. This problem creates an inhibition on the part of many wrongfully injured parties, to the extent that many people are deprived of their right to compensation merely because they do not consult a lawyer to determine whether they have grounds for suit and possible compensation. This is a regrettable weakness in our adversary system, since it is rare that one has to pay a lawyer to learn from him if sufficient grounds for suit exist. Nevertheless, in one study half the people interviewed thought to the contrary. Moreover, once they do decide to inquire, they are then faced with the problem in the selection of a lawyer, and that, in itself, for many, has proven to be a frightening experience. Relatively few people know how to go about seeking counsel in a meaningful way, which will insure their acquisition of a competent attorney. Most people do not have any understanding of the criteria by which to evaluate, in advance, the probable competence of a lawyer. When a lawyer is finally retained, and litigation commenced, the injured parties (plaintiffs), all too often, remain in the dark about what they can do to help themselves, along with their lawyer, to lead their case to a profitable conclusion. The uninformed client may cause the loss of his case that should be won. But a client who is aware of the importance to assist his counsel will become a "good" client and can easily help increase the size of the ultimate award by 15 percent to 20 percent.

The public is not to be blamed for its lack of knowledge. The fault, rather, lies largely at the door of the organized bar, which has done little to inform members of the public about their basic legal rights in personal-injury cases; has given them virtually no guidance about how to recognize and avoid the incompetent attorney; nor has it made any effort to provide useful information about how clients can help themselves make their cases more likely a success. The reasons for this apathy, perhaps, rise from an elitism within the profession and a disdain for the very clients who allow lawyers to earn the handsome living they do; or there may be other reasons for this lack of communication between lawyers and clients, but the fact remains that the Bar has shirked this important public duty. During 1979, the Philadelphia Bar Association instituted a Community Activation Program, in which the Association leaders sought input from numerous community organizations that were asked for criticism and input as to how the legal profession can improve its service to the public.

INTRODUCTION

Among the most common complaints about lawyers was a lack of communication, an apparent disrespect for the clients they serve, and a weak effort displayed by most lawyers to keep their clients informed as to the progress of their own cases. This experiment by our Bar Association was viewed by the traditionally conservative American Bar Association as an important innovative attempt to bridge the gap between lawyers and their clients, and consequently, the Philadelphia Bar Association was awarded a prize for excellence.

What the Bar has not been able to do over the years has been done by one who is not a lawyer. John Guinther is a veteran investigative reporter and author and, in *Winning Your Personal Injury Suit,* he has written an accurate and eminently practical book that is must reading for anyone who has suffered an injury at the hands of another, who has lost a family member that way, or, indeed, for any member of the public who wants to know more about his or her legal rights and what to do about finding a good attorney for any reason. As a lawyer, I am chagrined that the Bar has ignored the task Mr. Guinther has accomplished. However, his point of view, as a lay person, gives his book a unique quality that it could not have obtained had it been written by another attorney. We, as attorneys, inevitably sit on our side of the desk and see the world—including clients—out of our eyes. Mr. Guinther, however, sits on the other side of the desk, and as is apparent, in his book, he always had only one question in mind, the public's question: If this happened to me, what should I do?

He has found most of the answers to that question, and in the areas of the law to which a simple answer is not possible, he graphically discusses what is most often true and how the reader can make an informed and intelligent judgment. Such problems—both with the law and with one's lawyer—can become complicated, and he doesn't oversimplify them, but he does clarify them and does it in language that is lucid, demonstrative, and free from legal jargon. It is a book that the wise plaintiff's lawyer will provide to his clients for them to read so that he can have "good" clients to assist him in their personal-injury cases. It is obvious, therefore, that Mr. Guinther has given the public what it needs and what it hasn't before received, a candid and forthright step-by-step tour through the personal-injury legal system. Some lawyers are going to find it too direct, but it must be noted that this book was not written as a witch-hunt or exposé about the legal system. Mr. Guinther's accomplishment is no small achievement, and he is to be applauded and read.

Mr. Guinther has achieved two important goals—namely, he has given the public what it needs to know, and he has, by that process, also informed lawyers about what their clients need to know so that a client and an attorney can form a true "partnership" in their respective functions toward a successful conclusion of the client's claim for redress.

In that sense, not only should *Winning Your Personal Injury Suit* be must reading for the public, but also equally mandatory for attorneys. They may not be happy about everything they read in it, but for attorneys who are sincere in their desire to help their clients and be helped by them—thereby providing greater income for each—the book offers insights that will improve their own practice of the law. Recent law graduates would obtain an enormous benefit by reading this book early in their careers. We are creatures of habit and if young lawyers, who frequently survive on personal-injury cases until they build a general practice, would read this book diligently, they may not have to learn by bitter experience the importance of client rapport, trial preparation, open communication and their duty to the public. The end result for all readers will be a better and more enriching association for the parties on both sides of the desk.

LEON KATZ
Judge, Philadelphia Court of
Common Pleas; former Chancellor,
Philadelphia Bar Association

Acknowledgments

Without the help of many people, the writing of this book would not have been possible. They are responsible in large part for its truth, but for none of its errors. Included among those to whom appreciation must be extended are a number of individuals—attorneys, former plaintiffs, former defendants—who gave freely of their time and opinions only upon the guarantee that their names would not be used. They know who they are, and to them many thanks.

Special thanks are due to the following attorneys: Leon Katz, former chancellor of the Philadelphia Bar Association, whose critique of the entire manuscript contributed in a major way to its accuracy; and William Keller, David Shrager, M. Mark Mendel, and S. Gerald Litvin, who also devoted many hours of their time to providing editorial guidance and correction of the contents of individual chapters.

Mr. Litvin, who was the attorney for the plaintiff in the "flaming nightgown" case, described in Chapter Seventeen, also supplied the jury interrogatory reprinted in Chapter Six, along with several trial briefs and related research material that were of immeasurable help in providing understanding of the basic legal principles governing negligence and strict-liability tort law.

Appreciation is also extended to the following attorneys, who, like those already mentioned, gave hours of their time in answering questions about both the theory of personal-injury law and its application on a day-to-day basis: Marshall A. Bernstein, Benedict Casey, Nathan B. Feinstein, Robert Fellheimer, Joseph Foster, Joseph Frieri, Joseph Gallagher, Gerald J. Haas, Elwood S. Levy, William Loftus, William J. McGettigan, Max Millman, Joseph Sebastianelli, Carol Shepherd, Frederick Smith, A. Grant Sprecher, Gary Tilles. (None of these attorneys should be assumed to be among those whose opinions are quoted anonymously throughout the book.) Also, thanks for special help to C. Thomas Bendorf, department director, Association of Trial Lawyers of America, and Kenneth Shear, executive director, Philadelphia Bar Association.

The study of contributory- and comparative-negligence statutes in Appendix I is based primarily on a study published in November 1978 by the *Villanova University Law Review*, Villanova, Pennsylvania. For the study of no-fault automobile-insurance laws and the accompanying table in Appendix I, a major source was *Automobile No-Fault Insurance* (Chicago: American Bar Association, 1978), extrapolated from a data analysis by Kemper Insurance Group.

Martindale-Hubbell Legal Directory Law Digests, 1979 (Summit, New Jersey: Martindale-Hubbell, Inc., 1979) provided supplementary aid in the compilation of the study of no-fault laws and acted as a primary source of information for the study of immunity statutes and statutes of limitations depicted in Appendix I. Also of major help in determining the status of sovereign-immunity laws was a 1978 in-house study of the subject by the Association of Trial Lawyers of America. The study of immunity laws governing municipalities is based on The New World of Municipal Liability, prepared by Floyd, Kennedy and Associates, Inc. for the National League of Cities. A 1977 pamphlet published by the American Insurance Association acted as a useful subsidiary source to Martindale-Hubbell in compilation of the study of the statutes of limitations.

In addition to Martindale-Hubbell Law Digests, the following texts were consulted during the course of the research for this book: *Restatement of the Law Second, Torts Second* (St. Paul, Minnesota: American Law Institute, 1965); *Corpus Jurus Secundum,* Volumes 25 and 25A (Brooklyn, New York: American Law Book Company, 1964); *U. S. Code Annotated* (St. Paul, Minnesota: West Publishing Company; and Brooklyn, New York: Edward Thompson Company, 1966). Also, Jacob A. Stein, *Damages and Recovery: Personal Injury and Death Actions* (Rochester, New York: Lawyers Co-Operative Publishing Company; and San Francisco, California: Bancroft-Whitney Company, 1972, 1977; Roland F. Chase coauthor 1977 supplement).

Foreword

When you think you have been wrongfully injured by someone, you may have sufficient grounds to bring a lawsuit against that party. From it, you will hope to recover your out-of-pocket costs in medical bills and any loss of income the injury cost you, and often you also will be able to receive many thousands of dollars in tax-free income that represents a net profit to you from the injury.

In contemplating bringing suit, you will rightfully have many questions about the personal-injury legal system, which—theoretically, anyway—is there to pay you when you are in the right and to protect the defendant from you when you are in the wrong. The system is an old one, its basic rules largely unchanged for more than a thousand years, but time hasn't done much of a job to perfect it; you could be exploited by it, cheated by it, sometimes overpaid by it, more often underpaid, and sometimes not paid at all when you should be.

The purpose of this book is to help you understand that system and to show you when to use it, how to use it, and how to obtain from it every dollar that is due you.

The book will describe when you should sue and when not; also when you can't sue legally, and the money-providing alternatives to suit that are sometimes available.

When the decision is to sue, the book will show you how to obtain a qualified lawyer to represent you. No step in pursuing your case is more important than finding the right attorney. The difference between a good one and a bad one can be thousands of dollars for you and in some cases hundreds of thousands.

The book also describes how to make a fee arrangement with your lawyer that is to your financial benefit, and points out how you can avoid being defrauded by the lawyer and what to do should serious problems arise between the two of you.

The book further describes, in detail, the steps you can and should take to develop the evidence in your case. By following these guidelines, you can help yourself win the maximum amount of money, not just some of the money, that is due you.

Knowing how best to act as a witness on your own behalf—either at a pretrial deposition or at trial—is also a matter of crucial importance to you. Not only will your performance often determine whether or not you will win your case but also how much you will win, and therefore practical tips on how to be a good witness are included in the chapters ahead.

One of the most thorny problems you are likely to face in your case is represented by the defense settlement offer: Should you accept it? Or else, should you reject it and try to get more money by going to trial? The factors you should consider and the options you have available in making that decision are discussed.

But just as you could be injured at any time in such a way that gives you grounds for suit, so could you be accused of causing an injury and become a defendant in a suit. A chapter of the book, therefore, describes how you can protect your legal interests should that happen to you.

One attorney who was interviewed for this book remarked, "To be ignorant of the law is to become its victim." He might have added, "To know one's rights and not know how to exercise them is to be no less a victim." To the extent that the book provides both knowledge and the ability to use that knowledge, it fulfills its goals.

(Note: In references to attorneys throughout this book, the masculine pronoun is used, in part for simplicity's sake, but also because the personal-injury bar, especially on the plaintiff's side, is almost entirely dominated by male attorneys, much more so than in almost any other field of the law.)

Contents

	Introduction	ix
	Acknowledgments	xiii
	Foreword	xv
1	To Sue or Not to Sue	1
2	How to Find a Lawyer	17
3	How to Hire a Good Lawyer	35
4	Your Money and Your Lawyer	57
5	The Battle Is Joined	67
6	Winning at Settlement or Trial	79
7	Damages Equal Money	104
8	Making the Most of Your Loss of Income	114
9	How to Document Your Medical Expenses	128
10	Getting Compensated for Your Pain, Suffering, and Mental Anguish	138
11	Getting What's Due You	148
12	When Your Lawyer Is a Lemon	158
13	The Defendant in Trouble	171
14	You and the Law	185
15	Negligence	203

16	INTENTIONAL INJURIES	219
17	STRICT LIABILITY	231
	APPENDIX I	244
	APPENDIX II	266
	INDEX	283

WINNING YOUR PERSONAL INJURY SUIT

1

To Sue or Not to Sue

You may have grounds for a personal-injury suit when you have been injured as a result of:

> *Negligence* (i.e., someone's carelessness or incompetence); or a *deliberate* attempt to hurt you, including physical blows, harrassment, libel, or slander; or someone's failure to meet a *strict duty* to provide for your safety, even though there's been neither negligence nor a desire to harm you. (You are most likely to have this grounds for suit when you have been injured by a *defective* or *dangerous product*.)

When any of these conditions is proved, the defendant is *liable* to you and must pay you for your medical expenses, your income loss, and your pain and suffering. (Taken together, the injuries and the money you receive for them are called your *damages*.) If the injury caused death, members of the immediate family or the administrator of the estate may bring the suit.

The defendant in your suit ordinarily will be the person who injured you. However, if that person was acting in the capacity of an employee of someone other than your employer, you may, with some exceptions noted below, name the employer as a defendant. You may name as many defendants in your suit as you believe responsible.

Even though you have sufficient evidence to bring suit, there are situations in which your suit won't be permitted or won't be successful:

> You may not sue your spouse for the costs of an accidentally inflicted injury, although, in some jurisdictions, you may sue if the injury was deliberately inflicted. All other members of a family may sue one another.
>
> You may not bring suit against a very young child or its parents, unless the parents could have prevented the injury caused by the child. Once a child has reached the so-called "age of reason," usually between the ages of ten and twelve, the child may be sued, and so may the parents.
>
> You may not bring suit for an injury if the only way the defendant could have avoided it was by committing an illegal act.
>
> When an accidental injury occurs while you are at work, you almost never may sue your employer or a fellow worker for causing it, although you may sue an outsider who causes you a job-related injury. Payment for most employer- and fellow-employee-caused injuries is covered by workmen's-compensation insurance.
>
> In states with no-fault insurance laws, suit may be brought against the party that injured you in an automobile accident, but usually only when the cost of the injury exceeds the no-fault insurance coverage.
>
> Certain government agencies and charitable institutions are immune from suit, but their employees are not.
>
> Every state has a deadline—called the *statute of limitations*—beyond which suit may not be brought. Therefore, if you live in a state with a two-year statute, you must file suit within two years of the date of the injury or two years of the date you first knew you were injured.
>
> Although it is not a bar to bringing suit, in some jurisdictions, in certain kinds of cases, you cannot win if the defendant can prove that you—to any degree whatsoever—contributed to causing the injury. In many other states, however, you can still win, but the amount of your award will be reduced by the degree to which

the jury thinks you were at fault. *Never* decide on your own not to bring suit because you think you may have been partly at fault; only your lawyer can determine that.

Often, as a plaintiff, you will need to know more about your right to sue than has been stated here. For a further discussion of personal injury law in general, see Chapter Fourteen; for laws governing negligence, see Chapter Fifteen; for intentional injuries, Chapter Sixteen; and for product and other strict-liability suits, see Chapter Seventeen.

HOW TO TELL IF YOUR SUIT IS "WORTHY"

Any wrongfully inflicted injury is known in the law as a *tort*, a word you're likely to hear your lawyer use even though he may not explain it to you. That a tort has occurred doesn't always mean that it's a good subject for suit. Most lawyers reject cases in which an injury is medically insignificant, because the money they can earn won't be worth the time they would have to put into the case. In other words, you may want to sue, but you won't be able to find a lawyer to take your case. Some minor injuries, however, have serious side effects, and when that happens, they are eminently suit-worthy.

Not considering side effects, ordinarily the following physical injuries are either suit-worthy or not: A broken wrist, yes, but a minor and quickly healed sprain, no; a broken finger may be worth suit if it has harmed you occupationally, but ordinarily a broken toe is not worth suit. Almost all other fractures are worth suit. Internal injuries may or may not be worth suit, depending on their initial seriousness and their long-range effect on your health. Worth suit is any injury that results, permanently or temporarily, in the loss of use of any of your senses or that causes you paralysis, brain damage, or neural damage. Injury that causes the loss of your ability to have sexual relations is worth suit if the impairment is permanent, but it may not be if it is temporary. Injuries that are not readily provable medically (back problems and so-called "whiplash" are the most common) may be worth pursuing, but the loss ratio for plaintiffs is high. Injuries that manifest themselves solely in psychological terms—neurosis, psychosis, depression—are worth pursuing when medically documented. Loss of a tooth is not usually worth pursuing, loss of a whole set of teeth is. Disfiguring injuries are worth pursuing whether or not the disfigurement is visible when one is clothed, although visible disfigurements are usually worth more money than ones that are normally hidden. Any kind of injury that leaves you permanently crippled, including a permanent limp, is worth pursuing, but injuries that have as their sole effect a temporary limp usually are not worth the effort to sue.

HOW TO TELL IF THE DEFENDANT IS WORTH SUING

It is almost always a waste of time to sue an uninsured defendant *unless* it is a government agency, a public carrier, a large corporation, or some other entity or individual known to have substantial assets to pay for any judgment that results from the suit.

An uninsured but otherwise apparently suit-worthy individual may not, even so, be worth suing when that person holds assets in joint title. You cannot, for instance, force the sale of a defendant's home to satisfy a suit when that property is co-owned by his or her spouse. Collection only becomes possible when the property is sold, and even then it is limited to the defendant's share of the proceeds.

An uninsured defendant who is ordered to pay on a suit may declare bankruptcy, freeing him from his obligation to you, or attempt to hide assets through any number of fraudulent devices (including transfer of title of property to someone else). You may become aware of the fraud and take legal steps to undo it, but you should be aware that this can be a lengthy, sometimes quite expensive, and typically fruitless effort. When all else fails, defendants with sizable judgments against them have been known to disappear.

HOW TO TELL IF THE SUIT IS WORTH PURSUING IN TERMS OF THE PROBABLE NET AWARD

No one can foretell with absolute certainty what the result of a suit will be; however, once your lawyer has investigated all the elements of your claim, including your out-of-pocket costs and those that are reasonably likely to befall you in the future, he will be able to give you a fairly accurate estimate of the cash worth of your case and you should always obtain this figure. The amount could be expressed in terms of what a jury will probably award, or as the size offer that should be accepted to settle the case. Since the odds are overwhelming that, if you are to win, it will be by settlement, rather than by trial, the settlement figure is the most important one to use.

Let us suppose, for instance, that your lawyer tells you he can probably get $9,000 for your case through settlement. To figure your net award, first deduct the lawyer's fee. The lawyer will be representing you on a *contingency* basis, meaning he gets no fee from you at all if you lose, but a pre-agreed percentage of any of your winnings. In your case, we will assume it is one third. Therefore, you must deduct $3,000 from your $9,000, leaving you with $6,000. Next, the lawyer tells you that the cost of pursuing the suit (filing fees, investigation costs, witness fees, and the like) will be $1,500, payable out of your award. With that deduction, your net award is now $4,500. However, assume you also had $3,000 in medical bills paid by Blue Cross, an amount that must be repaid to it from your award. Deducting that from the remaining $4,500, you now see that your most probable net award is $1,500, and it is this figure, not the gross figure, by which you should decide whether or not suit is worthwhile.

In making your decision, however, always bear in mind that all the money you net from your suit is yours to keep: awards in personal-injury suits are not subject to taxation.

The repayment you are required to make to Blue Cross—called a *subrogation* claim—requires some explanation. It is an explanation that some lawyers won't make to their clients, or at least they won't until the case is almost ready to be settled, for fear that, if a client learns too early that he owes this money, he or she will back out of the suit and the lawyer will lose a lucrative fee. (Said one lawyer: "I wish you wouldn't tell your readers about subrogation claims; it's just too technical for them to understand.")

In fact, some clients, when they learn about subrogation laws, are not only shocked but outraged. As they see it, they pay a hefty bill to their medical-insurance plan each month in the expectation that most of their medical and hospital bills will be paid for them, and they don't think they should have to repay anything. However, as the law interprets it—and that's what counts—if the plaintiff hadn't been wrongfully injured, the medical-insurance plan wouldn't have had to put out any of its money, and so the wrongdoer owes the money, payable out of the plaintiff's award.

Subrogation claims aren't limited to medical-insurance plans. By the same legal reasoning, a workmen's-compensation insurer has the right to collect from the plaintiff's winnings any money it gave the plaintiff in connection with the injury, as does Social Security for Medicare and Medicaid payments, and often a state or city welfare department is permitted reimbursements for money it provided when the injury forced the plaintiff onto public assistance.

However, with only the rarest of exceptions, you don't have to worry about having to pay any of your award back to an income-maintenance or a health-insurance company. (These are companies which, in return for your premium, pay you for wages you miss due to an illness or injury, or flat amounts to cover part of your medical costs.)

Subrogation payments are due only if you get some money from the defendant. Thus, if you are wrongfully injured and don't sue, neither Blue Cross nor any other party that might otherwise have subrogation rights can collect from you. Similarly, if you sue and lose, you owe none of these claimants anything.

The amount you have to repay a subrogation claimant is limited by the size of your net award. In other words, if, after paying your lawyer, you are left with $4,500 but Blue Cross is owed $5,000 in medical bills, the most Blue Cross can take from you is $4,500. Or, if you owe Blue Cross $3,000 and a workmen's-compensation insurer another $3,000, the most the two can collect between them is $4,500.

The news isn't always completely bad, however, on the subrogation front. As we shall see, there can be occasions when the subrogation claimant will waive part of the money due it.

Deep and Shallow Pockets

A *shallow-pocket* defendant is one that has the ability to pay, usually via insurance, but not an ability to pay an amount sufficient to cover the full costs of the injury. A *deep-pocket* defendant is one whose ability to pay exceeds the reasonable value of the suit.

The implications of the two kinds of pockets are many. Consider, for instance, the fate of Mr. Blake.

While driving his car during the course of his employment, Blake was struck from the rear by another car, driving his head against the windshield and causing deep cuts that required plastic surgery. His body was simultaneously rammed against his steering wheel, fracturing ribs and causing serious internal injuries. Blake couldn't work for a year; his loss of income was $20,000, of which $13,000 was covered by workmen's-compensation payments. His medical bills amounted to $20,000, all but $2,000 of it covered by Blue Cross/Blue Shield. The driver of the car that hit Blake carried $25,000 in accident liability insurance and lacked the assets to pay for any verdict above that amount.

Considering the seriousness of his injuries and his resultant pain and suffering, Blake has a case most attorneys would estimate as conservatively worth $150,000 for settlement purposes. However, he is confronted with a shallow-pocket defendant. Should he bring suit, the most he can hope to win is the $25,000 available in insurance, less his attorney's fee and any litigation-related expenses. Assume that leaves him with a net of $16,000. But even that money isn't his, since he owes the subrogation claimants $31,000. Although they can't collect more from him than he nets, their claims eat up his entire award and apparently make suit pointless. However, at this point, the subrogation claimants, knowing they can't collect a penny unless Blake sues, will want to give him incentive to litigate and will do so by waiving enough of their claims so that he will see some money for himself from his suit. Let us therefore assume the subrogees waive 60 percent of the amount due them. In that event, Blake's settlement mathematics look like this:

Insurance Available	$ 25,000
Less legal fees and expenses	− 9,000
Remainder	16,000
Less subrogation payments	−12,400
Remainder	3,600
Less Blake's other medical bills	− 2,000
NET TO BLAKE	$ 1,600

Now let us suppose that Mr. Blake was injured exactly the same way while a passenger on a city-owned subway train that collided with another train. This time Blake has a deep-pocket defendant, since the municipality's ability to pay is limited, theoretically, only by its tax revenues. Let us assume, therefore, that following negotiations between his lawyer and the city, Blake agrees to accept an award of $150,000. Further, assume that Blake is paying his lawyer a one-third fee, that he has $3,000 in other suit-related expenses, $2,000 in unpaid medical bills, and $31,000 owed to subrogation holders:

Total Settlement	$ 150,000
Less lawyer's fee	− 50,000
Remainder	100,000
Less expenses	− 3,000
Remainder	97,000
Less subrogation claims (assuming no percentage waived)	− 31,000
Remainder	66,000
Less Blake's other medical bills	− 2,000
NET TO BLAKE	$ 64,000

(In a case similar to this, the plaintiff rejected a settlement offer of $160,000, took the case to trial, and won $325,000. When all his bills were paid, his net profit from his injury was $185,000.)

Sometimes there will be deep- and shallow-pocket defendants in the same case. To show how this can happen, suppose the injury-prone Mr. Blake was crossing the street when he was knocked down by the negligently driven car. His leg was fractured and he was taken to a hospital, where a resident set the bone. The doctor bungled the job. The leg had to be rebroken and reset. Blake faced an extensive period of therapy and will always walk with a limp. The driver of the car carried $25,000 in insurance. The hospital carried $1,000,000 worth of insurance per malpractice claim.

Under the law, the driver can be held responsible not only for Blake's original injury but also for the derivative injuries he received at the hospital. However, the driver's insurance pocket, which was more than amply deep to pay for the cost of a leg fracture, is shallow in terms of the devastating consequences to Blake of the hospital's malpractice. Blake's case is now worth, conservatively, $100,000, and he therefore will sue the shallow-pocket driver only for the cost of the broken leg and sue the deep-pocket hospital separately for malpractice, as is his legal right.

The depth of a defendant's pocket also has relevance in injuries less serious than the various ones suffered by Mr. Blake. For instance, if your case has a predictable settlement value of $20,000 to $25,000 and there is only $25,000 in insurance, your lawyer has little room to negotiate, whereas if there is $50,000 available, he might be able to get you a settlement closer to $30,000, and so on.

When the injury is minor, however, the depth of the pocket is usually irrelevant. If Blake had received no injury worse than a broken leg in any of the examples, the maximum amount he could have gotten from either the shallow- or the deep-pocket defendant would have been around $10,000.

THE BIG BAD DEFENDANT

Your chances of winning your suit are often at their best—even when your case is weak—when you have a "target" defendant; that is, one against whom the public (and hence any jurors) are likely to be prejudiced.

Target defendants include: units of government; utilities; almost any public transportation company, from a bus line to an airline; most large national corporations (especially automobile manufacturers and oil companies); hospitals (but not doctors); and generally, any company or institution, with either a local or a national base, with whom the jurors or their friends are likely to have had unfavorable experiences. The defendant itself need not have a bad reputation to become a target defendant, as long as it belongs to a category that is unpopular; for instance, if we assume that most people, rightly or wrongly, think that most auto body shops are not honestly run, then all body shops, honest or not, become target defendants.

Since there has never been any thorough study undertaken to determine why juries make the decisions they do, it is not clear that the target-defendant theory is anything more than a form of bias itself. In fact, to the extent that any creditable statisics are available, it appears that target defendants win a substantial percentage—more than half in cases brought against hospitals—of the suits that go through trial. This anomaly, however, might in part be explained by target defendants' practice of settling doubtful cases precisely because they are afraid of a prejudiced jury verdict. Therefore, they go to trial only on those suits in which the evidence is overwhelmingly in their favor.

Consider, for instance, the Bramwell case. A motorist, Mr. Fritz, stopped at Bramwell's gasoline station to have his tank filled and got out of his car to go to the rest room. Bramwell called out to him to watch for a grease spot that was directly on the way to the rest room but could be sidestepped. Fritz made it to the rest room safely, but on his return stepped on the grease spot, slipped, fell, and fractured his skull.

This is a difficult case. By stating that he warned Fritz of the grease spot, Bramwell was admitting he knew of its prior existence—in other words, it didn't just happen at that moment, not giving him time to clear it away—and in so doing was confessing his own negligence. But Fritz also has his legal problems. Quite apart from any warning Bramwell may have shouted to him, he obviously managed to avoid the spot that was in his path while on the way to the room, and a jury is likely to believe that he therefore should have been aware of it on his return and negligently failed to watch where he was going. Should the jury believe that, under contributory-negligence law, the verdict must be for Bramwell.

What will happen in this case, however, may be less determined by its facts and the legal interpretation of them than by who owns the gas station. If it is Bramwell, then he probably has a good chance of prevailing at trial, because a jury will have no reason to be prejudiced against him. However, if Bramwell only manages the station and it is owned by an oil company, Fritz is likely to get a substantial settlement offer from the oil company's insurer. Because its customer is a target defendant, it will fear the jury will interpret all the evidence as favorably as possible to the plaintiff.

But what of the insurance companies themselves? Do you, as a plaintiff, gain because the jury believes the defendant is insured? (Although a jury isn't permitted, under the law, to be told that a defendant carries insurance, from their practical knowledge of the world, most jurors will assume its presence.) When they do, according to some lawyers, they treat the insurance company itself as a target defendant.

This view was summarized by one attorney: "Damn' right, they're target defendants. Particularly the auto insurers. The public hates them. They figure they're overcharged by them, don't get good service from them, and are likely to get their policies canceled for no good reason at all. Believe me, when a jury gets a chance to stick it to an insurance company, they're going to do it."

Most other attorneys, however, disagree, at least in part. The consensus view was expressed by one lawyer this way: "Juries, in my judgment, are likely to take insurance into consideration only when it's a very close call. A typical example would be those cases—and they're fairly frequent—when the verdict depends on whose unsubstantiated word is to be believed, the plaintiff's or the defendant's. In those instances, the tilt will be to the plaintiff on the theory that the defendant, because he's insured, won't be hurt financially by the verdict and they might as well take some money out of the insurance company's deep pocket and put it in the plaintiff's. Other than in cases like that, I really don't believe juries think about insurance. Almost all of them try to come to their verdicts on the merits of the evidence."

Because of the lack of meaningful studies of jury psychology, there is no way of knowing which, if either, of these views is correct. Beyond doubt, as a plaintiff you will never be hurt by a jury's belief that your opponent is insured; there is not, however, enough evidence to suggest that you should ever proceed with a lengthy lawsuit when you have a weak case, solely on the basis that the defendant is insured.

ARE YOU A SYMPATHETIC PLAINTIFF?

When lawyers talk about sympathetic plaintiffs, they don't have in mind those who merely make a good appearance in court and will come across as credible to a jury. That, they hope, will be true of all their clients. What they are thinking of, rather, are plaintiffs who *because of what has happened to them* and *who they are* will naturally engender the jury's good will.

The ideal plaintiff, in this sense, is the severely injured small child. As one famous lawyer is supposed to have said, "Give me a brain-damaged eight-year-old and I don't need any facts."

While that remark had best be interpreted hyperbolically, attorneys agree that the sympathetic plaintiff is much more likely to prevail against adverse evidence than will others, and that the sympathetic plaintiff probably wins substantially larger verdicts and larger settlements than does the average plaintiff. (By this theory, the biggest winner of all will be a sympathetic plaintiff who has a deep-pocket, target defendant.)

Although children (the younger the better and the more maimed the better) are always considered to be sympathetic plaintiffs by lawyers, even here there are distinctions. Several lawyers said they have observed that little white children usually do better than black ones, and that children who survive an injury get larger awards—in part because they are right there in the courtroom, where the jury sees them throughout the trial—than those who perished.

People who have been severely scarred or severely crippled will often win suits on sympathy when the facts might not warrant it, and will usually win larger verdicts than those who have been as seriously injured but not visibly so.

Some lawyers also say widows are more likely to provoke sympathy than other women, and women may get a more sympathetic jury than do men, although girls not more so than boys. This type of sympathy, however, to the extent it actually exists, is not sufficient, lawyers agree, to recommend bringing a suit that should not otherwise be pursued on its merits.

HOW TO GET MONEY WITHOUT SUING

When a lawsuit, for whatever reason, is not for you, you can still sometimes get reimbursed for your injury in small or (occasionally) quite large amounts.

Most often, this occurs when you have been involved in an accident in which an insurance company's customer may have been at fault, and the company voluntarily offers you a small sum of money if you will then sign a paper agreeing to waive your right to sue.

A typical instance is Jane Brown, who suffered a sprained wrist while a passenger in a car involved in an accident. The insurer for the responsible driver offered her $500. Ms. Brown saw her doctor, who told her that her pain would pass away in a week or two.

Ms. Brown should accept the money. At the maximum, her injury is worth $1,000, and to obtain that she would have to hire a lawyer. Since any attorney who would accept a case this small is almost certainly going to charge a 50 percent fee to make it worth his while, she is no better off with his services than she would be if she took the money when it was offered. And she may be worse off; the company could withdraw its offer and dare her to sue. If it turns out the customer wasn't at fault, she gets nothing; if the customer was, she now has whatever costs her attorney encountered in pursuing her claim as well as his fee to pay out of her tiny award.

Sometimes you will receive a cash offer from an insurance company when you received no injury at all in the accident. In so doing, the company may not know you weren't injured, or it has decided that, regardless of the absence of injury, it is prudent to spend a couple of hundred dollars on you now in order to forfend the possibility of spending several thousand fighting a false claim you might make later. Even though you haven't been injured, legally you have every right to accept this money as long as you did nothing to solicit it.

When you have been injured, a voluntary offer ordinarily should be rejected and you should get a lawyer when: you believe the insurance company's customer was at fault, *and* you have no or little contributory fault in causing the accident, *and* your doctor cannot assure you your injury is insignificant and transitory.

Occasionally, the voluntary offer of payment by an insurance company means you have a suit-worthy injury when you thought you didn't. Illustrative is the experience of a plaintiff who eventually netted $18,000 from his injury: "About two or three days after the accident," he recalled, "this guy from the insurance company called on me at my house and said he had this check all made out to me for $750. He said the company wanted to give me that money 'for my trouble'; that was the phrase he used. Well, my shoulder was still bothering me, but I didn't think there was anything seriously wrong—I hadn't even been to a doctor—and I was really tempted to take the money. But I thought to myself, 'Well, maybe if they're offering me $750 now, they'll up it a little if I hold off.' So I told him that if they doubled it, I'd take it. So he said, 'No way; this is all I'm allowed to offer and if you don't accept it now, the offer is withdrawn.' So I said, 'No, that's not enough; see what you can do.' Well, he got kind of angry and indicated to me that I didn't know when I was well off, and secretly I agreed with him, but I'd taken my stand and I didn't know how the hell to back off. So, for about a week nothing happened, and I figured I'd blown $750. Then he called me back. He'd been talking to his boss, he said, really fighting for me, he said, and they were now willing to offer me $1,000. So I thought to myself, 'Whoa. How come they're offering me another $250 just because I'm a greedy SOB? Maybe they're worried about something I don't understand.' It was then I decided to get a lawyer, and, boy, am I ever glad I did."

As happened with this plaintiff, an increased voluntary offer by an insurer almost invariably means you should get legal advice.

Generally, too, see a lawyer when a voluntary offer approaches or exceeds $1,000. Consider that as a signal that your injury is worth a great deal more than that.

When your injury is minor or the circumstances of it make victory unlikely, you may still be able to get some money by threatening or filing a suit you have no intention of pursuing. The insurance company doesn't know what your true intent is and may not care. Just as it will often voluntarily offer payment in a preclaim stage to avoid later expenses, so will it now offer you a sum to avoid the expense of defending against your claim. The money offered will, at the least, cover your out-of-pocket medical expenses, and that's better than getting nothing. Your lawyer will know when this approach is viable and will also recognize when the insurance company's offer should be accepted.

In certain kinds of automobile accidents, litigation against your own insurer may be worthwhile.

For instance, if you live in a state with a no-fault insurance law, following an accident claim, you may believe that your insurer has not paid you the benefits to which you believe you are entitled or has cut them off prematurely. When that happens and you cannot obtain satisfaction on your own, it could be fruitful to engage an attorney to litigate against your insurer to obtain the proper amount due you. The attorney will be paid a percentage only of the additional money he obtains for you; you pay him nothing if he fails.

When you carry an uninsured-motorist policy—in some states, this is required by law—your carrier pays you when you have been *wrongfully* injured by an uninsured driver. Some insurers are more recalcitrant about paying off on these policies than are others, and you may need a lawyer to help you collect.

When you have both no-fault and uninsured-motorist coverage and are injured by an uninsured driver, it is particularly advisable to get legal help, especially when your injury costs exceed the amounts payable under *either* policy. The governing laws are varying and complex, and it is the rare lay person that can exploit them to their full profit potential. An astute attorney, however, can, and in some instances he will be able to obtain payments for the same element of injury under *both* policies. If, in addition, you are eligible for workmen's-compensation payments—as when you have been hit by an uninsured driver while going about the duties of your job—you further increase your possible sources of revenue, duplicative and otherwise.

The moral of all this appears to be: When in doubt, get a lawyer. True enough. However, there are lawyers and then there are lawyers. Obtaining the right one can be a major problem.

2

How to Find a Lawyer

If you're like most people, you probably have no idea about how to find a lawyer who handles personal-injury cases.

Aside from the overwhelming likelihood that the lawyer you eventually hire will be a man—fewer than 2 percent of those who handle these cases on a regular basis are women—you don't know what you will encounter as you begin your search, and you may enter it with considerable trepidation.

Much of your worry may be based on what you have heard about personal-injury lawyers in the past. Their reputation is not a good one. Twelve former plaintiffs who were interviewed recalled hearing that these attorneys were "ambulance chasers," "crooks," "fast-buck artists" who "cheat everybody," and so on.

Despite these bad impressions at the outset, however, nine of the twelve reported they had good experiences with the attorneys they finally engaged. Typical comments: "A wonderful man, sympathetic, warm," "fought like a tiger for me," "treated me with absolute integrity," and one rueful compliment: "I wish he had been a crook; I might have won more money."

Since there is evidence that one of the happiest clients actually got poor representation and one of the unhappiest got a surprisingly good result on her case, these comments have to be treated with caution. After all, the fact that you have a lawyer who is warm and sympathetic and fights like a tiger for you is no necessary proof that he is competent nor that the apparent laziness or other faults of a second attorney signal that he is a bad one.

Your preliminary worries about how to go about finding a lawyer and your fear that you might not recognize the right one when you see him, therefore, are hardly groundless. Nevertheless, in beginning your search for counsel, you do have some pluses working on your side that often aren't present for clients who have other kinds of legal problems. Your major advantage is the contingency-fee system, by which you pay the lawyer only if you win. As a result of it, he has no motive to encourage you to become a client when your case is weak, as can occur when dealing with a lawyer who gets his fee up front or on an hourly rate.

Because of the contingency fee, too, it is normally to the interest of your lawyer to work hard on your case. He knows that the greater his effort, the larger amount of money he will win for you and for himself. While, as we shall see, there are some exceptions to this general rule, it does provide a motivational factor for your lawyer that he might not have were he paid in advance.

Finally, the personal-injury lawyer has good reason to treat you well because of what you can do for him in the future. Most lawyers either work for big firms that have partners who go out and solicit business from corporate clients, or else, if they're in private practice, over the years develop a core of small clients (local businesses, labor unions, civic groups, and the like) on whom they can count for a good income each year. That's not so with the personal-injury lawyer. Once a case is done, the client's gone and not likely ever to return. However, the lawyer knows that clients who win their cases like to talk about them and about their lawyer. The result, from the satisfied client, is good word-of-mouth advertising for the lawyer and the referral of new clients to him from the old ones.

While all these factors are working on your side as you begin your hunt, they don't necessarily guarantee it will be a successful one. No magic formulas can be offered that do that. However, as you begin to look for a lawyer, there are some questions to which you should find the answers, some warning signs to watch out for, and some basic information you should have about the types of lawyers who handle this kind of litigation.

It is worth your time to do the job right, to lengthen the odds in your favor. Not only is the good lawyer more likely to win your case than the poor one, but he is—with your help—also going to win more money for you than will the lesser one.

Should you choose a lawyer recommended by a friend or a relative?

This is the most common way used to find a lawyer and is far from the worst one. With it, you know you are approaching an attorney who has given legal satisfaction to someone whose judgment you trust.

Nevertheless, be selective in how you get these referrals and careful in how you evaluate them. Recommendations of lawyers are somewhat like those for restaurants; they are offered with great enthusiasm but with no guarantee that the enthusiast's taste will agree with yours. Moreover, just because a lawyer did a great job for your friend's divorce doesn't mean he'll get the maximum result in your personal-injury case. Finally, be sure that the recommending source has actually had legal experience with the lawyer named; just because somebody's "heard" that a lawyer is good doesn't mean a thing; the originating source of that encomium might be the praised lawyer himself.

Should you hire a lawyer recommended by your employer?

The average employer is more likely than the average employee to know how to find a good attorney. A sympathetic boss may even set up the appointment for you. If the lawyer does some work for your boss, or hopes to, he's likely to take your case more seriously than he otherwise might.

All that's to the good, but there can be difficulties. For fear of offending your employer or, in some instances, even jeopardizing your job security, you may find you have been pressured into hiring and keeping a lawyer you don't trust. Consider the implications of that possibility before turning to the boss for help.

Should you select a lawyer who is a friend?

Not a good idea. The best relationship to have with an attorney is a professional one, and that's just about impossible when your lawyer is also your friend. You have entered the suit to get money for your injury, and you don't want your judgment about your case—including the possible judgment to dismiss the attorney—inhibited by your friendship with him or by worry about the unpleasant repercussions that problems with him could cause in the social circle in which you both move. For the same reason, it is never a good idea to hire a relative to represent you.

Lawyers who are friends or relatives, however, can be excellent sources for finding the right attorney for you.

Should you select an attorney who has previously handled a legal matter for you successfully?

Maybe and maybe not. This lawyer might take your case regardless of a lack of experience in personal-injury work, either because he needs the money or it doesn't occur to him he could lose—lawyers are rarely lacking in strong egos—and either possibility could spell trouble for you.

The chances are good, however, that the lawyer will recognize his limitations, and when he doesn't think he should take your case he will send you to someone he considers reputable. Don't worry about imposing on his time for this purpose. As one of his satisfied clients, you are a source of recommendation to him for future business, and he therefore will want to keep you happy by helping you with your present problem.

Should you engage a lawyer who regularly does legal work for you?

This situation most commonly occurs when the plaintiff owns or manages a business that requires the services of an attorney. If you are in this position, it is not a good idea to ask this lawyer to handle your personal-injury case. You may find that, while he's good on business law, he's a loser on your private litigation, and what do you do then? Keep him on one and fire him on the other? Keep him on both? Fire him on both? These are the kinds of problems you don't need. However, the lawyer who handles business matters for you should be able to recommend a good lawyer and has the motive to do so.

Should you hire a lawyer recommended by your union?

If your union is the kind that exists to serve the officers' interest, rather than the rank and file's, you can be quite sure that any law firm the union recommends will reflect that attitude, and your case—unless it's a big one—won't get much attention.

Should you hire a lawyer because he's well connected politically?

The stereotype of the political lawyer is the cigar-chomping ward heeler in the double-knit suit skulking through the danker passages of a city hall on his way to fix a case. And undoubtedly, some lawyers with significant political connections fit that description. Nevertheless, there can be cases, most particularly (and perhaps exclusively) those involving government agencies, in which the political lawyer can perform legitimate services that less-well-connected lawyers can't. The political lawyer is likely to know who the decision-making people are when it comes to settling a case and will be more conversant than other lawyers with the inner workings of the bureaucracy. Considering how frustratingly difficult it can be to get satisfaction—or even an answer—from some government agencies, the political lawyer can be a force on your side who meaningfully evens the odds.

However, always avoid the lawyer, political or not, who indicates he can fix your case. Quite apart from other questions that that proposition raises, it tells you the lawyer is dishonest, and dishonest lawyers rarely limit their dishonesty; they almost always cheat their clients, too.

Should you hire a lawyer recommended by your doctor?

This is a good bet that is often overlooked. However, be aware that some doctors steer patients to lawyers, occasionally on a fee basis, but more commonly under a reciprocity system in which the lawyer, for his part, sends his injured clients to the doctor. This doesn't necessarily mean that the lawyer to whom you will be steered isn't a good one, but it does raise questions of a financial self-interest on the doctor's part of which you have a right to be wary. For this reason, if you use this selection method, confine your inquiries to your family physician or some other doctor with whom you have a continuing relationship, professionally or socially, and always ask only for the name of his personal lawyer. This attorney may not handle injury cases himself, but he will usually be able to send you to someone good who does.

Should you choose a lawyer who, according to newspaper accounts, has just won a big verdict in a personal-injury case?

This might mean he's a good lawyer, but you have no way of knowing that another lawyer wouldn't have gotten an even bigger verdict.

Are law-school professors a good source for finding a lawyer?

Yes. Law professors usually know who the good lawyers are in their community. You might even happen upon one who has a private practice, and should he be willing to take your case, you probably need look no further. The only trouble with this excellent search method is that it may not work. Most professors don't see that helping the general public find competent legal counsel is part of their job, so you had better be prepared for a rebuff.

If you decide to try it anyway, always contact the professor by phone at the law school. When you don't have anyone's name, ask for a professor who teaches tort law. Should you be able to reach him, be flattering—you've heard of his fine reputation—but also be brief and businesslike. Don't sound desperate; he'll think you came to him only as a last resort. Should he suggest you call the local bar association, as he probably will, tell him you tried that and it didn't work. (Tell him that even if you didn't try it, since it probably won't work.) At that point, he may help you or he may tell you to write him a letter. Don't bother. That's just to put you off. The chances of getting a response are almost nil.

Will a bar association help you find a good lawyer?

They'll try. Whether they will do you any good is another matter. City and county bar associations usually have a lawyer-recommendation service for the public. Probably the most commonly used title is Lawyer Reference Service. The number will appear in the yellow pages of the phone book, usually prior to the listing of individual lawyers.

The quality of the aid offered by these services varies widely. Bar associations that take their duties to the public seriously, such as those in Philadelphia and St. Louis, maintain lists of attorneys by areas of expertise. Some, including Philadelphia, also provide, at minimal or no cost, the services of a staff attorney who will listen to your problem and give you an opinion as to whether or not you have grounds for suit.

In most parts of the country, however, the principal purpose of the service is to drum up business for the bar association's members. Names are given in alphabetical rotation without consideration to the caller's needs. Such services may be better than nothing, but not much better.

Even the best of these bar-association services are unlikely to lead you to the top lawyers in the field. Lists are limited to lawyers who want their names given out, and for the most part these are young ones looking to the service to help them build their practices. While many of these individuals will be capable of handling a routine personal-injury case and some can handle difficult ones, they may not be able to get as much money for them as will the more experienced attorney who isn't listed. As a result, if your case is one that is complex or has a considerable dollar potential, the Lawyer Reference Service is ordinarily a poor selection method to employ.

Should you ever select a lawyer at random from the phone directory?

It's usually a waste of time. Many of the lawyers you contact won't handle personal-injury cases. Many of those who do will refuse to speak to you. That includes most of the best ones, who accept clients only if they have been recommended by someone they know. It's not impossible to get a reputable attorney this way, but you are lengthening the odds against yourself.

Should you select a lawyer that advertises?

Advertising, by itself, makes the lawyer neither competent nor incompetent. However, it would be very unusual for attorneys who are considered by their colleagues to be outstanding in this field to advertise. The top lawyers don't need the business advertising can bring. They are already sufficiently busy with the cases that come to them on referral by previous clients and by other lawyers.

One word of warning about legal advertising: Some attorneys advertise that they are "specialists" in certain fields. Don't be misled. There is no such thing as specialization in the law as there is in medicine. A medical specialist is one who has undergone advanced training in the area of his interest and then has passed an examination by which he becomes *board-certified* to practice his specialty. Not so with lawyers. Once a lawyer has passed the bar examination in his state, he can practice any branch of the law he chooses except patent and copyright law, without any further training and without passage of any competency test. Consequently, when a lawyer advertises himself as a "specialist," that's his opinion, not necessarily anyone else's, although, as we shall see, there are certain highly skilled lawyers who are recognized as "specialists" by other attorneys.

Many lawyers, incidentally, are aware of the difficulty the public encounters in finding competent counsel to meet their legal needs, and for some years now the American Bar Association has been considering adoption of a board-certification program for attorneys similar to that used in medicine. Should this reform be instituted—and there is considerable opposition to it within the bar—it will be many years before it could become effective, and even then there is some question that the certification system will be able to prevent lawyers from advertising themselves as qualified in fields for which they have not passed the tests.

Should you hire a lawyer who personally solicits your business?

This is what is known as "ambulance chasing." Your chances are almost nil that you will get a competent lawyer this way.

WHEN A LAWYER SENDS YOU TO ANOTHER LAWYER

Should the first lawyer you see send you to another lawyer, do not assume you are being shunted aside or that the lawyer's refusal to take your case indicates it lacks merit. The opposite is more often true.

The first lawyer may reject you because he doesn't handle personal-injury work. Or if he does, he may have no room, at the moment, on his schedule for you. Or—and this happens frequently—after discussing the case with you, he realizes it presents complexities that move it outside his area of competence.

When a lawyer sends you to another lawyer, he will not charge you a fee for doing so. At least he shouldn't; find out before the meeting if there is to be a charge, and generally avoid any lawyer who makes one. In meeting with you, the lawyer is not giving you free time just to provide you with a service. Rather, he almost always hopes to make money from your case, although not from you personally. His income will be derived from the lawyer to whom he sends you. This lawyer pays him a percentage of his own fee, almost always one third. For instance, if you win $27,000 and pay your lawyer one third of that, he then sends $3,000 of his $9,000 to the lawyer who sent you to him. The referring lawyer makes nothing if the suit is lost.

This may sound like fee splitting, but it is not, at least not according to the American Bar Association. The Bar Association has denounced fee splitting, and any lawyer who engages in it can be censured or even disbarred. However, splitting a hair if not a fee, the Bar has ruled that *co-counsel* fees are ethical. Under this arrangement, the lawyer who does the referring, theoretically anyway, becomes your lawyer along with the lawyer to whom he sent you, and can—as we shall see—have continuing duties to you.

As co-counsel, the referring lawyer's name will appear on every legal paper associated with your case, although you may never see him again and he may never give your case another moment's thought from the time you leave his office until the time he gets the other lawyer's check. (One attorney gleefully recalled that he garnered $70,000 this way through a medical-malpractice suit on which he spent a total of ninety minutes.)

While one may easily become appalled (or jealous) when contemplating this staggeringly easy way that lawyers have of making huge sums of money for doing little or no work, for you as a plaintiff the only question is, Are you benefited by it or are you harmed?

Some critics believe the co-counsel system is costly to the plaintiff. An attorney, they point out, who is regularly returning one third of his fees to a referring counsel has a sizable drain on his annual income, and to compensate for it must charge all his clients higher fees than he would if the system didn't exist. Therefore, if there were no referral fees, a lawyer who presently charges a client one third would now be able to net the same income by charging 22 percent, in that way meaningfully increasing the client's share of the award.

However, even were legislation somehow to be passed that made referral or co-counsel fees illegal, and which simultaneously forced lawyers to lower their charges commensurately, it is not certain that most clients' interests would be served.

The difficulty is that abolition of the co-counsel system means the referring lawyer loses his financial incentive to farm out cases to lawyers he believes are the most competent to handle them. While, undoubtedly, some attorneys would continue to refer cases without a fee, the large majority probably would not. They would either refuse to talk to a client who has the kind of case they don't handle—thereby removing from the client a major means of access to good counsel—or they would charge the client several hundred dollars in a consultation fee he might not be able to afford and only then refer the case to someone the client might not want; or—and this is what would happen most frequently—the lawyer would decide to keep the case, rather than send it to a lawyer with greater skills. For the client, the result could be a lower fee but also a lesser net award. For instance, the inferior attorney, keeping a case because he can't earn a referral fee on it, might get the client $10,000 at a 22 percent fee, while a better lawyer, under the referral system, would have gotten the same client $15,000 at a one-third fee. The client is more than $2,000 poorer.

The great virtue of the co-counsel system for the plaintiff, therefore, is the incentive it gives the referring lawyer to get the case to a lawyer who has the capability to get the maximum out of it for himself, for the client, and for the referring lawyer.

There is a secondary virtue as well that won't come into play in many cases, but when it does it can be important: Even though the referring lawyer is, in effect, a sort of absentee landlord on your case, he is still one of your lawyers, and if you have problems with the lawyer to whom he sent you, you can go back to him and ask him to help. Not only does he have a legal and ethical obligation to do so, but his financial interest in your case guarantees that he will.

While lawyer-to-lawyer referrals usually work out to the client's benefit, the system, like any other, is not without its hazards. The lawyer may be overrating the ability of the lawyer to whom you are being sent, or you have been sent solely because the lawyer is a friend or someone to whom he owes a favor. There's not much you can do to prevent this happening to you, but you can somewhat improve the odds that it won't by asking the lawyer to give you the names of not just one but several lawyers he thinks can help you. You should be wary of any lawyer who would refuse to do this.

You are *never*, in any event, under any obligation to accept the services of a lawyer to whom another lawyer sends you. If you decide you don't want that lawyer, that is the end of it. You owe nobody anything, and you can go on to find another lawyer in any way you wish.

HIGH-VOLUME LAWYERS

These are the ones most people have in mind when the term "negligence lawyer" is used. As the name indicates, the high-volume lawyer generates his income by resolving large numbers of suits each year. In order for him to do that, most of his cases must be relatively easy ones that he knows from past experience can be settled with a time investment that nets him the kind of hourly rate he requires to operate his practice profitably. For instance, a lawyer may decide that in terms of office overhead and desired take-home pay, he needs a gross income of $100,000 a year. He assures that cash flow by accepting each year, on referral, fifty cases that are sure winners and will eventually provide him with an average income of $2,000 each. Economically, this is a much more sound approach for him to take than to accept ten cases that will provide $10,000 each but that necessitate a larger time investment in total than the fifty cases would have.

This does not mean that high-volume lawyers accept only low-value cases, although some do limit their practice in that fashion. Many high-volume lawyers, whether in solo practice or partners in big firms, prefer referrals on large cases, and will even take some difficult ones. The criterion, therefore, is not the size of the case or even necessarily its difficulty—although that is a major factor—but, rather, the predictable net income expressed in predictable time investment.

As a consequence, a plaintiff whose case doesn't fit the high-volume lawyer's economic system may have a winnable case rejected and could have difficulty obtaining counsel at all.

To illustrate, let us first assume that your injury could have a $100,000 award potential, that the defendant is provably liable, and that there is ample insurance to pay. Because of the large amount of money it has at stake, the insurance company will probably fight the suit vigorously in an endeavor to prove that you aren't as seriously injured as you claim. As a result, the high-volume lawyer will have to spend considerably more time on your case than he would on a comparable $5,000 case that the insurance company won't see as worth the effort to fight seriously. However, assuming he is charging you a one-third fee and further that he values his time at $100 an hour, as would be typical, that means he can afford to spend more than 300 hours on your case and still show a profit on it. ($100×300 hours=$30,000; one third of $100,000 potential is $33,333.) Since a case of this kind probably will be settled at close to the dollar maximum within one hundred hours, the lawyer has a two-hundred-hour margin to work with before the case becomes doubtful. Your suit, therefore, is highly desirable and you will have no difficulty obtaining a lawyer.

Now, however, suppose you have a $100,000 case but you also have a contributory-negligence problem which, when analyzed by a high-volume lawyer, leaves you with a better-than-even chance of winning. Will he accept your case? Some high-volume lawyers will pass it by. They can foresee the insurance company's fighting it all the way to trial, bringing their own investment in the case into the hundreds of hours which, coupled with the real potential of a loss at trial, is time that could be more profitably spent settling other cases that are sure winners. Due to its dollar value, you will still probably be able to get a lawyer for your suit, but you may have to do some shopping before you do.

But suppose your case has only a $10,000–20,000 potential and you have the same kind of contributory-negligence problem? Now, even though the high-volume lawyer may recognize he has sufficient skill *probably* to win the case if he spends enough time on it, the chances are great he will reject it. The time investment compared to the dollar earnings no longer make it worth his while. Thousands of plaintiffs each year cannot obtain competent legal counsel in cases that could be won for this reason alone. (They might finally be able to obtain a hungry and marginally skilled lawyer, but that means their chances of winning anything more than a token award are sharply reduced.)

Although most high-volume lawyers provide a good quality of legal service, their bad reputation among the public is not entirely unearned. If you find yourself in the clutches of the wrong kind of firm, you could lose thousands of dollars on your case, not because the lawyer is incompetent—that's rarely the problem—but because, in his way of moneymaking, it is *not* to his interest to do a good job for you.

Assume, for instance, that your case is one that has a settlement value between $5,000 and $7,500 but that the latter figure is obtainable only if your lawyer will develop the evidence carefully and spend an extra five to ten hours doing some hard bargaining with the other side. Most lawyers will make this effort as a matter of professional integrity, even though their fee return in terms of hours spent is less than they would prefer. Not so if your lawyer views your case as just one piece of product on a legal assembly line. As with any factory operator, this lawyer wants to get the maximum amount of product off the line in the minimum amount of time. For that reason, his cases are rarely exploited to their full dollar potential. As he sees it, it is far better to settle two cases in ten hours for $5,000 each than get one client $7,500 in the same amount of time. Obviously, the more cases the high-volume firm of this kind can shovel through the settlement process at one time—and it may have a dozen or more simultaneously with one insurance company—the more money it makes for itself and the more money its clients lose. Only when the firm's business is slack will its clients benefit, because only then will the lawyer spend client-profitable extra hours on cases.

It's possible, of course, that your case is one of those that's going to produce about the same amount of money no matter what is done with it, in which event the assembly-line lawyer will do as good a job as anyone. For instance, unless there has been some aggravating circumstance, a broken ankle is typically worth around $5,000, a simple fracture of the arm $3,000, and so on, and the best lawyer in the world is not going to get any more on such a case than will any other lawyer. Indeed, some clients benefit inadvertently from the assembly line. Law firms that settle their cases in this fashion—it is almost unheard of for them to take a case to trial—usually enjoy excellent relations with the insurance companies they nominally oppose, as well they should, since they don't force the company into expensive and time-consuming hard bargaining on a case-to-case basis. As a result, to maintain this mutally profitable relationship, the insurer will sometimes give the assembly-line operator, without cavil, a little more than a small case is worth. Thus, if it is part of a package of settlements, you might get $5,000 on a suit that otherwise is worth $3,000 or $4,000.

When your case is one that becomes more valuable in direct relationship to the amount of time that is put into it (and that's true of most suits), you will want to avoid the high-volume factory, but it may be difficult to do so. These firms don't announce their intentions to their clients beforehand, nor do they wear a mark of Cain emblazoned on their stationery (which, as with their offices, is frequently quite impressive). By following the guidelines offered in Chapter Three, however, you should be able to meaningfully reduce the probability that you will find yourself victimized in this fashion.

WHEN TO HIRE A "SPECIALIST"

Product-liability and medical-injury cases can create unusual problems for a plaintiff, requiring the services of an attorney of markedly high skills. Unlike the average automobile-collision or fall-on-the-sidewalk case, in these injuries cause and effect can be difficult to discern and difficult to prove: For instance, was the paralysis a patient suffered the result of incompetent surgery or was it an inherent risk in the procedure performed? Was a patient's brain damage the result of an anesthesiologist's negligence or did it occur because the patient had an unpredictable allergy to the anesthesia? Was it the manufacturer's fault that a product caused an injury or was it the purchaser's due to some misuse of it?

These questions, while barely touching upon the complex issues that can arise, nevertheless, point up how imperative it is that a client with a medical or a products case obtain the services of an outstanding attorney.

And the more serious the injury the greater the need. The key factor here is the amount of insurance available. Because manufacturers and medical people know they are capable of causing the greatest kind of harm to the public (paraplegia, quadriplegia, blindness, irreversible brain damage, severe burns, multiple loss of limbs, and so on), they purchase large amounts of insurance to protect themselves. The insurers providing this coverage therefore face much larger losses in a major malpractice or products case than they would for the same injury caused under less-well-insured circumstances.

For instance, the driver who leaves his victim paralyzed may carry only $25,000 in insurance, and his carrier is going to be happy to get out of the case for that amount; settlement won't be difficult; a superlawyer isn't needed. When, however, it is a hospital patient who has been left paralyzed, the hospital's insurer could face payment of a million dollars. On that kind of case, rather than letting a claims adjuster handle it, the insurer will engage the best law firm available and will spend whatever money is necessary to develop evidence that will exculpate the customer, either by blaming the victim or by trying to shift blame onto other defendants who may have been named and who also carry large amounts of insurance, with each of them also having hired outstanding legal counsel. If the case is going to be settled, the negotiating sessions won't be perfunctory, as they will in the small case, but instead lengthy, hotly fought, with the receipt or denial of tens of thousands of dollars for the plaintiff entirely dependent on the skill of his or her attorney. Should the negotiations collapse and the case go to trial, the plaintiff's attorney must then have the ability to match the well-financed and multifaceted attack the defendants will wage either to win or to obtain as low a verdict award as possible.

Fortunately for the plaintiff with a major malpractice or products suit, lawyers can be found—or at least they can in almost every metropolitan area—who have the expertise to research, litigate, negotiate, and when necessary, try these cases.

As a lay person, you will ordinarily not be able to find your way to one of these true legal specialists on your own (they never advertise), but you can be confident that when your case seems appropriate, a referring lawyer, who is going to get a fee for so doing, will see to it that you get to one.

Once you have managed to find your way to one of these superlawyers, however, there is no guarantee your case will be accepted. Lawyers of this degree of skill reject about seven of every ten cases sent to them. This does not mean the superlawyer is only looking for sure winners. While he will reject any case he thinks can't be won—and because of his expertise, he'll be a better judge of that than the referring lawyer—he earns his living by taking on tough cases against opponents he knows will be formidable, which means he also knows he is sometimes going to lose. When he does, his loss, unlike that of the average negligence lawyer, can be large. For example, the attorney in a product injury case that resulted in a $2.9-million verdict spent $52,000 on courtroom exhibits alone, an investment he would not have recouped had he lost at trial. The time investment is no less substantial. This lawyer and his staff put approximately four years in total man-hours into the effort. The specialist therefore will take great care in selecting his cases, rejecting not only those that probably can't be won but also those in which the dollar potential does not repay the gamble of time and money involved. In essence his economics are not qualitatively different from those of the negligence lawyer, but quantitatively they are.

Should a specialist reject your case, always find out why. When the reason rises from the award potential alone, you now know that your case is viable legally and that another attorney, perhaps of lesser standing but still of considerable ability, might find it attractive. Ask the specialist. He may know someone.

If, however, he is rejecting your case because he thinks it unwinnable, it's important for you to know that, too. You may want to seek a second opinion. The lawyer who sent you to the specialist probably knows a second one of equivalent qualifications, and this one may see something in the case that the other one didn't and will accept it and win with it. A rejection by a second specialist, however, should be considered by you to be authoritative.

(You might, of course, eventually be able to find some lawyer who will try to shake some money from the insurance company tree for you. But don't count on his succeeding. The insurance company has its lawyers, and they know when you have a losing case too.)

GENERAL PRACTITIONERS

Little can be said generically of these lawyers in terms of their ability to litigate personal-injury suits. Some of them are youngsters who take every kind of case they can get, just to make a living. Others are much more experienced, but of minimal competence, who've turned to general practice because they haven't been able to succeed in more lucrative branches of the law. Still others adopt general practice because of the accident of geography; the typical small-town lawyer fits that description. Then there are the legal GPs of extraordinary ability who have selected their field solely because they find the variety of cases it offers intellectually stimulating.

One way, oddly enough, that you will often be able to know that the lawyer you are considering is a general practitioner—aside from asking him, which is the best way—is by the size of his office. Few of these lawyers belong to large firms; instead they are individualists who either practice solo or with one or two young associates; occasionally, they share space with a colleague like themselves.

Although the general-practice lawyer may be able to handle your personal-injury case adequately or even quite well, there are a few considerations you should weigh before engaging one.

The first is legal knowledge. The average GP, unlike the average negligence lawyer, will not keep up to date on recent court decisions on personal-injury cases, may not be aware of the nuances in the interpretation of complex relevant statutes, won't attend seminars on personal-injury law, and for all these reasons may not recognize either the problems or the opportunities that your case presents.

The second is experience. Unlike the GP, who handles personal-injury work only occasionally, the negligence lawyer, through osmosis if nothing else, is the more likely of the two to recognize the significance of a piece of evidence, knows how to evaluate damages, and will—or should—have far-more-well-honed negotiating skills when the time comes to deal with the insurance company on settlement.

WHO'S BEST FOR YOU?

On balance, when you have the need and the opportunity to be represented by a malpractice or product-injury specialist, do so; that's the best you can get. When the choice is between a *good* GP and a *good* high-volume lawyer, ordinarily choose the latter. However, even an average GP is preferable to representation by a high-volume legal assembly line.

This summary, however, begs its own question: By whatever route you got there, how do you know that the lawyer in whose office you find yourself is a good lawyer? The answer is that often you don't and possibly you never will. However, there are criteria that can be applied to help you select a counsel who will handle your litigation competently and treat you well and honestly.

3

How to Hire a Good Lawyer

Regardless of the size and difficulty of your case, there are certain basic qualifications you require in your lawyer.

First, he must be someone who has the legal ability to handle your case. This criterion ordinarily is not difficult to meet. Almost every attorney who regularly represents personal-injury plaintiffs has the basic skills, and the overwhelming majority refer out cases that go beyond their areas of competence.

Second, you want a lawyer who enjoys a good reputation. Estimates of his integrity, therefore, are important; you don't want to have dealings with a lawyer, no matter how skilled, who you have reason to think may attempt to cheat you.

Integrity, however, is only one aspect of reputation. *You also want a lawyer whose abilities are respected by his opponents,* the defense attorneys and the insurance companies they represent. Insurance companies, for instance, keep dossiers on plaintiff attorneys. They know which ones are unlikely to work hard for their clients, and those who will never take a case to trial. When they see that you are represented by a non-fighting attorney—or perhaps one with whom they have had no previous dealings—they are likely to offer you considerably less than your case is worth. On the contrary, when the attorney's name appearing on your suit is one known to them as a hard, skilled advocate who will go to trial when the circumstances warrant it, your chances of getting a substantial settlement offer are markedly improved, even when your case does not appear to be a strong one.

Moreover, the better your lawyer's reputation the greater the amount of respect with which he will be treated by the judge in the case. The influence of the judge may be a subtle one, but it is not any the less beneficial to you for that. When highly respected Lawyer A is representing you, rather than fast-buck Lawyer B or nonentity Lawyer C, your attorney's brief, his objections, his analyses of the applicable laws, sometimes even the degree of latitude he is permitted in questioning witnesses, is accorded a judicial liberality that the lesser attorney doesn't command.

Such paragons of legal skill did not earn their reputations through idleness. Almost invariably, they are seasoned courtroom battlers; they know how to present a case—and themselves—to a jury in the most favorable way. Their opponents, recognizing this, are loath to engage them in head-on confrontations before a judge and jury, a factor that by itself can add thousands of dollars to a pretrial settlement of your case.

Quite apparently, lawyers whose skills have gained them this kind of reputation are also busy lawyers and unlikely to accept small cases. If yours is a minor one, however, it is always possible that a topflight lawyer will accept your case for his firm, your suit to be handled by a young associate whose work is supervised by the paragon, and this should be acceptable to you.

To learn the reputation and judge the ability and character of a lawyer whose name has been given to you, there is some research you can do, some questions you should get answered, some observations you should make, and some factors you should ignore because although they may seem important in prospect, they have no practical significance. By making use of the guidelines that follow, you will meaningfully increase the chances that you and your case will end in the hands of the right lawyer:

Attempt to obtain from a disinterested attorney an opinion of the prospective lawyer's ability and general reputation among his peers. A disinterested lawyer is one who rarely or never handles personal-injury work himself, and should be someone who has at least an implicit obligation to be honest with you, perhaps because he is friendly with you or with a member of your family, perhaps because he is doing other legal work for you or for your employer. Occasionally you may find that if you have had dealings with Community Legal Services or some other citizen advocacy group, that one of their staff attorneys or an attorney on the board of directors will either know or be able to find out about the qualifications of the lawyer to whom you have been recommended.

This research method won't always be successful. If you are a resident of a large city, the lawyer whose opinion you are seeking may know nothing about the lawyer whose name has been given you. If that happens, don't assume the source's lack of knowledge means your prospective lawyer is not a good one. However, if your source gives the lawyer a strong recommendation, consider that a *major plus*.

Remember, however, that even a lawyer with whom you are quite friendly is not likely to openly criticize another attorney. Lawyers denigrate other lawyers about as frequently as doctors do other doctors. Nevertheless, if you listen carefully to the way your source phrases his comments, you should be able to learn what he really thinks, and perhaps pick up additional valuable information along the way.

Illustrative is the experience of one former plaintiff: "I knew this assistant district attorney," he recalled, "not well, but we both belonged to the same swim club. So I asked him about this lawyer who had been recommended to me by a guy I worked with. He said he'd never heard of him, but he'd check him out for me. I didn't think he would, but he turned out to be a nice guy and did. He called me and said, 'I understand he's competent to handle personal-injury cases.' Somehow, that didn't sound exactly like a ringing endorsement to me, so I said, 'Would you say he's as good as X?' mentioning another lawyer whose name had been given me. So my friend says, 'I would think either man would be competent, although I suppose there are those who would think Y or Z might be more knowledgeable.' Well, sir, you can bet I wrote down Y and Z, and I called them for appointments the next day. I hired one of them, and he did one hell of a good job for me."

As happened here, by employing this system properly, you not only learn the reputation of one lawyer, but, in the process, you may get the name of a better one.

Check the lawyer's reputation in the Martindale-Hubbell Directory, available in most large public libraries.

Published annually, these huge volumes contain the names of all practicing attorneys in the United States. After some lawyers' names will be found code letters. The letter *a* means the lawyer has been rated by his colleagues as "very high" in terms of legal ability; *b* means "high," and *c* means "fair." The letter *v* following a lawyer's name indicates he has been rated outstanding in terms of his ethical standards. Consequently, the best rating any lawyer can get is *a v*. Consider the presence of a favorable code next to your lawyer's name as a *plus*. Do not, however, consider the absence of a code as a minus; many lawyers are never rated by Martindale-Hubbell.

When you meet the prospective lawyer, look at the certificates on his wall.

Consider it a *major plus* if one of them says he is a member of the College of Trial Lawyers. Only 1 percent of all attorneys in this field belong; membership is predicated on the highest reputation for ability and integrity. However, since so few lawyers are admitted to the College, do not consider its absence a minus.

Consider *irrelevant* a placard showing that the attorney belongs to the American Bar Association; anyone who pays dues can join, and a number of excellent lawyers belong to the rival National Lawyers Guild. Many plaintiff attorneys also belong to the Association of Trial Lawyers of America, another dues-paying body that mostly engages in lobbying; do not confuse it with the College of Trial Lawyers.

Occasionally, on a lawyer's wall you will see a certificate that states he is a member of the Order of the Coif. This is a scholastic society that permits entry only to those who were outstanding law-school students. If your lawyer belongs, consider that a *plus*; do not consider its absence a minus. While it serves as an indication that your prospective lawyer is a bright fellow and learned in the law, it does not necessarily follow that he has the investigative and negotiating skills or the ability to conduct a trial that are the hallmarks of the best plaintiff lawyers.

Do *not* be impressed by a certificate that states the lawyer has been admitted to practice before the supreme court of your state or even the United States Supreme Court. That's window dressing. Consider only as a *minor plus* a certificate showing the attorney graduated from a law school you recognize as prestigious. It does show he was smart enough (or had enough money) to get through a good school, but that's all. Many of the best plaintiff lawyers graduated from the lesser law schools. (If your lawyer is middle-aged or older and Jewish, it is quite possible he didn't get admitted to the prestigious law school because of the quotas on Jewish admissions prevalent in these institutions until as recently as twenty or thirty years ago. The same biased policy was applied against blacks and women by many schools until even more recent years.)

At the meeting, ask the lawyer about his outside activities.

Consider it a *major plus* if he tells you he teaches part time at a law school or has conducted continuing-education seminars for attorneys already in practice. Consider it a *minor plus* if he tells you he is chairman of a bar-association committee; consider membership on a committee irrelevant. Consider it a *plus* if he is active in the American Civil Liberties Union or some other citizen rights group. You need not agree with the goals of these organizations, but bear in mind as a client you may be looking for a lawyer willing to fight an establishment interest—a big corporation, a big government, a big insurance company—and a lawyer's activity in citizen advocacy efforts suggests he has an ideological as well as a monetary interest in protecting everybody's rights. (Members of the National Lawyers Guild, mentioned above, also fit into this category.)

Consider *irrelevant* memberships in charitable or social organizations. The lawyer probably joined them, at least in large part, to meet people who could become clients.

Ask the lawyer if you can speak to any of his previous clients.

Of nineteen plaintiff lawyers interviewed, only one could recall a client ever asking for such references, although all but two said they would be willing to provide them. Naturally, the lawyer will only give you the names of former clients he thinks will give him high marks. But call these people. It's possible they don't share the lawyer's opinion of the work he did for them. Don't, however, accept as true everything bad a former client says about a lawyer. He may really have done an excellent job and the client doesn't realize it. However, consider it a *major plus* when the comments are uniformly favorable.

Ask the lawyer about his experiences in trying cases in court.

Consider it a *major minus* if he doesn't want to answer this question or if he puts it off with some remark to the effect that he prides himself on his ability to settle cases. As noted above, the lawyer who doesn't try cases is usually held in low regard by his opponents, and his clients get less money as a result.

Should the lawyer tell you he is an experienced trial attorney, then, in asking for references, be sure to have him include clients whose cases he took to trial. Talk to these people. Even though they are lay people, their impressions of the lawyer's trial skills will often be surprisingly helpful to you. Consider it a *major minus* if the lawyer won't give you the names of any clients whose cases went to trial.

Be aware that in some law firms a division of labor occurs, with one attorney handling a case through the negotiation stage, another doing the trial work. This is a perfectly acceptable practice, and if it is one followed at the firm of the lawyer whom you are interviewing, you have the right to obtain the names of clients whose cases were tried even if not by the attorney to whom you are speaking.

Regardless of the source, treat cautiously any comments about the lawyer's personality.

A person's reputation for ability and character is one thing, personality another. Consider as a *minor plus* any volunteered favorable comments. Do not, however, consider negative comments as a minus. You may be told that the lawyer in question is arrogant, overbearing, an egomaniac, impossible to live with, and so on.

All that may be true and it doesn't sound very pleasant, but those may be the very characteristics you will want in a lawyer when he is out there fighting in your behalf.

Your own reaction to the lawyer's personality, however, is relevant.

Some people simply don't like each other, and if you have a strongly negative reaction to a lawyer at a first meeting, you are probably best advised to look elsewhere. When personal animosity is present, confidence rarely follows, and without confidence in your lawyer, the decisions you are going to have to face during the course of your litigation, many of them difficult at the best of times, may become impossible to reach objectively. (An exception to this general rule would be a product-liability or medical-malpractice specialist; with him, the quality of the representation he can offer supersedes any other consideration.)

Do not consider significant your reaction to an attorney's apparent legal knowledgeability.

The irrelevance of this criterion was summarized by one plaintiff's lawyer: "By nature and by training, we lawyers," he said, "are great talkers, and we have the added advantage of knowing that when we talk to a client, no matter how little we know, the client knows even less. Take me. I've been a lawyer for thirty years, and during that time I doubt if I've handled more than one or two estate cases. But give me ten minutes and I'll have you convinced I'm an absolute ace in the field. Now, if I mislead you about my qualifications and you hire me, I run very little risk and you run a lot. My advice, the way I handle your affairs, could cost you and your heirs thousands of dollars, even hundreds of thousands, but the law is so complex and your ignorance of how it can be used to your disadvantage so complete, that you will probably never realize my mismanagement, and it could be decades, if ever, before the heirs catch on. So my advice to any prospective client is this: 'Don't be impressed by the verbal legal pyrotechnics of the lawyer you're interviewing. He does it to impress you, and it's mostly bullshit.'"

Your reaction to the general progress of the meeting is relevant.

By the end of it, do you feel the lawyer understands your case? Do you feel his questions have helped you understand your case better? Do you sense he is the kind of lawyer you would like asking questions of your opponent? Consider it a *major plus* if you answer these questions yes.

When you ask him questions, does he answer them willingly? Directly? Does he answer them in language you can understand? Does he seem to sense when you are unclear about something and voluntarily offer a further explanation? Is he willing to explain the applicable law to you? Does he do all this without making you feel you are imposing on his time and patience? If the answers to these questions are yes, consider that a *major plus*.

Do you, on the contrary, feel, by the end of the interview, that somehow you've not managed to get across to him what you think your case is about? Do you sense he has made an assumption about your case at the beginning and that his questions have been directed at proving that assumption, rather than keeping his mind open to the possibility of special facts that make your case different and perhaps more profitable? Does he allow the interview to be interrupted by a series of phone calls? Do you feel patronized? Made to feel ignorant or stupid? Consider it a *major minus* when the answer to any of these questions is yes.

The lawyer's youth and apparent degree of experience may or may not be relevant.

On a routine case, the young lawyer will often display an enthusiasm and willingness to work hard that might not be shared by a more experienced, if jaded, colleague. The zest could pay off in extra dollars.

Experience, nevertheless, does teach, and the veteran attorney should possess a degree of expertise in all aspects of litigation that you can't rightly expect from a younger one. When, therefore, your case presents substantial legal difficulties or has a large amount of money riding on the lawyer's skill, the attorney's degree of experience can be important.

A good parlay, and one that happens not infrequently, occurs when your case is assigned by a senior member of the firm to one of the young associates. The junior one brings his enthusiasm and willingness to work hard—to impress the boss, if for no other reason—and he has access to the senior members for advice should problems arise.

The lawyer's race and sex are usually irrelevant.

And it is not an issue that will often arise. As noted earlier, more than 98 percent of all lawyers who regularly handle plaintiffs' work in personal-injury cases are male; probably almost as many are white.

On the rare occasion when you might have such a choice, there is no evidence to suggest that race should play a role in the decision-making process. The black lawyer will do as well for the white client as for the black and vice versa.

Sex is a more difficult issue. There is some indication, though it is hardly compelling, that male lawyers in personal-injury cases may have unconscious biases toward their female clients that cause them to dismiss as "hysterical" the same reaction to an event that they would consider "reasonable" if a male client recounted it. If so, the bias may cause the male lawyer to ignore or undervalue a significant item of evidence. Whether one could conclude from this that female lawyers wouldn't have the same or analogous biases, however, is unclear. On balance, the lawyer's sex should not be part of the decision-making process unless it is an issue that is of importance to you, and even then it should come into play only when it is the single remaining element of choice between two lawyers of apparently equal ability.

The impressiveness of the lawyer's quarters is unimportant.

The grand office can mean the grand lawyer, but it can also mean he has a wealthy family who paid to furnish it for him. Or it could mean he got rich stealing from his clients.

The appearance of the lawyer's desk is also unimportant.

Some people think that a clean desk means a lawyer is neat, methodical, and well organized. Perhaps. But it could also mean he doesn't have any business, and in any event, it doesn't mean he has the qualities of skill, imagination, and diligence that you are looking for. One lawyer interviewed for this book had his desk piled so high with folders it was difficult to see past them; in order to sit down, it was necessary to clear a chair of still other folders. Completely unusable was his couch, littered as it was with magazines, yellowing briefs, and piles of old newspapers. Yet this attorney, a member of the College of Trial Lawyers, is considered one of the half dozen best medical-malpractice lawyers in the major city in which he practices.

Personnel practices and staff morale may be important.

You will find, for instance, as you get into your case, that many of your dealings will be with your lawyer's secretary; constant changes in that position can lead to frustrations, delays, and occasionally the mislaying of important papers.

Bad personnel practices can also lead to rapid turnover of the legal staff. You may discover, in the middle of your case, that the lawyer to whom it was entrusted is leaving. As a result, you are sent to a new lawyer when you were perfectly satisfied with the old one; or, alternatively, the lawyer who is leaving wants to take your case with him and you may want him to, but his ex-employer refuses to agree. When you get caught in the middle of that kind of tug-of-war, your case could be harmed, or, minimally, seriously delayed in its resolution.

Since people leaving jobs or the breaking up of partnerships can happen in the best-ordered law firms, there is no certain way you can avoid this happening to you. Nevertheless, there are some precautionary steps you can take. When you first visit the lawyer's office, be alert to the quality of his relationship with his secretary and anyone else with whom you see him in contact. Be aware, however, that any impressions you receive, positive or negative, could be misleading, so do not give them great weight. More important, you should ask the lawyer how long he has been in practice with his present partners, how long any associates have been with the firm, how long his secretary has been with him. The answers themselves may not be too important, but if he shows signs of uneasiness in his responses, you may have hit on a warning sign.

THE INTERVIEW WITH THE PROSPECTIVE LAWYER

The questions and answers that follow cover the major aspects of the interview, except for the details of fee arrangements, which are discussed separately in Chapter Four.

How should you prepare for the interview?

At the time the date for an interview is set, the lawyer or his secretary will tell you what records you should bring with you. The information requested varies from lawyer to lawyer, just as the amount of information available varies from plaintiff to plaintiff. Some plaintiffs don't even know who injured them (a common problem in operating-room accidents), and others may not have been present when the injury occurred (parents bringing suit for their children, survivors bringing a wrongful-death action).

Available in most cases, however, will be medical expense records, and these a lawyer will always want to see. From them, he obtains a first, important indication of the probable cash worth of your case. Although you may not receive specific instructions in this regard—some lawyers and their secretaries can be infuriatingly vague—when the lawyer talks about your medical expenses, he doesn't mean just those you owe or have already paid yourself. He wants to see them, but also bring along any records or copies of records of bills from doctors, hospitals, physical-therapy institutes, X-ray laboratories, convalescent homes, and the like that show amounts paid for the care by Blue Cross/Blue Shield or any similar medical-insurance plan. It doesn't matter whether you or your employer paid the premiums; the bills are part of your medical expenses. The same is true of any medical or nursing charges that have been paid by other individuals, such as members of your family or your employer. Records of loans you obtained to pay medical or other bills are also relevant, since the interest you paid on them can also be incorporated in your losses.

When you are the party whose injury is the cause of the suit, an excellent method of preparation for the interview is to write a chronology of the accident. Include all events immediately prior to it, even those that do not appear to you to have any direct relationship to the injury itself. Note, as best you can recall, the events immediately following, including any conversations you may have had (such as those with a passerby, a policeman, the defendant, a doctor or nurse at the hospital), questions you were asked, and your best recollection of how you responded. If, subsequent to the accident, you were approached by the defendant's insurance company, summarize the content of that conversation. Try to recall your emotional reactions—fear, panic, anger—both during the course of the accident and afterward, and the names of anybody to whom you may have expressed these feelings. Valuable also will be a description of the pain you suffered: Was it sharp? dull? shooting? aching? do you still have it? how often? Be sure to include all pains you have suffered since the accident; *do not try to decide on your own whether or not they are a result of your injury*.

Bring the chronology you have composed to the meeting with you. The lawyer won't want you to read directly from it when you first describe the events of the accident to him—he wants to get a feeling of how you express yourself without notes, since you won't be permitted them if you ultimately have to testify at trial—but afterward, you can use the chronology to make sure you have covered every point that seems salient to you. Should you and the lawyer subsequently agree on representation, he will undoubtedly ask you to leave the chronology with him. Although it can't be used as evidence in your case, it will be an important reference tool for him in locating witnesses, interviewing them, studying medical records and police reports, and in determining the amount of money he wants to demand for you.

By way of preparation, too, write out the questions you want him to answer and take that list to the meeting. Many of the questions you are planning to raise will be answered by the lawyer without your asking them, and others will become irrelevant, but before you leave, check your list and get answers to those that remain.

Will you have to pay the lawyer for his time at the interview?

You shouldn't. He is investing his time to learn if you are someone from whom he can earn money, and you are investing yours to see if he can help you get money. There's no more reason he should charge you than you should charge him.

However, since a few lawyers do charge for an interview, always check this out at the time you are setting the date for it. Don't go through with the interview if there is a charge. Don't go through with the interview if you are told you will be charged only if you *don't* become a client. That is an unconscionable ploy by the lawyer to put financial pressure on you to engage him, and you don't want anything to do with him.

There is one situation in which a lawyer properly may charge you for an interview in a personal-injury case. This occurs when, during a phone conversation with him in which you have briefly outlined your problem, he tells you he doesn't think you have grounds for suit. If, upon hearing that, you tell him you still would like to meet to get his advice, he will probably agree to do so, and he then has a legitimate right to ask for a consultation fee. If, at the end of the interview, he decides to take your case anyway or refers you to another lawyer, he will almost certainly waive the fee.

Should you go to the interview alone?

It depends. First, let us consider the position of spouses vis-à-vis one another in a personal-injury suit:

1. When both spouses are injured, as often happens in automobile accidents, the presence of both is imperative at the interview. Not only can both then help fill the lawyer in on the circumstances of the accident, but also both are needed to decide their common or separate rights. Often, the two should become co-plaintiffs in a single suit, but other times one spouse will have different grounds for suit than the other, and one might not have grounds while the other does. Only if both are present will the lawyer be able to determine the applicable law and the best procedure to follow.

2. If one spouse was injured, the other wasn't, and both were present at the accident, the uninjured spouse should always accompany the injured one, because he or she is an important witness and will often have a more detailed and objective view of what occurred than will the injured one.

3. If one spouse wasn't present when the injury occurred, it is still a good idea for both to be present. Frequently, the spouse who wasn't injured will have gone to the hospital after the injury

and subsequently consulted with physicians, and this spouse's information can therefore have evidentiary value. The uninjured one can also provide information about the injured one's pain and suffering, medications, and the like, in a detailed way that the injured one might not be able to recall. It also sometimes happens that one spouse is more eager to pursue the suit than the other. If so, the lawyer wants to know about that. It could mean that one spouse knows facts that make the suit unwinnable. More frequently, the reluctant spouse's reservations will turn out to be groundless, and the lawyer can then allay them, something he can't do if the reluctant party is the uninjured spouse, who isn't present. In any event, it is always better for both to be present to hear what the lawyer has to say; there'll be far fewer later misunderstandings that way.

4. If one spouse wasn't injured in the accident and wasn't present when it occurred, that spouse may, even so, have grounds for suit, and should therefore be present at the meeting. There are several situations in which this can occur, but it is most common when the injury has made it impossible for the injured party to continue sexual relations with his or her spouse. In that event, the uninjured spouse probably has grounds for suit based on loss of consortium.

5. When suit is brought on behalf of an injured or deceased child, the presence of both parents is usually necessary. In these cases, the parents may have grounds for bringing suit on their own behalf as well as on the child's. When the parents are no longer married to each other, the grounds could still exist, but their interests may no longer be identical and they should consult attorneys separately. For instance, let us suppose your child was injured while living with your ex-wife and you paid the child's medical bills but are behind on your support payments. You have good grounds for suit to obtain reimbursement of the medical payments, but it might be to your ex-wife's interest to oppose you in order to get that money for herself.

There could, of course, be times when it would be unwise to have your spouse accompany you. You may have something to hide. Whether you will succeed or not is another matter. On this point, an attorney recalled a client who was seriously injured by a car while in the company of his mistress. "He was scared," said the attorney, "that if he sued, his wife would find out, and scared that if he didn't sue, considering he had such a good case, that she'd get awfully suspicious for that reason. Well, in the long run, he sued and won $50,000; his wife found out and she sued him for divorce; cost him $50,000. I guess you could say he broke even."

When you aren't married, it is usually best to attend the meeting alone. You may feel more comfortable having a friend with you, and that is fine, but leave that person at the lawyer's office door. His or her presence at the meeting could inhibit you from giving the lawyer important, confidential information that you would not hesitate to express in the company of a spouse.

A different situation is raised when the accompanying person is an attorney. In a co-counsel situation, you always have the right to have the referring attorney with you when you meet the lawyer to whom he has sent you, and often the new lawyer will suggest that the referring attorney be present. When that referring attorney or other lawyer is someone you trust—based either on friendship or on your previous professional dealings with him—it is ordinarily a good idea to have him along. By so doing, you now have at your side someone who is professionally competent, who is interested in your welfare and not the other lawyer's, who will be able to ask pertinent questions that might not occur to you, and who will later be able to give you sound advice as to whether or not you should engage the attorney you have just interviewed. Under any other circumstances, however, there seems no cogent reason why, from your view, a referring attorney should be at the meeting. The whole purpose of his presence probably is to put pressure on you to sign with the lawyer he has recommended. In any event, the choice is yours. If you don't want the referring attorney present, say so and that will be the end of it.

How much will the attorney want to learn about you and your accident?

He'll want to obtain a fairly complete biography of you. He'll want to know your job history, your job skills even if they aren't being used in your present occupation, your educational attainment, income both before and after the injury, your medical history prior to the accident, your recreational activities, and so on. The information he gleans this way helps him evaluate the effects the injury had on your earning capacity and on your enjoyment in life, factors that are important in determining the total cash value of your case.

When the discussion turns to the facts of the injury itself, some lawyers prefer to let the prospective client tell the story from beginning to end without interruption, going back over it point by point only after it is completed. Other lawyers, however, insert questions as they occur to them. The questions can be sympathetic, principally intended to help you articulate what has happened to you, but they also can became sharp and apparently antagonistic.

Should that happen, don't assume the lawyer has suddenly found some terrible legal flaw from listening to your recountal and is about to reject you as a client. The chances are, rather, that his previous questioning has made him conclude you have a good case, and the tougher questions are now inserted to see how you would stand up under cross-examination. Many clients with good cases make bad witnesses, and if you are one of those, he wants to know that from the start in order that he can develop strategy that will minimize exposure of your weaknesses to the other side.

How much of the truth about your injury should you tell the lawyer? How much does he want to hear?

Your lawyer wants you to be truthful in response to every question he asks you, but he doesn't necessarily want to hear the truth about everything.

The problem, which can be a serious one, usually arises when the plaintiff was partly at fault in causing the injury, a factor that can result in loss of the case in some jurisdictions and sizable reduction of the award in others. Often, clients, possibly because they're not aware of the law or simply because they think they should tell everything, blurt out the harmful information to the lawyer. At that point, ethically, a lawyer cannot advise a client to change the story. (This isn't to say that some attorneys won't do just that.) By encouraging perjury, the lawyer, if his malefaction is discovered, is subject to disbarment, conceivably even to criminal charges, or to malpractice charges by the client if his wrongful advice can be shown to have caused the client to lose the case.

But there's also another possible scenario. Sometimes, the client knows enough about the law to realize there may be a contributory-negligence problem and—fearing the lawyer won't take the case if he knows the full truth—hides facts that, if they were known to the lawyer, would allow him to get around them and develop a winning case anyway. When the lawyer isn't told, both he and the client are now standing on a time bomb that explodes when the defense, which has learned of the contributory negligence, introduces it—often at trial, when it is too late for the plaintiff's lawyer to successfully counter it.

Of course, there is also always the possibility that the defense won't learn of the contributory negligence or—and this is much more likely—suspects it but isn't able to prove it, because the case essentially is based on one person's word about what happened against another's.

On this complex issue, the following excerpt from an interview with an experienced plaintiff's attorney may be helpful:

Q. What do you do when a prospective client gives you information that is harmful to his case?

A. I evaluate it. It's important to know. Not all negative information is completely harmful. It won't necessarily ruin the case. With it, I know the kind of problem I have, the way the case has to be developed.

Q. But suppose the client hasn't said anything harmful yet, but you can tell by the way he is going in his story that he probably has a contributory-negligence problem?

A. Yes, that sometimes happens. Well, what I do—what can be done is this: You can interrupt the client as he seems to be reaching that point, and you say to him, "I think I ought to explain to you at this point what the law is." And then, and then I might, just hypothetically, I might say, "Now, that means that if the light was red when you crossed the street, you probably don't have a case. But if it was green, you do."

Q. What happens then?

A. Well, it varies. The client might say the light was red anyway. Then we have to deal with that. Maybe it'll mean I can't represent him. Other times, he'll say, "Well, that's not what happened here. The light was green." And so on. Maybe he's telling the truth, maybe he isn't. But that's no concern of mine. I can now presume he's telling the truth and we go on from there.

Q. And if he does blurt it out, the harmful thing, and you turn down the case and he realizes what's happened, and he goes to another lawyer—

A. He may be more circumspect in the way he tells the story to the second lawyer. That's possible, yes.

A plaintiff who eventually won a gross award of $15,000 on his case had his own experience with historical revisionism and a red light: "When I first told the lawyer about it, I told him the truth. I was so dumb—I mean, you know, the car was speeding and it was his fault I got hit, and, hell, everybody goes against lights once in a while, so I didn't think it mattered. Anyway, he sits there like a big owl while I'm telling him all this, his eyes half closed, his hands folded, and he doesn't say a word. Then, when I'm done, he asks a lot of questions before he gets back to that light, and he says to me, 'You say you think the light was red when you started across the street?' 'Yes, sir,' says I. 'In other words, you think, right now you think, the light *probably* was red?' 'Well, it—' says I, but he puts up his hand and says, 'Isn't it conceivable, think carefully now, that the light may have been green?' Then I see what he's getting at, and obediently I say, 'Yes, now that I think about it, maybe it was.' Well, I can assure you that was the last time that light was even 'maybe' green. From then on it was green, I'll tell you."

Exactly how one handles this kind of pirouetting about with the facts of a case—"rearranging the truth," as one client hopefully put it—is a matter that can only be determined by one's conscience (and by the desperation of one's need for money).

However, one rule should not be violated: When the lawyer pursues the possible contributory-negligence problem, you have to assume he knows what he is doing, and you should answer him as accurately as possible. The same is true of your responses to his other questions. The thoroughness with which you recount your story could mean the difference between victory and defeat in your suit.

Should you decide not to hire an attorney after an interview, is he obliged to keep confidential all the information about the accident you have given him?

Yes. He also has an ethical duty not to represent or advise the opposing side should they come to him. A lawyer who violates a confidential relationship in this fashion would risk disbarment and could be sued for malpractice.

Will the lawyer tell you, at the conclusion of the interview, whether he wants to accept your case?

With only rare exceptions, yes. He will then ask you to sign a contingency-fee agreement, by which you authorize him to represent you.

In so doing, he may be aware that your case presents substantial legal or evidentiary problems and that subsequent investigation will make it necessary for him to advise you to drop your suit. In that event, you owe him nothing. Nevertheless, he will prefer to have you sign the agreement, because he knows that if you leave his office without having done so, the chances are it is the last he'll see of you; you'll go to another lawyer, who will take your case right away.

Consequently, you may find yourself under some pressure to sign. Don't do so unless you are convinced this is the lawyer you want. You can abrogate the agreement later, but the lawyer could then bill you for the time he has put into the case other than for the interview itself.

Will the lawyer tell you how much your case is worth?

It depends. Let us suppose, for instance, that your injury is a broken leg and that it occurred six months prior to the time you decide to see a lawyer; by that date, you should know from your doctor as well as your own observations of your medical progress whether you are recovering at a normal rate and whether there is any likelihood of long-range crippling effects from the injury. Assuming progress is normal, the lawyer—based on your version of how the injury occurred—probably will be able to give you a reasonably accurate dollar recovery range for your suit at the interview.

On the contrary, if you are not recovering normally, a whole range of possibilities exists—including the possibility that your failure to recover may be the result of medical malpractice, suggesting a different defendant from the one who originally injured you—and a reputable lawyer will not want to offer, at that point, even a guess as to the dollar value.

Similarly, if, instead of six months, it is six days from the time of the accident that you consult a lawyer, there is no conceivable way he can know, any more than you or your doctor can, what your actual recovery prospects are. The most he can legitimately tell you is that, assuming a normal recovery, your case may have a *minimal* value of so many dollars.

The more complicated your case is, the more difficult an estimate becomes. A relatively minor injury could be worth a great deal of money when the causation indicates gross negligence by the defendant. But, even in that situation, the lawyer has only your version of the facts to go with, and further investigation may reveal contributory negligence on your part or some other set of facts that lessens the case's original apparent worth.

As a prospective client, therefore, you should never make your decision on engaging an attorney based on what he will or won't tell you about the cash value of your case. Remember, an attorney would not be considering accepting you as a client unless he foresaw, from the version of the events you gave him, a case that was worth his while monetarily. And that usually means it will be worth your while too.

When estimates are given, never base your choice of counsel on the results of a bidding war; i.e., don't choose Lawyer A over Lawyer B solely because A names a higher figure than B. You should, on the contrary, consider it a *major minus* when an attorney voluntarily talks in big-dollar terms or makes glowing promises: "We're going to be in this together, you and I," one former plaintiff recalls her attorney telling her, "and get these bastards. I wouldn't settle for a penny under $100,000." She got $15,000.

No reputable attorney will engage in that kind of huckstering for business.

Once you have signed on with a lawyer, you have then, however, the right to obtain a realistic assessment of its value. This will occur usually within a month or two of your first meeting, when the lawyer has completed his preliminary investigation. If, upon hearing that figure, you decide not to go ahead, you can then drop your claim without any financial obligation to him. (This is a different matter from signing an agreement with one lawyer, dropping him, and going to another; there, as will be discussed further in Chapter Twelve, you have a financial obligation.) Assuming you decide to go ahead, the estimate you have received gives you a measure by which you can evaluate the acceptibility of any settlement offers the defense makes. Always bear in mind that the first estimate the lawyer gives you can increase or decrease in value as your case matures, dependent upon the development of the accident evidence and changes in your medical condition.

What should the lawyer tell you about your chances of winning any money?

A reputable lawyer never guarantees a win. Avoid a lawyer who does. The lawyer's willingness to accept you as a client is the only "guarantee" you need or should receive that you have a case that can be won.

What should the lawyer tell you about the legal steps that will be taken in your behalf?

A great deal. You should be informed—in language you can understand—about which legal papers will be filed, when, and what their purposes are. You should also be informed of the probable steps the defense will take to counter your claim, when they are likely to do it, and what role, if any, you will be asked to play in responding to them. Further, the lawyer should advise you of the probable amount of time it will take to resolve the case, the various decisions (including accepting or rejecting settlement offers) that you will be expected to make, and the likely points in the case in which these decisive moments will arise. Some of the information he gives you will be of no further value to you, but since you don't know in advance what you'll eventually need to know, it is wise to cover every possible base at the beginning.

What information about your case should you have in writing?

The financial arrangements must be in writing; all of them. In addition, you may find it useful to have the lawyer provide you with a memorandum outlining the future steps he has discussed with you.

This is not an imposition on your part; a reputable lawyer will never object to putting into writing anything he has told you orally, and you can consider it a bad signal if the lawyer you are interviewing refuses to do so. Any timetable discussed, however, is tentative and will probably not be met. An exception is the date on which the statute-of-limitations deadline for filing suit on your case is reached. Miss that and you lose.

Assuming you decide to have the lawyer represent you, what should you find out about future contacts with him?

Ask him when you can next expect to hear from him. Four to six weeks is typical; by that time, he should have completed his preliminary investigation of the case, made contact with the opponent, and have some news for you. A lawyer's occasional failure to contact you by a prescribed date is not a cause for worry, but repeated failures to do so or repeated failures to return your phone calls should be treated with great suspicion and may indicate you should find another lawyer.

After the early stages of your case, any six-month period that goes by without a contact from him warrants a call from you. The lawyer probably has nothing to report, but there's no harm reminding him that you are keeping an eye on your own affairs. In any event, always call him when some aspect of your case comes to your mind that you have not previously mentioned to him. It could be important.

Assuming suit hasn't already been filed, one time you should always call the lawyer is when the statute-of-limitations deadline is near. Don't assume he hasn't forgotten it.

4

Your Money and Your Lawyer

When you decide, during the course of your interview, that the lawyer before you is the one you want to have represent you, the time has come to talk money. In your newfound enthusiasm for him and your eagerness to get your suit going, your temptation, at this point, may be to agree to everything he tells you about the fee, particularly when he explains that his services won't cost you a penny until and if you win.

But this, above all, is the time to be careful. Some fee arrangements are much more to the plaintiff's interest than are others, and it will be up to you to recognize what's good and what's bad and what to do about it.

In certain instances, the fee arrangement suggested should be rejected in totality, and you should go on to find another lawyer who will offer a better deal. However, many times—although the lawyer won't present them to you that way—the terms are negotiable, and by bargaining with the lawyer on them at the outset, you may eventually get a net recovery thousands of dollars larger than you would have had you not made the effort.

This chapter describes what you should know about contingency fees and how to make the best deal for yourself.

THE CONTRACT

Ordinarily, only the client signs the contingency-fee agreement. The document, nevertheless, is a legal contract that places obligations on both sides. Under its terms, you empower the lawyer to represent you for an agreed percentage of any award you receive and to reimburse him, from the award, for any expenses he incurred while pursuing your litigation. For his part, the lawyer agrees you owe him no fee if the case is lost, and—although this won't be stated in the agreement—he takes on the duty to provide you with competent professional services. This means that if he should fail to take legally recognized appropriate steps in the furtherance of your case or should act unethically toward you, he can be sued by you for breach of contract or for malpractice.

There is no standard wording for a contingency-fee agreement. The forms vary from law firm to law firm. Do not sign the document if it does not contain every oral agreement you and the lawyer have reached. Always ask for and retain a copy of the contract. Should worse come to worst and it becomes necessary to sue the lawyer, you will need the contract as proof of the agreement between you.

Contingency-fee arrangements are offered on either a *flat* or a *sliding-scale* basis. Under the flat system, the lawyer gets the same percentage of the award regardless of the stage at which the suit was resolved, the time put into it, and the amount that is won. The flat percentage offered most commonly is one third. Some lawyers, however, charge flat fees of 40, 45, or 50 percent.

A typical sliding-scale fee arrangement works as follows: The lawyer receives 25 percent of the award if the case is settled prior to filing suit, one third if settled prior to trial, or forty percent if the case goes to trial.

The cost of appeals from a trial verdict varies. A sliding scale, at that point, may escalate to either 45 or 50 percent, regardless of whether it is you or the defendant making the appeal. Most flat-percentage lawyers won't charge extra if the appeal is made by the defendant, but some will require a separate fee paid in advance if it is their client who wants to appeal; charges of $1,000 are common, plus the cost of obtaining a transcript of the trial proceedings (at least another $750, also paid by the plaintiff in advance). The appeal fee arrangement may or may not be incorporated in the original contingency percentage. Therefore, ascertain in advance of signing the agreement what charges, if any, the lawyer imposes in an appeals situation.

In some jurisdictions, downward sliding scales have been enacted into law. The New Jersey system is typical. There the lawyer is permitted one third of any award up to $50,000, 20 percent of the amount over $50,000 up to $100,000, and 10 percent of the amount over $100,000. Thus, if you receive a $150,000 award in New Jersey, your lawyer's fee will be $31,667 ($16,667 on the first $50,000, $10,000 on the second, and $5,000 on the third.) By comparison, in an unregulated state, you would pay him $50,000 on a one-third basis, or $75,000 on a 50 percent fee.

Elsewhere—including New York—in any kind of personal-injury suit that goes through trial, the judge has the right to reduce a plaintiff attorney's fee if he thinks it is too high.

In cases in which the United States Government is the defendant, under the Federal Tort Claims Act the plaintiff may be charged no more than 20 percent if the case is settled at an administrative hearing held by the agency involved, and no more than 25 percent if suit is filed.

Most of the time, however, arrangements between client and lawyer in a personal-injury suit are not subject to fee limits or review by an outside body. As a client, therefore, usually you are on your own to strike the best bargain you can.

ARE YOU BETTER OFF PAYING A FLAT OR A SLIDING SCALE?

When you have a choice between two apparently equally competent lawyers, one of whom charges a flat percentage and the other an upward sliding scale, *choose the flat-percentage lawyer* when his fee does not exceed 40 percent. (The only possible exception, and even this is debatable, occurs when the top of the sliding scale equals the flat percentage; e.g., Lawyer A charges a flat 40 percent, and Lawyer B charges 25, 33⅓, and 40 percent.)

The flat scale is preferable because it makes it more likely you will get disinterested advice from your lawyer at each step of the proceedings and because you can make decisions on settlement offers on their merits, without concern over the percentage the lawyer will charge.

For instance, let's suppose Mr. Haley's attorney charges him 25 percent if he settles his claim prior to filing suit, one third if settled after suit is filed, or 40 percent if it goes to trial. Immediately prior to the deadline for filing suit, Haley's lawyer tells him the other side has offered $6,000 to end the claim; he urges Haley to reject the offer. Meanwhile, Mr. Braddock, whose lawyer is working on a flat one-third basis, receives a similar offer on his case and his lawyer also urges him to reject it.

Haley, in this example, has no way of knowing if his lawyer is urging him to reject the offer because it should be rejected or is doing so only to force Haley to file suit, thereby increasing the lawyer's share from one quarter to one third. Braddock, on the contrary, knows he's getting objective advice, since his lawyer's percentage of the proceeds remains the same no matter what he decides.

An even more difficult problem can occur with the sliding scale when the choice is between agreeing to a settlement and going to trial.

For example, Mr. Judson's lawyer charges him one third if his case is settled prior to trial, 40 percent if it goes to trial, and 45 percent if the verdict is appealed. His lawyer has advised him that a $25,000 jury verdict is within reach. Immediately prior to the scheduled date of trial, the lawyer tells Judson that the defense has offered $20,000 to settle the case. He recommends that Judson accept the offer. Mr. Wilson, whose case is similar to Judson's but whose attorney is working on a flat one-third fee, receives the same offer and his lawyer makes the same recommendation.

Both Judson and Wilson have a crucial decision to make: Should they take the money in hand or gamble that a jury—which might give them less or nothing—will give them more? At the best of times, reaching the right conclusion is not going to be easy, but Judson's problem is much more complex than Wilson's. Unlike Wilson, with his flat-fee lawyer, Judson has to consider not only the wisdom of going to trial but the effect it will have on his net award; he has to figure how much more he will have to earn at trial on a 40 percent fee to his lawyer than on settlement at 33⅓ percent; in addition, he has to consider that even if he happens to get a large award at trial, it may be appealed, and then he'll have to pay his lawyer 45 percent instead of 40 percent.

lawyer for the expenses he has advanced? It is difficult to say that something never happens, but it would be extremely rare for the lawyer to try to collect his expenses following a loss. Most contingency-fee agreements are silent on the subject, and when they are, you are free of any legal obligation to repay. Should an agreement contain a repayment proviso, you usually will be able to get the lawyer to cross it out. He wouldn't be taking your case if he weren't fairly confident of victory, and he's not about to lose you as a client over a problem he thinks will never arise.

But even when the contract does require repayment, few lawyers ever try to enforce their collection right. The effort is, as they know, usually a futile one. The client either lacks the money to repay, or—unhappy at his loss—refuses. In the latter instance, the lawyer's only option is to sue the client, and few want to go to that expense over several hundred or even several thousand dollars. (If nothing else, it's bad publicity for a lawyer to become known as one who'd sue his own clients.) A lawyer's most feasible method, therefore, of handling the unreimbursed-expense problem is to deduct it as a business loss on his tax returns.

PAYING YOUR OWN EXPENSES

Many plaintiffs are unable to pay medical bills and other costs associated with their injuries until they win their suit. Almost invariably, under the terms of the contingency-fee agreement, the attorney pays these bills from the plaintiff's share of the proceeds. He deducts his fees and expenses first, and then the amounts due on the bills. In addition to any suit-related money the plaintiff owes personally, the lawyer also pays the money due Blue Cross and other subrogation claimants.

When the lawyer takes on the bill-paying responsibility, legally he removes it from your shoulders. Therefore, should he subsequently fail to pay bills for which he has deducted amounts due, the creditors can collect from him, not from you. They may try to collect from you, however, and succeed, or at least make your life miserable, unless you can prove, by having retained your contract and the distribution sheet showing the deductions, that the obligation is the lawyer's.

It is, however, rare for any problem to arise on this score. In taking on payment of your bills, the lawyer is protecting his own interest. Most of the money due will be to doctors or hospitals, sources with whom he has regular contact as part of his personal-injury practice, and he knows that if he fails to see that they are paid, his reputation among them will suffer and with it the cooperation he can expect in future cases. For this reason, he will probably reject any request you make to pay these bills yourself; he's afraid you won't and he'll get the blame for it.

HOW TO MAKE MONEY ON DEDUCTION OF THE LAWYER'S EXPENSES

At the time of distribution of funds, the lawyer's first deduction from the gross award will either be the contingency fee or the reimbursement for his own expenses. *Which deduction he takes first can be a matter of paramount financial importance to you.*

To illustrate, let us assume that a jury awards you $30,000 on your suit. Your lawyer is representing you on a one-third contingency-fee basis. His expenses, pretrial and at trial, come to a total of $6,000. You have no additional bills that must be paid.

Observe the difference in your net award depending on the point at which he repays himself his expenses:

CONTINGENCY FEE FIRST
Total Award	$ 30,000
Less lawyer's fee	−10,000
Remainder	20,000
Less reimbursement of expenses	− 6,000
NET TO YOU	$ 14,000

EXPENSES FIRST
Total Award	$ 30,000
Less reimbursement of expenses	− 6,000
Remainder	24,000
Less lawyer's fee	− 8,000
NET TO YOU	$ 16,000

Note that the lawyer who takes the contingency fee first has not cheated you. He has taken no more than his agreed-upon one third; it is just that, by so doing, he has made himself an extra $2,000 and you have lost $2,000.

Despite its obvious financial benefits to them, a number of lawyers interviewed stated they did not believe it was proper to take their fee first: "When I do that," explained one, "it is as though I were paying myself a one-third commission on my own expenses, and that's just not right." However, it is probably safe to say that the majority of lawyers disagree with this pro-plaintiff reasoning.

Contingency-fee agreements are often vague on when expenses are to be taken, probably purposely so. Therefore, unless the agreement specifically states that the expenses are to be deducted first, you should discuss the subject with the lawyer *prior* to the signing of the agreement. Remember, when the wording is ambiguous, it is he who will be interpreting its meaning, and you will have no recourse if he says on distribution day that it means he takes his commission first.

Since there could be anywhere from several hundred to many thousands of dollars at stake for you, the fight for favorable wording is worth the making, and you should seriously consider not engaging an attorney who will refuse to agree to your demand. You may, in fact, get what you want simply by asking for it. The lawyer presumably wants your case, and he may not want to risk losing you as a client over that issue.

Revealing on the subject was the following discussion with a lawyer whose contingency-fee agreements specifically state that the legal fee is to be deducted first and expenses afterward:

Q. . . . but suppose the client asks you to change it so that expenses are deducted first?

A. Oh, that's negotiable. That kind of thing is negotiable.

Q. In other words, you might agree?

A. That's—yes, I might.

Q. Well, how often would you say that clients have asked you to make that kind of change?

A. Offhand, I—well, yes, there was—I guess it's happened a couple times. But it's very rare. You see, what you must understand is that clients hardly ever ask those kinds of questions. I suppose they assume that anything that's in the contingency-fee contract is the law . . . that's—that there is some kind of law that regulates it and it can't be changed. And the other thing is that clients are nervous at that time. Most of them hardly read the agreement before they sign it.

Still another area in which you can sometimes negotiate to increase the size of your net award concerns interest earnings. In almost every jurisdiction, a plaintiff is entitled to interest on the award either from the time the suit was filed or from the date it was resolved until the date the check in payment arrives. The amount can be considerable. For instance, if you win a $50,000 verdict and the defense appeals, and two years later your award is upheld, you are due 5–6 percent (depending on the going bank interest rate in your community) for that two-year period.

The question is, Do you get all the interest, or is the attorney entitled to take his contingency-fee percentage from it? It can certainly be argued that since the attorney had to wait for his money just as you did, he deserves his share of the interest. However, it could also be argued that he deserves his share from your award only and that the interest payment is a separate item to which only you are entitled. As with the lawyer's expenses, this is an issue you should discuss prior to signing the contingency-fee agreement. Some lawyers will insist they get their share of the interest; others will agree to give you the entire amount. You have everything to gain and nothing to lose by broaching the subject.

The following, therefore, is the wording you should ask to have included in the contingency-fee agreement:

I (We) hearby agree that the compensation for my (our) attorney(s) for services shall be determined as follows:____percent of the fund resulting from the settlement or verdict *after* reimbursement of all legal expenses and costs incurred by counsel and advanced in my (our) behalf has first been deducted, and after any interest payment on my (our) award shall have first been paid to me (us).

5

The Battle Is Joined

Occasionally, your personal-injury claim will come to a quick and happy conclusion when the defense offers you a sum that is agreeable to you to end your case. Most often, however, that's not going to happen and you will have to file suit. The way you handle yourself in the earliest stages of the suit will determine not only *if* you're going to win but *how much* you're going to win.

Your opponent will be, typically, a high-powered insurance company and its no-less-high-powered lawyers. Your first battle with the enemy will consist of a rearguard action of fighting off its attempt to weaken or destroy your case by spying on you.

HOW TO PROTECT YOURSELF FROM THE GUMSHOES

Normally, unless your case has a probable value of less than $5,000, you can assume you are going to be investigated, and the more serious the injury you allege, the more intensive and long-lasting the investigation will be.

Never think that just because you are telling the absolute truth about what happened to you and just because you know that the defendant was absolutely at fault, that the insurance-company investigation can't harm you. The defense may be perfectly aware of who was at fault, but that is not going to stop it from wanting to find some bits of evidence that can be twisted to indicate you were partly to blame. But even if that's not its goal, even if it is convinced that its customer is going to be found liable, the insurer—to cut its losses—will still want to try to show that you aren't as seriously injured as you claim, and in doing that, it is not necessarily going to be interested in the truthfulness of the information it turns up, but, rather, how the information can be presented to a jury to impugn your credibility.

You often will be the object of surveillance. If your claim is sufficiently big, the insurance company will hire detectives to follow you around and secretly film you in the hope of showing you going about some activity that you shouldn't be able to perform in terms of your injury. The film record is admissible as evidence at trial.

On the insurance company investigator's hit list will also be your neighbors, friends, relatives, an ex-spouse, your employer, fellow employees, and anybody with whom you do business regularly.

These people will rarely be told the true reason for the questions they are being asked about your health, financial position, family relationships, or state of mind. Most often, instead, those contacted by the detective will be told that you are the subject of a routine check because you have applied for insurance or for a new job and often that their names were given by you as references. Some of these gumshoes are not above giving the impression they are police officers, government officials, and sometimes FBI agents who want information about you for a "security clearance."

Your financial status will frequently be of interest to your enemy. Were you in deep monetary need at the time of the injury? Had you just been turned down for a bank loan? If so, that might be evidence to suggest—just as any domestic problems you were having might be—that you were worried, preoccupied, at the time of the injury, and as a result probably weren't paying sufficient attention to what you were doing. On such thin grounds, defendants have been known, despite all the concrete evidence against them, to be able to suggest the plaintiff was contributorily negligent, and the defendant, therefore, wins.

There's no way you can stop the insurer from investigating you, but there are some steps you can take to make its job harder.

Obey your doctor's orders concerning physical activities, especially those that might be viewed by outsiders.

You don't know to whom they might be talking. By the same token, don't do any loose talking yourself. Even if it is true, there's no need to regale your friends with stories about how rapidly you have recuperated from your injury; you may hear them telling that on the witness stand, testimony that could have a sharply adverse effect on your pain-and-suffering damages. In personal-injury cases, it's better to be a slow healer than a fast one.

Do not, however, worry about engaging in activities for fear they might look peculiar if an insurance company investigator learns of them, *as long as* they are activities permitted or recommended by your doctor.

His testimony will rebut any allegations that are made. Neither should you worry about engaging in forbidden activities when you have no choice but to perform them (carrying heavy groceries, putting out the trash, etc.). The fact that you were forced to perform hurtful activities adds to your damages; it doesn't subtract from them.

Alert people who might be contacted by the investigator.

Ask them to refuse to answer questions about you from anyone they don't know. If you are doubtful about someone's cooperation, an appeal to self-interest often works; the last thing most people want to do is testify in someone else's case, and you could point out to them (and you won't be lying) that anything they tell the investigator they may have to repeat under oath at your trial.

Ask people to let you know if they have been contacted.

Find out from them the kinds of questions the investigator was asking. Sometimes this will give you a lead about the direction the defense investigation is taking, what it knows and doesn't know, and what it is trying to find out. Report to your lawyer anything you learn along this line. It could help the two of you in plotting your case strategy.

Be alert to the possibility of becoming a victim of subterfuge yourself.

You may, for instance, receive a phone call from someone purporting to represent a well-known polling service and find yourself suddenly answering questions about your hobbies, your health, and your physical activities. The pollster is probably an insurance-company detective. Or the detective may come to your house, representing himself as a government employee who is required to ask you questions because you have been selected for jury duty. Note, for instance, how the following exchange could be used against you:

Q. We don't want anyone serving on a jury who will have to be excused for reasons of illness. How would you describe your state of health?

A. Oh, it's good. Fine.

The way the question was phrased was designed to make you think of "health" in terms of illness. Because you don't consider your injury—perhaps a broken leg—a sickness, and certainly not one that would make it impossible for you to serve on a jury, you answer innocently and truthfully. At trial, however, the defense may be able to show that, just a few months after your accident, you were stating that you had no health disability. Your pain-and-suffering damages are diminished.

When you have a suit pending, therefore, turn away any stranger who seeks personal information from you, or tell that person you will speak only after you have made a credential check. If the party is an insurance investigator, that is the last you'll hear from him (or her; many insurance companies employ attractive young women solely to interview male plaintiffs). Let your attorney know of any unusual contacts. He'll call the insurance company and order them to cease their harassment of you.

Almost invariably, that will be the end of it, at least as far as attempts to trick you personally are concerned.

Always tell your lawyer if there is any event, directly or indirectly associated with your injury, that could embarrass or harm you if revealed.

Insurance companies piously maintain that it is not the purpose of their investigations to turn up scandalous information about plaintiffs to force them to drop their claims, and perhaps they are telling the truth, although it is often difficult to perceive what other purpose some investigations have. In any event, even though the scandalous episode may have ceased prior to the injury, this does not mean that an insurer· can't or won't make use of it.

A defense attorney has a right to ask you questions, either at deposition (see below in this chapter) or at trial, about your activities prior to the accident. They help show your state of mind at the time, providing testimony that could prove fault on your part. This means, for example, that if you are a man and were in the company, immediately before the accident, of a woman who wasn't your wife, there is a real possibility that that information could come out at trial.

Therefore, if the circumstances of your injury, or a *possible* interpretation of a circumstance, is such that you don't want it known either publicly or to members of your family, discuss the problem in detail with your lawyer at the outset of your case. Don't wait, hoping the insurance company won't find out; you had best assume they will. Lawyers are resourceful, and if your attorney is given advance warning of a problem, he will often be able to develop tactics that protect what has to be protected.

THE MEDICAL GUMSHOES

Although, as a plaintiff, you may or may not be subjected to a gumshoe-style investigation of the circumstances of your case, you will almost certainly be subjected to a medical one. You can't object to it. The defense, under the law, has an unchallenged right to choose its doctor to conduct a physical and—when the circumstances of the suit warrant it—a psychological examination of the plaintiff.

The examination usually takes place within a few months of the filing of suit. However, if, as is common, your case drags on for a number of years and you are claiming continuing adverse medical effects, the defense may require a second examination close to the eve of trial.

Insurance companies employ doctors for this purpose. They are handsomely paid. Earnings of $100,000 a year or more just for examining plaintiffs is not uncommon. With this large source of income at stake, it is not surprising that these doctors usually find what their masters want them to find, either that the plaintiff is faking, exaggerating the seriousness of the injuries, or—and this may be most common—that the pain complained of has a source other than the injury.

On this last point the experience of a plaintiff we'll call Mr. Stanley is typical. At the age of fifty, Stanley suffered a broken shoulder in an automobile accident. Although the fracture healed properly, he complained of bursitis pains in the shoulder area. He was examined by an insurance-company doctor, who X-rayed his shoulder and neck. Subsequently, the doctor reported back to the insurer that Stanley was suffering from a severe degeneration of the upper spine that predated his injury and that this condition—not the shoulder fracture—was the cause of his bursitis.

In ordering the X rays of Stanley's neck, the insurance doctor was confident they would show what they did; most people of Stanley's age develop deterioration of the spinal column, the natural result of the wearing of bones against one another over a lifetime. Since, occasionally, this kind of neck condition can produce pains similar to those Stanley was feeling, the doctor provided his employer with a medically reasonable alternative diagnosis for the cause of Stanley's bursitis. He did what he was paid to do, and even though, as a doctor, he might not believe his own diagnosis, he will get more work as a result of it. (The jury may not believe him either; it may decide that it is more logical to think, as Stanley's own doctor will testify, that the bursitis was brought on by the fracture; but that's not the insurance doctor's concern; his insurance-company check is.)

Although, as a plaintiff, there's no way you can forfend happening to you what happened to Stanley, there are steps you can take that will make the insurance-company doctor's task more difficult.

To begin with, your lawyer will never permit you to go to the examination by yourself. He, or one of his associates, will accompany you right into the examination room and stay there with you until it is completed. *When the doctor asks you questions, follow your lawyer's lead.* If he objects to a question, don't you answer it, no matter how innocuous it sounds to you. *Never volunteer information* to the doctor, the receptionist, or the nurse. If you are asked how the accident occurred, you need say nothing more than "an automobile accident," "a fall," or whatever it might be. They have no right to know anything more than that. Remember, if you tell the doctor a version of the accident that is in any way different from the circumstances you are alleging in your suit, the doctor can testify to that in court.

During the course of the examination, the doctor will probably touch those areas of your body in which you are alleging you are suffering pain. Even though the examination does not produce pain at that moment, *you should tell him that he has hit a painful spot.* Otherwise, he will report back to the insurance company that you are presently suffering no pain in the injury area.

The doctor also may examine areas of your body that are unassociated with the injury site. In so doing, he is looking for a medical excuse to claim a non-injury cause of your present difficulties. Don't help him by asserting you feel pain in those areas.

The insurance company's medical examination can also serve another purpose. In conducting it, the doctor will be looking for possible long-term medical effects of the injury, which, if they materialize, could substantially increase your award. When his findings indicate such effects, he won't tell you, but he will tell his employer, who may, as a result, want to try to settle the suit before you become aware of the problems the examination has uncovered. You should therefore be suspicious of any settlement offer that follows a physical examination of you by the defendant's doctor. It is a signal to consult your own doctor.

Your lawyer has a right to demand a copy of the insurance-company doctor's diagnosis. You need not, therefore, fear that his findings will be sprung on you as a surprise at trial.

HOW TO HELP PREPARE YOUR CASE

Your ability to help develop the evidence in your case will be pivotal to its success. From the beginning of your suit onward, one of your jobs will be to document the costs of your injury, both financial and emotional.

The written chronology of the accident you have prepared is a good beginning, but that is all it is. During an accident, events can occur with astonishing rapidity, and it is probable that the main focus of your recollections is on the accident itself. Nevertheless, somewhere inside your memory are all the other events, sensations, emotions, and actions you observed. They must be brought out; the buried moment can be the important one. Sometimes you can do this by going over the events by yourself, but usually the best way is for you and your lawyer to go over the details together, again and again.

Nothing is too insignificant to be mentioned. In one case, for example, it wasn't until her fourth meeting with him that a client finally mentioned to her attorney that just before she was struck by a car she had "the feeling" it was "chasing after me." Her bizarre reaction gave the attorney his first hint—and as it turned out, the first hint the driver had too—that the accident may not have been caused by driver error. As a result, the attorney launched a new investigation that showed evidence of a steering-mechanism failure, allowing him to name the car's manufacturer as defendant. Its insurer eventually settled the case for $150,000, or $100,000 more than would have been available in insurance if the driver had been the defendant found liable. Subsequently, the lawyer asked his client why she had not immediately told him about her feeling that the car was chasing her. She said, "Well, it didn't fit. I knew he wasn't deliberately trying to run me down, and I was afraid you'd think I was just hysterical if I told you something crazy like that." The woman's fear of what her lawyer would think of her had nearly cost her $100,000.

To jog your memory, it is often a good idea to return to the scene of the accident, preferably—if it occurred out of doors—at about the same time of day. By so doing, you may observe environmental details (the presence of a traffic light, an obstruction, a curve in the road) that you were unaware of or had forgotten in the fright of the accident itself. Often, what you see won't be important in itself but—by process of association—will release from your memory information that will prove helpful. Other times, your observations will have a more immediate and dramatic impact, explaining actions on your part that would otherwise make you appear to have been negligent. In one such instance, a woman, upon returning to the scene of the accident, for the first time realized she hadn't started across the street from where she had previously been sure she had, but, rather, ten feet farther along, her memory being refreshed by seeing a mailbox. The difference was the difference between winning and losing her suit. If she had crossed where she thought she had, she probably should have seen the approaching car, but from the mailbox position, her view would have been blocked, just as she had all along maintained.

MEETING THE ENEMY FACE TO FACE

During the pretrial period, the defense has a right to question you, and any witnesses you may have, about the circumstances of your injury. You have the same right to question their witnesses. These question-and-answer sessions will usually take place within a few months after suit is filed and rarely more than a year later. (Both sides see it as being to their advantage to get witnesses while their memories are still fresh.)

The questioning can be written or oral or—in the large majority of cases—both. The written questions, called *interrogatories,* should not be of any worry to you. Your lawyer will tell you exactly how to answer them and which questions not to answer; often he will write the actual responses for you. (The purpose of the interrogatory is to establish those areas of the suit on which there is no dispute; e.g., both sides agree that the injury occurred on such-and-such a date, place, time, that the victim was hospitalized with certain injuries, and so on. Statements made in an interrogatory are admissible as evidence should the case go to trial.)

In minor cases in which there is no serious dispute about the facts, the oral questioning may be omitted. If you are demanding a substantial amount of money in your case, however (and generally anything from $10,000 on up fits that description), you can be just about certain you will undergo this form of grilling, known as a *deposition*.

The deposition will be your first face-to-face meeting with the other side, in the person of its lawyer. It will take place in that lawyer's office, putting you at a psychological disadvantage. You will, however, be accompanied by your lawyer, whose role will be to protect you from having to answer improper questions.

Anything you say at the deposition can be used against you should your case go to trial. Thus, if you give one version of the injury and its medical effects at the deposition but a slightly different one at trial, the defense lawyer can then have a field day with you as he quotes from the transcript of your deposition and asks you whether you were telling the truth under oath at the deposition or whether you are telling the truth under oath now, at trial. The differences don't have to be significant ones; defense lawyers know how to seize on small points and make them seem important, misdirecting the jury from the truth in the process.

But the prospect of the deposition being used against you at trial isn't the only problem that can face you. Plaintiffs have been known, under smart questioning at these sessions, to blurt out, usually without realizing it, admissions of fault. Should that happen to you, your case at best loses much of its dollar value and may be, to all intents and purposes, lost.

Not only bad things can happen to you at deposition; so can good ones. If you acquit yourself well, the defense lawyer may be forced to reevaluate your suit and begin to move, for the first time, toward making you a realistic settlement offer.

The deposition therefore is one of the most crucial battles in which you will engage the enemy; often, it will be the most important. For it, you should be well prepared by your lawyer.

On the same day as the deposition, and never further removed in time than a day or two before it, he should go over with you every question he thinks it likely that you will be asked and the responses you should make. By the end of that briefing, your feeling should be one of confidence. If it is not, or if the lawyer fails to prepare you at all, *refuse to go through with the deposition,* and you should also, at that point, seriously consider changing lawyers. Or, if your attorney is a member of a firm, complain to a senior partner and demand you be briefed by someone who is more knowledgeable.

Eventually, you are going to have to undergo the deposition, but nothing can happen to you by postponing it once. Your lawyer, not you, will just have to make an excuse for your absence.

For a deposition, the following general advice should prove useful.

Answer only what is asked you. Do not add to your answers in order to explain them more fully. It's not your job, and not to your interest, to provide detailed information to the other side. The extended answer, no matter how innocuous it seems to you, can open the way for other, more difficult questions. You may, for instance, have a contributory-negligence problem of which the defense is uncertain; your volunteered answer could provide the defense attorney with the clue he is looking for.

When you don't know the answer to a question, say you don't know it. Don't guess. Your guess could be quoted back to you, to your disadvantage, at trial.

When you don't understand a question, don't respond to it on the basis of what you think it means. Good lawyers often ask vague or ambiguous questions in the hope that they will lead to an admission—or a seeming admission—that can be turned to their advantage at trial. Therefore, never hesitate to ask the lawyer to clarify the question, and don't answer it until you are certain of its meaning. Your lawyer will come to your aid on this.

When your lawyer interrupts a question, don't answer that question. If you have already started to reply, immediately fall silent. Your lawyer's interruption means either that he thinks the question is legally improper or else he senses you are about to say something harmful to yourself, and he wants to give you time to collect your thoughts. In so doing, he will often rephrase the question in a way that will suggest to you—if you listen carefully—how you should respond. Never resume answering a question until and unless your lawyer gives you permission to do so.

Remember that the defense lawyer is your enemy, the major person standing between you and the money you think you deserve. This doesn't mean that you have to worry that he will try to browbeat you at the deposition. That hardly ever happens, and if it should, your own lawyer will quickly put a stop to it. The danger to you is much more likely to rise from the opposite direction. The defense lawyer will almost always be polite; he will be low-keyed, even friendly in his approach, often giving you the impression that he wants to believe you and that if you can convince him of your truthfulness by answering his questions candidly and fully, he will then recommend you be paid. Don't believe it. He's trying to disarm you. He knows from past experience that you are approaching the deposition with trepidation, fearful of an attack, and he hopes that when you realize that's not going to happen, because he's such a fine fellow, that your relief will cause you to become voluble and say things that will hurt your case. Therefore, concentrate always on the questions, not the nice way in which they are asked.

Never engage in a battle of wits with the defense lawyer. No matter how clever you are, you are on his professional turf, and there he's more clever than you. Similarly, never become aggressive; never become apologetic. A display of any of these attitudes is exactly what he is looking for, signals to him that you are the kind of person who can be baited at trial and likely to make a bad impression on a jury.

The final piece of advice encompasses all the others and is the one you should repeat to yourself on the way to the deposition: *Keep your answers brief. What you don't say doesn't have to be unsaid. What you don't explain doesn't have to be unexplained or reexplained at trial.*

6

Winning at Settlement or Trial

With the taking of depositions of all the witnesses in the case, the early battles between you and the defense have come to an end. It's possible there'll be no further ones, that a satisfactory settlement offer will be made almost immediately afterward. But don't count on it. Most of the time you are now in for a wait. It may be only months. It probably will be years.

The key to the delay is the case backlog in the court in which your suit is filed. Until your case makes its way up to the top of that list and is scheduled for trial, the defense has no reason to settle, even though it may know it is going to lose and especially if it thinks it's going to have to pay out a considerable sum. Much better, as the insurer sees it, to hold onto that money as long as possible, earning interest on it by investing it. In some states, an effort has been made to force insurers to settle losing cases quickly, by requiring them to pay a winning plaintiff interest on the award from the date suit was filed. While this provides a nice bonus for you as a plaintiff, these laws generally have not succeeded in accomplishing their goal, primarily because the plaintiff is paid at the going rate of interest, while the insurance company is probably earning at least double that on its investments. (In other words, if they're eventually going to have to pay you 5 percent but they earn 12 percent, why should they settle early and lose the 7 percent?)

Although in the sense of earning money on its money (actually your money), the defense benefits from the holding pattern, there are times when delay is in your interest. The final effects of many injuries don't manifest themselves for several years; or you may require a new operation or a series of them which could help you medically but could also leave you worse off than before. Under circumstances like those, you will not want to hurry your case to a resolution; and even when it reaches the top of the trial list, you may want to obtain continuances until your prognosis can be more accurately determined.

You could, however, also be among those plaintiffs to whom the delay period works a terrible hardship. You might have creditors hounding you for money; or your injuries may be such that you have been unable to work and you're facing bankruptcy or the dole. In your desperation, you will be tempted to urge your lawyer to reopen negotiations to see if there's any way he can get you some money. Often he can, but if you can possibly avoid it, *do not take this step.* As soon as your lawyer goes to the insurance company, it will recognize that you must be in bad financial straits and—far from taking pity on you—it will lick its chops and then offer you a ridiculously low amount. (Incidentally, do not expect your lawyer to tide you over with money while your case is in waiting; even if he were inclined to do so, he is not permitted to loan or give money to a client and could be disbarred if his generosity were discovered.)

There is, however, one judicial process that can sometimes bring a personal-injury suit to settlement quickly—often within a year of the date of its filing—and if yours fits the rules, it is one you should consider using.

HOW TO WIN THROUGH ARBITRATION

Arbitration panels for the disposition of personal-injury suits operate in almost every major metropolitan area in the country and in many less populated districts as well.

With only rare exceptions, cases selected for arbitration are those in which the plaintiff doesn't demand more than a minimum determined by the court system. In some places, only those suits valued at $5,000 or less by the plaintiff (as stated in the suit) are eligible for arbitration, although $10,000 appears to be the most commonly employed cutoff figure. Whatever the established ceiling, the arbitration panel cannot make an award in excess of it. The theory is that by diverting the minor cases into arbitration, the remaining major cases will move to their trial dates more rapidly, and by and large that is what has happened.

An arbitration panel typically consists of three private attorneys usually chosen by the court; they listen to the facts in the suit and then make recommendation for its proper resolution. (For their services, the arbitrators are paid a small sum, usually between fifty and one hundred dollars, allocated from public funds.) Although the findings of these panels are not binding, in about three quarters of all cases they are accepted. When rejected by either side, the case then goes on the trial list, usually at the bottom.

If your case goes to arbitration, you will find that the proceedings are informal compared to those that prevail at trial. The hearing is held in the office of one of the arbitrators, with the participants sitting around a table, the arbitrators at the head of it, the defense and plaintiff teams facing each other. Questions are asked of the various parties by the arbitrators, but there is no direct or cross-examination by the defendant's or plaintiff's attorney. Both sides can submit documents: suit pleadings, interrogatories, depositions, medical records, police records, and the like. The entire process rarely takes more than a couple of hours. Within a month or two, the panel submits its recommendations to the participants and usually to a judge temporarily or permanently assigned to the case.

For you, as a plaintiff, the great virtue of arbitration is the opportunity it gives you to get money quickly when that is to your interest. Should you reject the panel's recommendation, you can continue to negotiate with the other side. At this point, what frequently happens is that although one side or the other, or perhaps both, haven't agreed with the settlement figure recommended by the arbitrators, that amount nevertheless becomes the basis around which the new negotiations revolve, and a settlement usually quickly follows. Should negotiations ultimately fail, at trial a jury can award any amount; it is not bound by the arbitration ceiling.

Occasionally, however, even though your case is the kind that seems suitable for arbitration, your lawyer will want to avoid it, and will do so by having you ask in your suit for an amount of money that is above the arbitration limit. He does this because he recognizes that the insurance company is one that has no intention of settling through arbitration but, rather, is using the process to gain free information about your side of the case. You should also avoid arbitration whenever the final effects of your injury, in medical expenses and income loss, remains unknown.

HERE COMES THE JUDGE

Assuming your case isn't resolved through arbitration or any other step along the way, when it finally gets near the top of the trial list, it will have a judge assigned to it. This could be a judge who is already familiar with it from having ruled on pretrial motions, but, if so, that will usually be a coincidence. (There's one exception: cases filed in federal court are immediately assigned to a judge who stays with the case until the conclusion.)

The first step the judge will take is to call the opposing lawyers into his chambers for a so-called "pretrial settlement conference." Your lawyer will advise you when this is about to occur, and at that point you and he will spend time discussing the minimum figure you are willing to accept to bring your case to an end.

At the conference, the judge won't be particularly interested in the merits of the case. Rather, he wants to find out how far apart you and the other side are and determine if, through his intervention, a compromise can be reached. By so doing, the judge—and the court system—recognize that personal-injury suits are primarily private matters, that they don't have the impact on the security of the community that criminal cases have, and that therefore it's all to the good if they can be settled and not tie up a public courtroom and a judge and jurors who will have to be paid for their time.

If, by the end of the conference, the two sides are still in disagreement, the judge then sets a date for trial, usually one that is only a few weeks or a month in the future. By doing that, he knows he is forcing the issue. From your view, ever since your case started, you have probably been thinking about the day you might be sitting on the witness stand under cross-examination, a prospect that doesn't exactly thrill you but which until now has not seemed dangerous, due to its being sometime in the hazy future. Now it has a palpable date to it, and you may decide—and the judge hopes you will—to lower your demands in order to avoid the witness stand. At the same time, once the trial date is set, the period of profitable delay for the defense is over, and it (which knows the weaknesses of its case, just as you know yours) may well decide that it should increase its offer by a couple of thousand, rather than face the uncertainties and expense of trial. And the judge hopes that's what will happen too.

If the case remains unresolved by the eve of trial, the judge may call the lawyers in for a second conference. There, he may submit some figure he thinks is proper (even though his knowledge of the issues in the case remains dim or nonexistent). Or, as often happens, since the first conference, the lawyers have been seriously negotiating with each other and the difference has narrowed; at that point, the judge may simply urge them to split the difference. Some judges aren't very subtle about the pressures they lay at this time. As one plaintiff's lawyer recalled, "I've had judges say to me and my opponent, 'If you fellows aren't smart enough to talk your clients into settling this case, you know what you can expect the next time you come in front of me.'" This kind of threat may not settle the case then and there, but it often leads to one made literally on the courthouse steps the next day.

WHEN AND HOW TO SETTLE TO YOUR BEST ADVANTAGE

Regardless of the pressure laid by a judge or anyone else, as the plaintiff it is exclusively your decision to accept or reject a settlement offer, whenever and however it is made. You also have the right, in suits in which there is more than one defendant, to accept some offers and reject others. For instance, if you have named four defendants and three of them come up with figures agreeable to you but the fourth doesn't, you can proceed to trial against the fourth defendant alone.

It is always easy to reject a settlement offer that leaves you with little or nothing after your lawyer's bill and other costs have been paid. And it is usually easy to reject one early in the litigation that is substantially below the value you and your lawyer have placed on the case; such offers represent preliminary probes by the defense and will be increased as the trial date nears.

You should, however, always become worried when, *at any time* in the litigational process, your attorney urges you to accept an offer markedly lower than the figure you and he have previously agreed upon. He may have cogent reasons for doing so—such as the development of adverse evidence in your case—but if his explanations are not specific and satisfactory to you, you should consider the possibility that you have become the victim of a quick-settlement *quid pro quo* arrangement between him and the insurer. At that point, if you have a co-counsel, discuss the situation with him. The time may be at hand to change lawyers. This problem, it should be noted, occurs only very rarely and then usually only in cases that involve small amounts of money.

Somewhat more commonly, the *quid pro quo* is one between your lawyer and the defense lawyer. Insurance companies usually assign settlement or trial of a suit to a law firm that specializes in defense work in personal-injury cases. When it does so, the company gives the law firm a maximum figure to which it is allowed to go in making a settlement. One major standard the insurer uses to judge the outside law firm's competence is the amount of money it saves them in settling cases for less than the maximum. Since many law firms compete for this kind of business, the pressure on the one that has it can become substantial. As a result, when your lawyer and the defense lawyer are friendly or have done a sizable amount of business together, the following colloquy can develop:

Defense lawyer: Look, between us, I can go to the $25,000 policy limit on this one, but the company's really been on our backs lately, and we've got to start being heroes and save them some money or we might lose them as a client. XYZ has been promising them the sky [naming a firm that will be tough for the plaintiff's lawyer to deal with].

Plaintiff's lawyer: Them, huh? Well, I'd hate to see you guys lose out. What do you have in mind?

Defense lawyer: Do you think you can get your guy to go for twenty-two five?

Plaintiff's lawyer: No, but make it twenty-three. I can talk him into that.

Defense lawyer: You got a deal, friend. Don't worry; I'll make it up to you later, when the pressure's off.

And he will; you've lost $2,000 that some future, undeserving client will get.

This kind of deal, which almost always develops near trial date, can be almost impossible for you to protect yourself against. You should, however, be suspicious of it when the other side's "final" offer has come very close to the defendant's insurance maximum or when it lacks only one or two thousand dollars of the figure your lawyer has mentioned as a good settlement possibility. Since you can't prove what is happening—and in fact nothing may be happening—never at this point accuse your lawyer of wrongdoing, but you should reject the offer. Don't worry that your action will force the case to trial; you can always back down if you have to. Frequently, however, by taking a strong position at this late stage of the proceedings, you will find that the defense will come up with the extra amount.

Nevertheless, sometimes the final offer made by the defense remains substantially below the amount you have determined to be minimally acceptable, although it is one that does allow you, if you take it, to pay your bills and still have some money for yourself. At that point, the decision facing you can become excruciatingly difficult: Is it a good idea, you will wonder, to take the offer and that way *know* you are getting some money, even if not a satisfactory amount, or should you go to trial, where you might get a great deal more, perhaps tens of thousands of dollars more—dollars will be jumping in your head at this moment—or where you might get less or nothing?

No magic formula exists that, if applied, will lead you inevitably to the right decision. There are, however, factors to be considered, questions to which the most reasonably probable answers must be found, before you make a decision. They include:

What is your lawyer's advice and how much weight should you give it?

Assuming there is no reason to suspect any *quid pro quo* deals as described above, even so, when discussing with your attorney the advisability of accepting a settlement offer, bear in mind that he, like you, has a self-interest. In some senses, his stake in your case is more substantial than yours. Unlike you, he has already invested not only time but perhaps a sizable amount of his own money in furthering your action. By convincing you to accept an offer, he therefore is guaranteeing himself that his time has earned him a fee, that he will recoup his expenses, and that he won't have to venture any further money for witness fees and the like at a trial, in which everything will be lost if he doesn't win. (It is also possible, as we have seen, that your lawyer may be under extreme pressure to settle from a judge whose good will he needs for the future.)

When your lawyer urges you to reject a final settlement offer and take your case to trial, it usually means that in his professional judgment the odds strongly favor your winning a jury verdict substantially higher than the offer. Occasionally, however, a lawyer's recommendation to go to trial is based primarily on his conclusion that the fee he'd earn from the final settlement offer is so inconsiderable that he might as well take a chance on gaining a large fee from a jury verdict, even though there may be no better than a fifty-fifty chance he will win.

Either way, the lawyer's interest and yours are not identical. He, after all, has many cases, all of which can earn him money, whereas you have only your case to earn you money. Therefore, what appears a good gamble for trial to him—or even a nearly sure bet—represents a choice on his part that doesn't carry with it the same degree of risk it does for you, especially if you are faced with thousands of dollars in bills that could be paid if you accepted the settlement but that you have no way of paying if you lose the trial. (And remember, even if you win at trial an amount considerably larger than the settlement offer, you may still have to wait several years before you get your money, should the verdict be appealed. When your need for money is pressing, that is a legitimate consideration.)

Nevertheless, despite the fact that your lawyer's advice—for one reason or another—may not be disinterested, that does not mean it is not valuable. He is both more legally knowledgeable and objective about the merits of your case than you can ever possibly be. He understands not only the technical issues but also the system and the people with whom he is dealing. He probably knows the temperament, the ability, the prejudices of the judge. (Is he pro-plaintiff or pro-defense?) He probably knows the strengths and weaknesses of his lawyer opponent. He knows, better than you do, anyway, how a jury is likely to react to you personally and how believable it will find your story. Your lawyer's hardly likely to tell you when he thinks, from past experience, that you're the kind of plaintiff a jury's not going to find credible, but if he does think that, he's serving your interest as well as his own by guiding you away from trial.

On balance, therefore, assuming you don't have any specific reason to mistrust his judgment, your lawyer's recommendation on a settlement offer should be given primary and positive—but not exclusive—weight in your decision-making process.

What are the implications of the insurance factor?

Your lawyer will recommend and you should ordinarily accept a settlement offer at the face value of the defendant's insurance.

You should turn down the offer and go to trial only when your damages are substantially greater than the insurance amount available *and* you have a strong case on the evidence *and* the defendant has substantial assets that can be readily attached by a judgment for the amount of the verdict that is in excess of the insurance.

What effect will a probable jury verdict have on your award, compared to the award obtainable by settlement?

This can be the single most important determining factor for you. Your lawyer will be able to provide you any necessary figures. Concentrate on the net, not the gross, amounts.

For example: You and your attorney have placed a settlement value on your case of $20,000. The defense's final offer is $15,000. Your attorney has always said he believes that your chances of getting $20,000 at trial range from good to excellent, $25,000 fair, and $30,000 not out of the realm of possibility. His fee is one third if the suit is settled, 40 percent if the case goes through trial. Up to this point in the case, he tells you he has incurred $1,000 in out-of-pocket expenses; should the case go to trial it will be necessary to spend another $1,000 on witness fees. Based on this information, you can now compare the settlement and probable trial net awards:

SETTLEMENT OFFER

Amount	$ 15,000
Less attorney fee @ 33⅓%	− 5,000
Remainder	10,000
Less expenses	− 1,000
Net to You	$ 9,000

TRIAL VERDICT

(Despite your high hopes that a jury will give you a large verdict—and you fear that it will give you a small one or none at all—for these calculations, always work from the most probable jury award as estimated by your attorney in your original discussions.)

Probable trial amount	$ 20,000
Less attorney fee @ 40%	− 8,000
Remainder	12,000
Less expenses	− 2,000
Net to You	$ 10,000

In this example, you should accept the settlement offer. The $1,000 difference you will probably win at trial is not worth the risk.

Obviously, your problem becomes increasingly complicated as the difference between the net settlement award and the net probable jury award widens. However, *it is usually wise to accept a settlement offer from which the net amount you receive comes to within 10–15 percent of the most probable jury award net.*

Before accepting or rejecting a settlement offer, are there any other sources available to you from which the amount of your net award can be increased?

Very often, you can increase the net amount of a settlement offer by striking a deal with a subrogation-claim holder.

Let us suppose you have received a settlement offer of $15,000. After your lawyer's bill and your other expenses have been paid, including a $2,000 reimbursement to Blue Cross on its subrogation claim, your net award will be $7,000. At this point, you should ask your lawyer to contact Blue Cross and tell them you have received an offer that you will probably reject—whether this is so or not—but that you will accept it if Blue Cross will waive half its claim against you.

Blue Cross or any other subrogation holder on which you attempt this squeeze play will probably strongly suspect what you are doing, but the chances are that it will agree anyway. It knows, under the law, that should you take your case to trial and lose, it won't be able to collect a penny from you. Therefore, under the theory that half a loaf is better than none, it makes sense for it to waive part of its claim in order to guarantee it will get the rest of it when you sign the settlement agreement.

Some attorneys recommend that their clients not pay any hospital-insurance subrogation claimant until it can prove that it actually paid the money it claims to have paid. Since insurance plans like Blue Cross pay hospital bills, rather than individual patient bills *per se,* they often find it difficult or impossible to retrieve the necessary proof from their records and will let a disputed claim drop. Before you decide on a refusal to pay on this basis, however, you should discuss all the implications of the action with your attorney.

Sometimes you can increase the net size of your award by making a squeeze play on your own lawyer.

For example, you receive a $15,000 settlement offer and your lawyer tells you he thinks that's the best you can get. You realize that once the lawyer is paid his 40 percent and his out-of-pocket expenses and even after Blue Cross has been whittled down from $2,000 to $1,500, you still are going to net only $6,000. At that point, you tell the lawyer you are dissatisfied and want to reject the offer and go to trial. You indicate that if the offer were better by $1,000 to $2,000 you'd accept it.

Now you have the lawyer in a bind. He may suspect you are bluffing and decide to call you on it, telling you that he's sorry but there's nothing more he can do, so let's go to trial. At that point, you may decide you better back down. However, he also may fear that you aren't bluffing, and knowing the case could be lost at trial or result in an award of less than $15,000, he'll decide it's best to make a deal. He will therefore tell you that he, too, is disappointed in the size of the offer but thinks it should be taken, and to show you the sincerity of his belief, he is going to reduce his fee from 40 percent of the $15,000 to one third. Result: You get an extra $1,000.

It's hard to say what your chances of winning are in this kind of war of nerves against your own lawyer, since apparently very few plaintiffs have ever thought to try it. Several attorneys who were interviewed on this subject, however, agreed they have "occasionally" or "rarely" lowered their share of the prize money to encourage their clients to settle.

HELPING YOURSELF WIN AT TRIAL

When your case goes to trial, it can be decided either by a jury or by a judge. Some lawyers prefer to avoid a jury when the issues are complex legally, when they fear their client may incur jury bias, when they think they have a favorable judge, or when the judge has an outstanding reputation. However, since both sides must agree before the right to jury is waived, and since what strikes one side as favorable will usually be viewed unfavorably by the other, the overwhelming likelihood is that your case will be decided by jury, rather than judge, verdict.

The size of the jury depends on the rules of the jurisdiction in which you live. Twelve is the maximum; six is the minimum. The jury ordinarily won't have to agree unanimously on its verdict.

Either three-quarters agreement or one less than unanimity is common.

While the jury is being chosen, you will be present, sitting at a table next to your lawyer. Usually the judge won't be there. Both your lawyer and one for the defense are permitted to question prospective jurors in order to weed out those who may be prejudiced. Your lawyer normally will consult with you before deciding to "challenge" (i.e., dismiss) a prospective juror. Challenging jurors is hardly an exact science. Often it is based on nothing more than a hunch. However, ordinarily you won't want on the jury someone who works in the same business as the defendant or someone who has earlier been a defendant in a personal-injury suit. When the defendant is a large corporation, you will probably prefer a working-class jury to one that consists largely of executives. But even these seemingly reasonable standards don't always work out. The person who was once a defendant may feel he was mistreated by his lawyer or insurance company and will see your case as a chance to get even; the person who works in the same business as the defendant may be aware of practices in that business that he knows made your injury more likely, and so on.

One time you should *always* instruct your lawyer to challenge a prospective juror is when you recognize that you know the juror or that the juror is known to someone in your family or social circle. The presence of such an individual on a jury is inherently prejudicial to the other side and could lead to a reversal of a verdict in your favor if the defendant learns of it.

From the beginning of your trial on through to the end of it, *never* speak to a juror inside or outside the courtroom. *Never* discuss your case with your lawyer or anyone else where a juror could hear you. Either event could lead to the judge's declaring a mistrial, meaning that your case goes back on the new trial list and may not be heard again for many more months or even years. It is also possible, although this happens only under extreme circumstances, that by speaking to a juror you could be charged with the crime of jury tampering.

You also want to protect your own interests. Therefore, should you see someone from the other side contact a juror, immediately tell your attorney.

Beginning with the jury-selection process and continuing through the trial, it is a good idea to adhere to the following rules concerning appearance and deportment:

Dress conservatively.
Men should wear jacket and tie, the more muted the better. Women should wear skirts or dresses. Liberal-minded jurors aren't going to be upset about a conservative appearance, but conservative ones may develop a prejudice against a flashy or sloppy dresser.

Do not wear expensive-looking clothing or jewelry.
This doesn't mean that you want to appear like a denizen of Poverty Row—that could rouse the ire of a juror who thinks the world is full of welfare bums—but neither do you want to look as though you live in a penthouse before a group of people who are going to decide how much money they want to give you.

Don't chew gum.

Try not to appear nervous.
This advice holds true both when you are on the witness stand and when you are sitting next to your attorney. If the jurors were in your place, they'd be nervous too, but they aren't in your place and they are likely to interpret overt signs of nervousness as an indication you think your case is weak. Therefore, don't drum your fingers on the table; don't drink a lot of water (a sure giveaway); and if your palms are sweating, let them sweat or, if you dry them off, do it in such a way that the jurors can't see you do it.

Treat evidence damaging to your case calmly.
While this advice is more easily given than acted upon, it is important. When the jurors suspect that the defense has brought out a good point against you through one of its witnesses, their natural reaction is to glance at you to see how you are taking it. That's the time for you to be maintaining a calm, unconcerned expression. Never, at that point, begin to whisper frantically to

your lawyer, and never overreact by smiling at the bad news; that's what boxers do when they have been hurt in the ring, and the jurors will recognize your grin for the giveaway it is. (You will, incidentally, have been prepared for the introduction of damaging evidence by your lawyer before the trial begins; that's a good time for you to begin practicing your poker face.)

Always appear attentive.
Considering the monetary stake you have in the proceedings, this would seem to be unnecessary advice; nevertheless, not only can some parts of a trial become boring, but some plaintiffs develop bad body-language signs that make them appear inattentive even though they may not be. If you don't seem interested in what is going on, the jurors will wonder why they should be, or they may take your apparent lack of interest as a signal they need not pay attention, and an important point in your favor could get lost that way. Therefore: don't slouch; don't doodle; try to avoid yawning; don't look at your watch; don't stare at the ceiling or off into space.

On the witness stand

The foregoing advice holds true at every point during the trial. When you are on the witness stand, there are additional rules you should follow.

Before stating them, it is necessary first to set the stage. As the prosecutor in the case, your side is heard first, after your attorney and the defense attorney have made their introductory statements to the jury. This means you have the opportunity, through your testimony, to impress the jury with your truthfulness before the other side can put on any of its witnesses. The impression you leave with the jury is one that, consciously or subconsciously, will be the criterion by which they judge later testimony. The more favorable the impression you have made, therefore, the more likely they are to resist the later adverse testimony. (One good way, incidentally, to prepare for your trial is to attend someone else's. Just by watching, you will familiarize yourself with procedures and feel more comfortable with a courtroom setting when your day arrives. Your lawyer will know how to locate a personal-injury trial for you to watch and be able to answer any questions you might have about it.)

Your testimony will consist of several parts: First, on what is called direct examination, your lawyer will ask his friendly questions designed to bring out your case in its best possible light. Next, the defense attorney will cross-examine you. Once he is done, your attorney is allowed redirect examination, giving you the opportunity to explain points that appear to have damaged you on cross-examination. After that is concluded, the defense attorney is permitted a recross examination but only on points covered by your lawyer on redirect. Finally, at any time during the attorney questioning, the judge may intervene and ask you questions of his own, usually because he thinks the jury requires clarification on some point.

The chances are overwhelming that you will be nervous when you testify, no matter how certain you are of the righteousness of your cause. It is important, however, that you control your nerves, and one of the best ways to be able to do this is to have rehearsed with your lawyer the questions he is going to ask and those the defense is likely to raise. Keep these question-and-answer sessions going until you, not your lawyer, are confident of your ability to answer almost any question that could be put to you. You also have the right to study the transcript of your testimony at deposition, and you should do so. You almost certainly will be asked questions from it.

When you are on the witness stand under questioning by your lawyer, listen to him carefully. Sometimes, despite himself, he will ask a question somewhat differently than planned, and you don't want the jury to hear you giving an answer to a question from your own lawyer that isn't directly responsive to the question itself. Also, the defense lawyer may object to a question, and if he is successful your lawyer will have to find a way to rephrase it if the answer is important to your case. Concentrate on the rephrasing so that your answer doesn't sound as though it were given by rote.

Your lawyer will probably have a signal system worked out with you. Perhaps he will tell you that whenever he says, "Thank you," it means that you are to stop your response with what you have just said. Obey that signal. Never meander on, regardless of how brilliant your next remark seemed to you in prospect. Your lawyer is trying to keep you out of trouble. He knows that, most often, it is the volunteered or unnecessary answer, the one that goes beyond the question, that gets the client into trouble on cross-examination.

While your lawyer will probably have a good idea of the questions the defense is going to put to you, he can't know all of them, the order in which they will be asked, or how they will be phrased. Thus, his pretrial preparation of you will help you and give you a measure of confidence, but on cross-examination you are largely on your own.

The advice given in Chapter Five in connection with how you should handle yourself at deposition has analogous applications to cross-examination at trial. If you don't understand a question, ask that it be repeated, and if it is still unclear to you, the judge will ask the lawyer to rephrase it. When your lawyer objects to a question, stop what you are saying immediately. Do not answer unless you are directed to by the judge. Use the time, while the merits of the objection are being argued, to collect your thoughts. Your lawyer may have raised the objection solely for that reason.

When you don't know the answer to a question, say that you don't know it. Obviously, however, if you have already answered a similar question on your direct examination or at deposition, you cannot have a convenient lapse of memory on cross-examination. Or if you do, be prepared to accept the probability that the defense lawyer is going to leap on the discrepancy and your case will be damaged as a result.

Never engage in a battle of wits with the opposing attorney. Above all, never assume that when he asks a question, he is trying to trick you. He may be, but try to answer the question asked as best you can. By hesitating in order to speculate on the hidden meaning of a question, you may make the jury think you are being evasive.

Ordinarily, you will be permitted to explain an answer. Some lawyers will attempt to force a yes or no answer from you when it is impossible to accurately respond in that manner. When this happens, turn to the judge and ask him if he will allow you to continue your answer. If he rules that you can't, you have at least alerted your lawyer to questions he may want to ask you on redirect examination. But don't get upset if he doesn't. He may be aware that by allowing you to finish an answer, he is opening the door to other questions that could harm you.

It is probable that at some point in the cross-examination, the defense lawyer in a vaguely accusatory tone will ask you if you have gone over your testimony with anyone. Or he may ask you if you have read your deposition transcript prior to testifying. Don't try to evade these questions; in neither event did you do anything wrong. Simply answer, "Yes, my attorney and I discussed my testimony," and "Yes, I read my deposition testimony." Since you don't seem upset about saying that, the jury won't take any negative inferences from it.

Finally, remember that the worst that can happen to you as a result of cross-examination is that your case is weakened. You're not going to be thrown into jail for making apparently contradictory or unbelievable statements. Remember, too, that by the time your lawyer has had his opportunity on redirect examination of you and on cross-examination of the defense witnesses, the apparent weaknesses the defense has brought out in your case may become minor or nonexistent.

No matter who is doing the questioning, try to follow these guidelines:

Keep your voice up.

Nothing is more annoying to a jury than to have to strain to hear what a witness is saying, and they may eventually give up, greatly to your detriment. To combat the problem of the faint-voice witness, some courtrooms come equipped with witness-stand microphones. If that's true in your case, speak directly toward it but don't breathe into it or hunch yourself over in an effort to reach it; if it's not picking up your voice, a court attendant will see to it. Whether you are equipped with a microphone or not, try not to allow your voice to rise in answer to some questions and become tiny or mumbled in answer to others. Jurors are going to assume that the indistinct answer indicates a question you don't want to answer, or fear, and that is not an impression you ever want to give them.

Maintain eye contact with the jury.
Preferably, responses should be directed toward the jury, not the questioner. The jurors are not only listening to what you have to say but trying to decide what kind of person you are, and your willingness to look at them, especially when the going gets tough, will be a score in your favor. While this is generally good advice, don't follow it if it forces you to do something that is unnatural to you. Some people are comfortable in responding to questions only by looking at the person who is doing the asking, and if that is true of you, do it.

Correct your own mistakes.
It is possible, during either direct or cross-examination, that you may make a response to a question that is incorrect or likely to be misleading. You should immediately say, "May I correct what I have just said?" and then do so. It is far better you do this than wait and hope the defense attorney won't catch you up on it. If he does, he'll probably succeed in making you look like a liar.

Try to give definitive answers.
When you know the facts, don't couch them with phrases such as "I think that's what happened" or "In my opinion" or "Probably." Such qualifiers, which some people fall into the habit of using when they don't mean to, dilute the effectiveness of testimony.

Don't feign your emotions.
Some plaintiffs, when they get around to explaining how their injury occurred or describing the terrible pain and suffering they underwent, feel they should display the appropriate emotional response. If those emotions come pouring out of you without your willing them, don't worry about it; it's more likely to help than harm you. However, you'd best assume that the jury is going to be able to spot any theatrics on your part. If they do, they're going to hold them against you.

(More specifics on how you develop and give your testimony are discussed in the chapters that follow on damages. See especially the advice on pain and suffering testimony in Chapter Ten.)

A new settlement offer

This happens not infrequently during the course of a trial, and is most likely to be made after you have completed putting on your case and before the defense begins its. (Sometimes, however, a settlement offer will be made while the jury is debating its verdict.)

The new settlement figure—whether it's higher or the same as a previous offer; it will hardly ever be lower—will be proposed to your attorney by the defense attorney and take place outside the jury's hearing, sometimes in the judge's chambers with the judge present.

Rely on your attorney's advice as to whether or not you should accept the offer. You may be in for a bitter disappointment if he tells you to reject it and the jury comes in with less or nothing, but he's much more competent than you are to judge how the trial is progressing and what your odds are for an award larger than the offer.

There is, however, one rule of thumb that can sometimes be applied when the new offer is higher than any previous one: Strongly consider accepting it when it moves within 10–15 percent of your original maximum settlement demand. In other words, if you had been asking for $30,000 and the defense was offering $15,000 and is now offering $25,000 or more, you probably should take the money and run.

You and the defense case

After you have rested your case, and assuming it is not then settled, the defense puts on its witnesses. At this point, with your harrowing experience as a witness on your own behalf behind you, you may be tempted to relax. Don't. The jury can still see you, will still be making judgments of you.

Although your main duty at this time is to retain a calm, alert and poker-faced countenance, you can also use your time profitably by engaging in covert psychological warfare against the enemy. You do that by riveting your attention on each defense witness, focusing your unrelenting gaze on the witness's eyes. Most witnesses will find your stare disconcerting, especially if they aren't telling the truth. The more conscious you make them of you, the more nervous they become, their concentration disrupted. Since the jurors have no way of knowing what is causing the ill ease, they may decide it indicates the witness is evasive or untruthful; score one for your side.

When the defense concludes its case—and it will have been attempting to prove either that the defendant wasn't responsible for your injury or that you were partly responsible or that your injuries aren't as serious as you claim, or some combination of all three—then the time has arrived for your side to put rebuttal witnesses on the stand. That usually means you.

Your testimony this time will be considerably shorter than on your original appearance, often no more than five or ten minutes. In it, your lawyer may ask you to respond to allegations the defense has made. The defense is then permitted to cross-examine you, but only on those issues your lawyer has raised. By keeping away from areas where your case is particularly vulnerable, your lawyer thereby prevents the defense attorney from getting in a second lick at you. Your rebuttal testimony is your chance to make a final favorable impression on the jury, and you should consider it as the opportunity it is.

Once both sides have rested, the lawyers make their closing speeches to the jury. During his speech, the defense lawyer will almost certainly attack your credibility and try to recapitulate your testimony in the worst possible light. As he does this, the jury will be watching you for your reactions. Try to show none.

Then the judge takes over. He explains the applicable law to the jurors and gives them general instructions on how to weigh evidence ("If you believe this, you may infer that," and so on.) He tells them the questions they must answer to reach a verdict, and if the case is complex, they may be provided with an *interrogatory* sheet to help them. (For an example of a jury interrogatory, see pp. 102–3.)

The jury then retires and determines whether or not the defendant is liable, and if so, how much money to give the plaintiff.

However, in some jurisdictions, including federal courts, that is not what happens. These places provide for a so-called *bifurcated* trial. In it, the jurors first hear evidence on the cause of the injury and reach a verdict on liability. When that verdict favors the plaintiff, only then is evidence permitted about the costs of the injury; once that's completed, the jury retires a second time and decides on the amount of money to award. In a bifurcated trial, therefore, quite apart from any rebuttal testimony, you could have to testify two separate times, first to the facts of the injury and then, if you win on that score, on its effects.

Although this will happen only rarely, a jury's verdict in a personal-injury case (unlike a criminal one) can in most places be reversed by the trial judge as to the verdict or to the amount when the judge considers the award excessive.

A verdict, or a judge's reversal of it, can be appealed by either side. Grounds for appeal include, but are not limited to, issues of liability (the jury's decision was contrary to the facts or the law), size of the award (too large or too small), error by the judge in permitting or forbidding evidence into admission, error by the judge in the charge to the jury, and abuse of judicial discretion in changing the jury's verdict.

When a case is appealed, the court that hears it is called, in most states, the Superior Court. The decision of this intermediate court can be further appealed to the state's highest court, usually called the Supreme Court. (In New York, for reasons that defy logic, the lowest court is called the Supreme Court, and the highest court is called the Court of Appeals.) In federal cases, appeals are taken from the district court to the circuit court of appeals and ultimately to the United States Supreme Court.

Although every plaintiff and defendant has an absolute right to appeal before an intermediate court, neither the United States Supreme Court nor the highest court of any individual state is *required* to accept an appeal in a personal-injury case. Before it will do so, it must be convinced, on the basis of arguments—written or oral—made by the appellant that the case raises constitutional issues or matters of significant public or legal import that were ignored or improperly adjudicated by the intermediate court.

(How this is done varies from state to state, but typically, if the highest court has seven members, at least three of them must be convinced that a valid issue exists, before the entire court will agree to hear the appeal.)

In deciding whether or not you should appeal a losing case or one in which you think the award was insufficient, remember that, even when you have sufficient technical grounds for the appeal, the odds are against your winning, and the same is true for the defense when they appeal. Generally, although with the major exception of punitive damages, which will be discussed in the next chapter, appeals-court judges hold to the primacy of the jury as the finder of fact, and even when they disagree with the verdict will uphold it unless they believe an error of such magnitude occurred that the jury could not have reached a proper decision because of it.

When the appeals process ends in your favor, you are then entitled—almost everywhere—to a payment of interest, at the going bank rate in your community, by the defendant beginning from the date of the original verdict and concluding with the date the check is sent to you. (As noted earlier, in some places you are also entitled to interest from the date you filed the successful suit.) Make sure the interest money is included when your lawyer is dividing the proceeds with you.

Your case is most likely to conclude satisfactorily for you when you and your lawyer, from the very beginning of your association, have done a good job of developing and documenting what are known as your damages. These will be discussed in the next four chapters.

INTERROGATORIES TO THE JURY*

1. Was defendant XYZ Swim Pools, Inc., negligent?

    Yes ——— No ———

2. If you answered ※1 "YES," was this a "substantial factor" or a "substantial contributing factor" in bringing about the accident?

    Yes ——— No ———

3. Were the pool, deck, fencing or instruction manuals defective when they left the possession of XYZ Swim Pools, Inc.?

    Yes ——— No ———

4. If you answered ※3 "YES," was this a "substantial factor" or a "substantial contributing factor" in bringing about the accident?

    Yes ——— No ———

5. If you answered ※4 "YES," did the pool, deck, fencing or instruction manuals undergo substantial change, other than change contemplated by the instructions, after it left ABC Corporation?

    Yes ——— No ———

6. Did XYZ Swim Pools, Inc., expressly warrant that it would supply a pool with deck and fencing to encircle the pool completely?

    Yes ——— No ———

7. If you answered ※6 "YES," did XYZ Swim Pools, Inc., breach this warranty?

    Yes ——— No ———

8. If you answered ※7 "YES," was this a "substantial factor" or a "substantial contributing factor" in bringing about the accident?

    Yes ——— No ———

* When cases are complicated, such as this one involving an injury allegedly caused by a faulty protective fence around a home swimming pool, jurors are often given questionnaires to help them sort out the issues. (The

9. Was defendant ABC Corporation negligent?
   Yes —— No ——
10. If you answered ✻9 "YES," was this a "substantial factor" or a "substantial contributing factor" in bringing about the accident?
    Yes —— No ——
11. Were the pool, deck, fencing or instruction manuals defective when they left the possession of ABC Corporation?
    Yes —— No ——
12. If you answered ✻11 "YES," was the defect a "substantial factor" or a "substantial contributing factor" in bringing about the accident?
    Yes —— No ——
13. If you answered ✻12 "YES," did the pool, deck, fencing or instruction manuals undergo substantial change, other than change contemplated by the instructions, after it left ABC Corporation?
    Yes —— No ——
14. Was defendant DEF negligent?
    Yes —— No ——
15. If you answered ✻14 "YES," was this a "substantial factor" or a "substantial contributing factor" in bringing about the accident?
    Yes —— No ——
16. Was plaintiff John or Mary Doe, or both, negligent?
    Yes —— No ——
17. If you answered ✻16 "YES," was this a "substantial factor" or a "substantial contributing factor" in bringing about the accident?
    Yes —— No ——
18. If you answered ✻3 "YES," did John and Mary Doe know before the accident that the defect was dangerous and voluntarily choose to encounter the danger?
    Yes —— No ——

---

names of the plaintiffs and defendants in the suit have been changed; the plaintiffs, incidentally, won.)

7

Damages Equal Money

Your damages are the total sum, expressed in dollars, of the harm —financial, physical, and emotional—that you claim your injury has caused you.

As a successful plaintiff, you are entitled to be paid not only for your damages up until the time your suit is resolved but also for reasonably likely future costs.

During the litigation of your suit, your lawyer will ask you many questions about your damages. The better the lawyer the more probing and detailed will be the questions. But even the best lawyer is not a mind reader. What you don't tell him he can't know, and what he doesn't know could cost you money.

However, it won't always be your fault that the lawyer doesn't get as much information from you as he should. Some lawyers, probably the majority of them, spend an insufficient amount of time explaining damages to their clients. Often a lawyer will *think* he has made an ample explanation, but in so doing he has couched it in the kind of dense legal terminology that even the most sophisticated lay person can't be expected to understand, or, if understood, can't be expected to retain over the years that the case will drag on.

To help you understand how damages work, the first task, therefore, is to clear up the lawyer jargon.

You need be concerned, in the overwhelming majority of personal-injury cases, with just two grounds for damages. One is called *special* damages. The other is called *general* damages. Both are misnomers.

Special damages (or "specials," as your lawyer is likely to call them) do not, as the term would seem to indicate, have any relationship to unusual or extraordinary events in your case. Rather, special damages are those items which, under the law, must be documented (i.e., "specially" proved) before you can collect money for them. They include the income losses and medical expenses your injury caused you.

General damages, despite the name, are quite specific in their categories too. They include the pain and suffering from your injury and any accompanying mental anguish.

By their nature, general damages can't be documented in dollar terms. There is, after all, no mathematical system by which a pricetag can be put on your pain, no way to translate your suffering into dollars, no way to say you had a dollar's or a million dollars' worth of fear (mental anguish) as a result of your injury. Nevertheless, as the law sees it, when people have been wrongfully injured, it is the duty of the wrongdoers to make the victims "whole," that is, restore them to the position they were in, and that they reasonably would have been expected to enjoy in the future, had not the injury intervened. Since one's pain, suffering, and anguish can be as important a disruption to one's enjoyment of life as any financial costs from an injury, the law therefore dictates that the successful plaintiff be paid for these damages just as for the special ones. How that is done is up to the negotiating lawyers, or, at trial, a judge or jury.

If your case is settled, the final award might be only for the amount of the special damages your lawyer and the other side can agree is accurate. This usually happens, however, only when your case is a very weak one. When the opponent thinks you have a fair to good chance of winning at trial, there will be an extra amount for your general damages, a figure that, in small cases, can sometimes magically coincide with your lawyer's fee. However, in some strong cases with terrible injuries, the general damage award by settlement has exceeded a million dollars.

When negotiations fail and the case goes to trial, any award the jury gives you for your special and general damages is ordinarily made in a lump sum, so that you won't know how much you were given for each item separately.

Occasionally, you may be eligible for another award, one that is made separately from the general and special damages. This is called a *punitive* damage award.

Unlike the other damage terminology, punitive damages mean what they seem to mean. Their purpose is to punish the defendant, in part so that others will be deterred from doing the same thing. For this reason, punitive damages are sometimes called *exemplary,* i.e., to make an example of the defendant. To be eligible for punitive damages, the defendant must have acted in some particularly vicious, heinous, or grossly negligent way toward you. Probably more than nine of every ten punitive awards of any substantial size are made against large corporations, such as an automobile manufacturer that, through gross negligence, sells cars that have exploding gas tanks. The legal difference between gross and simple negligence, however, is probably most easily explained at a more commonplace level. Let us suppose you have been injured by a carelessly driven car; that is simple negligence. However, suppose further that the driver, after hitting you, drives off without offering aid or calling for a doctor, leaving you lying in the street; that is gross negligence.

Since punitive-damage awards can become very large—one recent one was for eight million dollars—you may hope that your lawyer will be able to get at least a bite of that kind of money for you. The chances are, however, that even if your case seems to merit a punitive award, your lawyer will not make a demand for it.

He may not tell you why, but he has good reason for making that decision. To begin with, when, as a plaintiff, you ask for a punitive award, the judge must then explain to the jury the difference between gross and simple negligence. Depending on the judge, that could be a confusing explanation, and if the jury decides the defendant's actions didn't rise to gross negligence, it could forget that the defendant was guilty of simple negligence and either not make an award to you at all or a much smaller one than you otherwise would have gotten. Secondly, as your lawyer should know, punitive-damage awards—especially those made against corporations or institutions such as hospitals—are almost invariably reversed on appeal. Judges, probably because most of them are pro-business, disapprove of punitive awards and will use any excuse they can find to set one aside. Thirdly, *punitive awards are never covered by insurance,* meaning it may be impossible for you to collect one when you get it. It would indeed be an ironic conclusion to your case if you got a punitive award that you can't collect, while the general-damage award—which you can collect, because it is covered by insurance—is made small because the jury thought it was taking care of you with the punitive award.

Therefore, don't become suspicious of your lawyer or think he's not doing the proper job for you because he tells you he doesn't think you should ask for a punitive award. His refusal doesn't mean he won't make use of the "punitive" elements in your case. He will. However, he will do it by regaling the jury with them in terms of the (insurance-covered) pain and suffering and mental anguish that these terrible events caused you. Like you, he wants to be able to collect on the money he wins, and by doing it that way, he will, and so will you. (This doesn't mean that there can never be legitimate grounds for a punitive demand—it may be the principal grounds for an award involving an intentionally inflicted injury—but, rather, that in the average case it is most likely to be counterproductive and is a demand you should never force on your lawyer when he doesn't want to make it.)

HOW SPECIAL DAMAGES ARE COMPUTED

Assuming you can meet the tests for proof that will be discussed later, your medical damages will be based on their cost, not on the amounts you have paid personally. Thus, your medical damages can include unpaid bills, bills you have no intention of paying, and bills that have been paid by others. For instance, you might have had $2,000 in medical expenses that were paid by your employer or by a relative, with neither party expecting to be reimbursed. Even so, you can claim the $2,000 as a medical expense.

Probable future medical expenses are normally based on percentage of likelihood. For example, if your doctor testifies there is a 50-percent chance you will eventually require an operation to relieve the aftereffects of an injury and that the operation will cost $2,000, you can make a $1,000 future-medical-expense claim. (The fact that an operation that costs $2,000 today might cost $3,000 by the time you require it is not admissible; awards for future medical bills are made on their current cost.) Should you never undertake the operation, that is nobody's business but your own. You never have to repay part of an award because you didn't use the money for the purpose for which it was given.

Medical bills you incur as part of the preparation of your case cannot be considered part of your damages. Excluded would be any examination your doctor gave you on the eve of trial to help bring his medical records up to date, also X rays or laboratory tests ordered at that time, also any witness fee you pay that doctor or any other doctor. X rays and other tests that were taken primarily to provide treatment for you are legitimate medical expenses even if the results of those tests are introduced as evidence at your trial.

Your income damages are computed on a gross-loss basis. Thus, if at the time of the injury you are earning a salary of $300 a week, with a take-home pay of $220, and you lose ten weeks' work, your loss of income is $3,000, not $2,200.

Awards for probable future loss of income are reduced to prevent overcompensation.

To explain, assume that, at the time of the injury, you were earning $20,000 a year and expected to work for another thirty years. The injury leaves you totally disabled. Discounting any other factors that might affect your future income, this means that you have lost at least $600,000 ($20,000×30 years).

However, should a jury award you $600,000 and you put that money in an ordinary savings account at 5 percent interest, you would earn $900,000 in simple interest alone, or a total of $1.5 million, over the thirty years, rather than the $600,000 the jury wanted you to have. The judge, consequently, will order the jury to reduce your award so that at the end of the thirty years, in principal and interest, it will produce $600,000. In the example given, your actual award would be around $300,000.

Since making the necessary computations are beyond the ability of jurors, to say nothing of lawyers and judges, an actuary will have to testify to show the proper reduction, with the going bank interest rate the one ordinarily used as the basis.

This so-called "reduction to present value" rule may not be a fair one—considering the probability that inflation, in terms of buying power, will reduce the $600,000 to $300,000 on its own in much less than thirty years—but it is the law almost everywhere.

The picture, however, is not quite so bleak as it might seem. As with your other income-loss awards, the one for future loss is based on probable gross earnings. Thus, a $30,000 award for future loss of income is $30,000 in spendable money, whereas if you had earned that same amount at work, you might have, after tax deductions, only $20,000 to spend.

HOW SPECIAL DAMAGES CREATE GENERAL DAMAGES

When, sometime early in your relationship with him, your lawyer tells you how much he thinks your case is worth, you may wonder how he arrived at that figure. Does he have a formula? Is he just guessing? Or is he going by experience, both his own and that of other lawyers, in order to come up with the figure?

The answer—usually—is some combination of all three. At the heart of his calculations, however, almost always are those documentable special damages.

They play their most significant role in suits that are settled by private negotiation. The main reason most suits are settled is the fear—shared by both sides—of what will happen if there is a trial. The key to the fear is the jury. Why juries come to the decisions they do is a mystery to lawyers, judges, and clients alike. In terms of the amount of the award, anyway, it is probably also a mystery to most jurors. As one was quoted as saying about a verdict: "I don't really know how we came to that figure. It just sort of grew."

Two cases studied in connection with this book point up what can happen. In the first, the plaintiff had less than $2,000 in medical bills and about $1,000 in loss of wages, and there was no evidence of gross negligence or of any other kind of aggravating circumstance in the causation of the injury, nor even unusual pain and suffering by the victim. Yet this plaintiff got a jury verdict of $35,000. In the second case, the plaintiff had $18,000 in documented medical bills, nearly $6,000 in loss of income, and severe and long-lasting pain and suffering. Yet this plaintiff received an award of only $26,000; he had earlier rejected a settlement offer of $50,000.

It is this unpredictability of jurors, especially in terms of the size of their awards, that makes both sides eager to settle cases privately. But, if lawyers have no way of predicting what a jury will do with a case when it goes to trial, how can they decide what a fair settlement figure will be, in order to avoid trial?

The question admits of no logical answer, but that doesn't mean that an answer hasn't been found. Although many lawyers deplore it and try to avoid it when they can, a system has developed for calculating settlements that is in use across the country. By understanding the system, you can evaluate the cash worth of your case for yourself and continue to revise that estimate as time goes on and new damage evidence develops.

The system is predicated on the assumption that—even though no one knows what any individual jury will do—the *average* jury, in making an award, will take the provable special damages and multiply them by some figure in order to come up with the total award. Although there is no credible evidence that even some juries perform this kind of bizarre mathematics, insurance-company actuaries think they do, and since it is their employers' money that is at stake in a suit, what they think is important.

There are two principal variations. One can be called the $3\times$ system, the other the $5\times$ system.

The $3\times$ system has the appeal of simplicity if nothing else. With it, to determine the basic settlement value of your case, multiply your special damages by three. Thus, if you had $3,000 in medical bills and $2,000 in loss of income, your case is "worth" $15,000.

In the $5\times$ system, the medical damages alone are multiplied by five and then all the specials are added to the product, giving a plaintiff with $3,000 in medical bills and $2,000 in income loss a case with a settlement value of $20,000 ($3,000$\times$5+$3,000+$2,000).

there can be extras for you. The most common is overtime pay. Any overtime you were earning—or were likely to be earning—and didn't earn because of your injury is a ground for compensation. Similarly, if you are allowed by your doctor to work regular hours but not allowed to work overtime for a given number of weeks or months, the overtime you lose during that period is compensable. To prove loss of overtime earnings, you *don't* have to show that you personally would have gotten the extra wages, only that it was available to other employees in your general job category during your injury and recuperation period.

By the same reasoning, if you were holding two jobs at the time of your injury and you can now continue—temporarily or permanently—with only one of them, the money you didn't earn from the second job is an income loss. In one case, a man was employed as an accountant at $400 a week for one company and as a part-time bookkeeper for a second company at $75 a week. His full-time employer paid his salary while he couldn't work, but the part-time employer didn't, and he lost twenty weeks of earnings from that source. His income loss, therefore, was $1,500 (20 weeks×$75).

Any money you would have earned from tips is also compensable. Your income-tax records will offer sufficient proof. If, however, you were injured shortly after beginning the tip-producing job, you may not have such a record; in that event, a jury will probably accept your estimate if it seems reasonable, although testimony from others in the same job about their tip earnings will be very helpful to you.

The fact that you don't return to your old job, even if you are capable of doing so, following your injury has no legal bearing on your right to claim the income loss whether from salary or any other source. The law's assumption is that you would have continued on that job during the recuperation period. Even had you already given notice of quitting or were about to be laid off when the injury occurred, you can still claim the loss on the basis that, had it not been for the injury, you would have been able to obtain other employment at least at the same income level. The same argument holds true if your employer went out of business during the injury period. However, if you had already left work and the defense can somehow show that you had no intention of resuming employment at the time of the injury, then you have no provable income loss.

Did you lose your job because of your injury?

This usually comes about in one of two ways: either you are unable to resume your old job due to your injuries or else your employer was forced to hire someone to replace you and now there is no opening for you. Your ex-employer's testimony on this point will be important for you in proving this allegation, as will medical testimony about the temporary or permanent effects of your injury in terms of your ability to work. Do not worry about the possibility that you might have been fired anyway or laid off because of cutbacks. The law isn't concerned about what might have happened had there been no injury, only what did happen because there was one. Ordinarily, earnings from any new job you get will be deducted from those you would have gotten from the job you lost. The law gets complicated here, however, sometimes to your benefit; see the discussion of the impact of reduced earning capacity due to an injury, later in this chapter.

When your injuries are such that you are unable to resume work at all, your income damages are based on the amount you would have earned until time of retirement. In most states, that is still the age of sixty-five. Thus, if you were earning $15,000 a year when you were permanently injured at the age of fifty-nine, your gross loss of income from your injury is $90,000, an amount that will be reduced, as we saw in the previous chapter, to cover future interest earnings on the lump-sum award.

As a consequence of your injury, did you lose fringe benefits?

This can be an excellent source for showing income loss. Take Mr. Fiedler as an example. He had worked for the XYZ Company for eighteen years prior to an injury that left him unable to resume his occupation. Since the XYZ Company's pension plan applied only to employees with twenty years of service, Fiedler lost out on $5,000 a year that way. His future income loss is $5,000 multiplied by his life expectancy after reaching the retirement age of sixty-five, as derived from actuarial tables. (This payment is in addition to any loss of income between the time of the injury and time of retirement.) To obtain this award, Fiedler will have to show that—had it not been for the injury—he would have kept his job for another two years.

Meeting this requirement will rarely present you with a problem. Since the award will be paid by the defendant, your employer loses no money by so testifying for you.

Further, if your employer has an "incentive-pay" program, you should learn its conditions and the average amount of money that others in your occupational category earned while you were injured. That money is a loss of income for you, even though your employer paid you your regular salary during your recuperation. The same holds true for bonuses. If they were given to others, but not to you due to your injury, you have an income-loss damage. The fact that a bonus or the incentive plan was voluntary on the part of the employer doesn't matter.

The issue is whether he paid it and whether you would have gotten it had you not been injured. (It will be a rare employer who will say you wouldn't have gotten it.)

Did your injury cause you to lose a promotion?

This is a claim that can be difficult to prove. For example, Mr. Smith was regional sales manager for the XYZ Company and believed he was in line for promotion to general sales manager, a post that paid an additional $10,000 a year. He was injured, and while he was recuperating, the promotion was given to another regional sales manager. Smith probably won't be able to prove his injury cost him the promotion, since the job apparently went to an equally qualified individual who might have gotten it even if Smith hadn't been injured.

If you find yourself in a situation similar to Smith's, you should not necessarily give up on this income-loss demand just because the odds are against you. It is possible that your employer will testify you would have gotten the job had it not been for your injury, whether that is a certainty or not. However, since there could be hundreds of thousands of dollars riding on this allegation, the defense is certain to fight it vigorously, attacking your employer's truthfulness in his testimony for you and attempting to show that the best-qualified person got the job. The result of this cross-examination could be an employer who is sorry he ever spoke up for you, who now realizes by his testimony he was indirectly attacking the ability of the person who did get the job, and you may, as a result, find your future with that employer highly limited. The gamble may be worth it, but consider the possible repercussions before undertaking it.

Sometimes the loss-of-promotion allegation is rather easily proved. Consider young Mr. Berry, who was hired as a machinery cleaner at the XYZ factory. Because of his injury, one of his legs was now shorter than the other, and although he could still perform the job for which he was hired, he was no longer capable of doing heavier, better-paid labor. If Berry can show that other machinery cleaners are routinely promoted to the work he now can't do, he can recover the difference between his present wage and the higher wage he would have received, multiplied by his probable future number of working years. That can be a tidy sum.

Even though your income after an injury is as great or greater than it was prior to it, did you lose the opportunity to earn even larger sums of money?

This ground for income loss is most likely to arise if you are self-employed or earn your living from commissions. Typical is the experience of a former plaintiff interviewed for this book whom we'll call Mr. Bramwell. A manufacturer's representative, Bramwell was earning $1,500 a month on commissions, prior to his injury. He lost work for twenty weeks. During that interval, as payments were made to him for sales completed before the injury, he averaged $1,800 a month. Subsequent to returning to work, he managed to maintain the $1,800-a-month average and within a year had upped it to $2,100. Bramwell, even so, decided to try to prove he had a loss of income.

To do so, using his appointment diaries for several years preceding and following the injury, he developed figures that seemed to show a substantial drop in sales from several customers during and following the injury period. Said Bramwell, recalling what he did: "There was no way of proving this 100 percent—who knows when a customer is going to buy?—but at least it looked like a loss and a continuing one and I figured it might confuse a jury enough that they'd take my word for it." Bramwell's case was further helped when, after doing some digging in the company records, he learned that a fellow salesperson had earned at least one hefty commission from one of his customers while he was injured. That added credibility to his other figures. Next, Bramwell obtained the agreement from two executives of one of his customers that they would testify they had given business to a competitor solely because Bramwell wasn't available to them during a crucial buying period. "I assured them I just wanted their word now, that the case would never go to trial; I think that encouraged them," said Bramwell.

Bramwell had gone to a great deal of work—which you may have to do if you face this or related kinds of situations—but it paid off for him. Despite the fact that his income was $3,600 more in the year following the injury than the one before, he now had evidence to suggest that the injury had cost him $18,000 over a three-year period. Faced with the possibility that a jury would believe the welter of paperwork Bramwell had accumulated as well as the damaging testimony of the two executives, the defendant's insurance company raised its settlement offer by $12,000 and the diligent Bramwell (who had good reason to think his two executives would refuse to testify if it came to the crunch) happily accepted the deal. His lawyer told him, "If I had more clients like you, I'd be a rich man." Commented Bramwell, with a sigh: "Not that that inspired him to waive his one-third fee on the extra twelve grand I'd snared. But that, I guess, is why he, unlike me, will be a rich man someday."

If you are the owner of your own business, did you lose income or profits as a direct result of your inability to work?

Another former plaintiff, call him Mr. O'Riordan, provides a case in point. He owned a sign-painting shop which, during the year prior to his injury, netted him a profit of $10,000; in addition to that, he paid himself $250 a week in salary. Due to his injury, O'Riordan had to hire a sign painter at $350 a week for one year, continuing to take $250 weekly for himself. Because his injury made it impossible for him to solicit new business for his shop, during the injury year O'Riordan's net profit declined to $3,000. O'Riordan, whose case was settled out of court, was eligible to be compensated by a jury for the total cost of hiring the new sign painter—or, in some jurisdictions, at least for the hundred-dollar difference in salary—and he was also eligible to be compensated for his $7,000 loss in profit.

The key to O'Riordan's right to recover the profit loss, and yours as a business owner, depends on your ability to produce convincing evidence showing that the success of your business directly depended on your presence on the scene. When that cannot be proved, an owner of a business ordinarily cannot use a decline in profit during an injury period as an item of damage. Moreover, if, as the owner of your business, your income from investment of capital declined while you were injured, that loss ordinarily is not recoverable either. The law considers investment income to be speculative and therefore not to be associated with the consequences of an injury, except when the injured party earned his or her living totally or largely as an investor, and in certain death cases in which the cessation of the investment income affected the estate.

Did your injury delay your entry into the job market?

This is one time that a person who has never worked a day in his or her life can show a loss of income. For instance, let's suppose that your daughter was a college student when she was injured and as a result missed a year of studies. Had it not been for the injury, she would have entered employment a year earlier than she did, and she is entitled to be compensated for that year's loss, usually based on her present earnings or her probable earnings in the field of her major. But that's not all. Because your daughter entered or is going to enter work a year late, she is also going to have one less year of employment before retirement, and that could affect pension benefits. She deserves compensation for that prospective loss too.

> Regardless of how you were earning your living at the time of the injury, did you have any special training or were you undergoing a course of instruction to give you new skills that you cannot now employ because of the injury?

When you fit this classification, your loss of earning capacity can sometimes become enormous. Consider Ms. McKenzie, a student at a conservatory of music, who was employed as a part-time waitress when she suffered an injury that caused permanent partial paralysis of her right arm. As a consequence, she could no longer hope to fulfill her ambition to become a concert pianist. Her loss of earning capacity is based not on her earnings as a waitress when she was injured but, rather, on the amount she might have earned as a concert pianist, less her probable future income from occupations she is still qualified to perform. The defense is not permitted to argue that McKenzie never would have become a concert pianist. That the injury deprived her of the chance to become one is the only relevant fact.

Before asserting this kind of claim (whether your ambition was to be a concert pianist, a secretary, an engineer, or whatever), you must be able to show that you had taken or were about to take concrete educational steps to fulfill that ambition before your injury made its obtainment impossible. A mere statement that you "intended" to become a concert pianist, etc., will not be sufficient.

> Regardless of how you were earning a living at the time of the injury, do you have skills that paid you more in the past or gave you a greater earning potential and that cannot now be used because of your injury?

This also can be a profitable question for you if you can answer yes to it. By way of illustration, consider Mr. Ridley, who was employed as a $13,000-a-year high school teacher when he was injured. Previously, he had earned $30,000 annually as an engineer at an aircraft plant, losing his job when the company's government contract was canceled. Because Ridley's injury, which led to partial permanent paralysis, made it impossible for him to regain employment as an engineer, his loss of earning capacity was based on his probable higher income from that profession, rather than the lower one from his teaching job. As it happened, Ridley was able to resume teaching; his award eligibility, therefore, became the difference between his earning capacity as an engineer and his earnings as a teacher, multiplied by his probable number of future working years.

Considering the dollar stakes here, it is worth your while to go back over your background, educational attainments, training, and jobs you have held, in terms not only of your earnings in them but their promotion potential, and even jobs you never sought but for which you were qualified. There may be one with a higher average earnings potential than your present occupation that may now be foreclosed to you because of your injury.

Even though you weren't employed when injured, did you intend to seek work using skills no longer available to you due to the injury?

Two examples will help explain your rights in this area. First we have Ms. Boyce, who worked as a registered nurse but quit her job to raise a family. At the time of her injury, she had two children, aged six and three. Many times she had expressed to friends —who were willing to testify for her—that she intended to resume nursing after her children no longer needed her full-time care. Because her injury left her right arm paralyzed, she could no longer hope to fulfill that ambition. Ms. Boyce has grounds to recover damages based on her lost earning capacity as a nurse.

Not so fortunate was Ms. Flowers. After graduating from college, she taught school for one year and then retired to raise a family. Her injury left her permanently paralyzed. When it occurred, her children were twenty-four and twenty-two years old and she had not yet made any effort to resume work. Although Ms. Flowers had a skilled occupation, she does not appear to have any provable loss of earning capacity, due to her failure to seek employment after her children reached maturity.

If your position is similar to Ms. Flowers', you should not necessarily give up on this allegation, but your proof problems are going to be difficult ones. Helpful would be any record you might have of taking courses during your unemployment period that either were intended to refresh your old skills or lead to new, marketable ones. (Self-help or hobby courses would not meet that criterion.)

It should be emphasized here that loss of earning capacity is not defined by the length of time you didn't work in a job for which you were trained, or even the number of jobs you held that didn't make use of your skills. The only legally relevant fact is that you had the skills or were training to obtain them with the intent of using them but cannot do so because of your injury.

If suit is brought on behalf of a child, did the injury affect its future earning capacity?

In most injuries involving children, this isn't an issue except in the sense, noted above, that it may have been sufficiently serious to delay entry into the job market. However, some injuries are of such magnitude (permanent paralysis, brain damage) that the child's future earning capacity is totally or nearly totally destroyed. Should this occur when the child is very young—or if it was injured prior to birth—there is no way of foretelling how much the child might have earned in adult life. In those cases, the usual assumption is that he or she would have graduated high school and had lifetime earnings on the average of all high school graduates at the time of the injury.

With older children, future earnings often can be more accurately and profitably predicted. In one tragic case, a fifteen-year-old boy suffered brain damage as a result of negligently performed surgery. Although the boy had a normal life expectancy, his earning capacity was destroyed. Prior to the injury, he had been an outstanding student, displaying particular aptitude in science. Frequently he had expressed to teachers, friends, and family his ambition to become a doctor. The evidence of the boy's special aptitude was admissible at trial, and his loss of future earnings was computed on that of the average income of doctors, rather than high school graduates.

If your suit is based on a wrongful death, what have been the economic effects of the victim's demise on the surviving family?

The grounds for bringing wrongful-death actions vary from state to state, with some states placing a ceiling on the amount that can be awarded (see Chapter Fourteen). The two examples that follow, therefore, are intended to illustrate only those grounds for compensation that apply in most jurisdictions; they may not be valid in yours, or else the limit on the total award you can receive is so low that a detailed compilation of losses is meaningless.

First consider Roger Heath, age forty-five, married, with three minor children, who was killed as a result of someone's negligence. At the time of his death, Heath was earning $25,000 a year, was eligible for an annual pension of $7,500 at the age of sixty-five, and was saving $1,000 a year in an interest-earning account. The family's loss of income from Heath's death will be computed on his lost earnings: $25,000 $\times$ 20 years $+$ $7,500 $\times$ his probable life-span following retirement (based on actuarial tables) $+$ income from the savings account which, it will be presumed legally, he would have continued to build in the future as he had in the past. From this total will be deducted the money Heath could have been expected, had he lived, to have spent on himself for food, clothing, shelter, etc. As is true of people who survive their injuries, the future-earnings award will also be reduced to its present value.

The economic losses suffered by Heath's family, however, are not limited to his earning capacity. As a father, he probably counseled his children and helped them with their homework; probably he did routine repair work about the house. Services such as these, which Heath performed without charge to his family, become cost items for the family in his absence. The value of his removed services, therefore, is a ground for recovery. The jury will decide how much worth, if any, to give each item.

Survivors of unemployed people who were wrongfully killed can also usually show a financial loss. For example, Martha Stone, an unemployed housewife with two minor children was killed as a result of someone's negligence. Her loss to her family economically is predicated on the worth of her services, including housekeeping, child care, educational functions, and the like—detailed charts of cash values of a housewife and mother's services are available to attorneys—plus any provable loss of earning capacity from paid work that her training made likely she would have engaged upon in the future for her family's benefit. As with Mr. Heath, deducted from these amounts will be the predicted cost for her own maintenance had she continued to live, and the award will be reduced to present value.

HOW TO DOCUMENT YOUR INCOME DAMAGES

Maintain your own records of loss of income.

You will have no choice but to do this if you are self-employed. However, it is also a prudent policy to adopt when you are an employee. Employers have been known to go out of business and to lose or destroy old payroll records. While your own income-loss log—noting every day you missed wages because of your injury—might not have the evidentiary value that an employer's would, it will, in conjunction with matching medical records, usually be sufficient to convince a jury of the accuracy of the figure you are demanding.

Although income-tax returns can often provide supporting documentation for a loss-of-income claim, they should not be relied upon completely, since they may not be revelatory. For instance, you may have missed a month of income due to your injury but received a raise the same year, making your total income for the year higher than for the year prior to the injury, thereby hiding the actual loss during the injury period.

Always advise your employer when you are taking time off work for reasons associated with your injury.

Even after you return to employment, there may be days on which you will lose income because you had to see a doctor for follow-up care or you simply weren't feeling well enough to work. The money you lose this way is as compensable as that incurred during the original injury period. Request your employer (or your shop steward) to note on your employment records that these absences were injury-related.

A jury may not find records developed this way credible when based on your word alone, but when they can be backed by your doctor's records that you actually did visit him on the dates stated and if he will testify that you probably did feel too unwell to work at various times when you didn't go to see him, then they can become important documentation.

If your injury caused you to lose your job, keep a complete record of all efforts you made to find new employment.

Jurors are not going to be impressed by a plaintiff who, although able to work, has sat around for years waiting for the time when they will give him some money. They will be impressed by a plaintiff who has made an honest effort to find work, even if that effort was unsuccessful.

Therefore, keep a list of all prospective employers to whom résumés were sent, dates of job interviews, the names of the persons conducting the interviews, and the results of the interviews.

Job-hunting efforts should include seeking employment in fields in which you have qualifications that were adversely affected or obliterated by your injury. Testimony from a prospective employer (or your previous employer) that you could not be hired (or rehired) due to your injury will carry great weight with a jury.

When you show that you were eventually forced, due to your injury, to accept a position that was not commensurate with your preinjury employment or skills, you have developed an important proof of loss of earning capacity. The fact that the new job pays the same or even higher wages than the pre-injury employment need not be harmful to your claim, as long as the job does not permit you to make use of your skills or lacks the opportunity for advancement that had been true in your employment (or training for employment) prior to the injury.

If you remain employed, do not go back to work before you are physically able to do so.

If you are a person who is a compulsive worker, who is desperately in need of money, or who fears loss of employment if an early return to the job does not take place, this advice is more easily given than taken. Nevertheless, in terms of increasing your award from your suit, the more time you miss from work, the more money you will be eligible for as a special damage and presumably the greater the multiplier effect that will have on your total award. An early return to work by you is also almost certain to be used by the defense attorney as proof that you weren't as seriously injured as you allege.

9

How to Document Your Medical Expenses

During the negotiation stage of your case, there is nothing to stop your lawyer from tossing special-damage figures—both income and medical—at the opponent, not all of them verifiable. The lawyer knows he might as well maximize them, since the opponent is going to try to minimize them, and the hope is they'll meet at some agreeable mid-point. Should your case go to trial, however, you are going to have to document your claims. We have already seen how this is done with income damages; the medical ones present a somewhat different problem.

For them, documentation alone is not enough. To be reimbursable to you, they must also be shown to be reasonable. For instance, suppose your doctor charged you $5,000 for an operation in connection with your injury and the defense learns that the going rate for this operation is $3,000. Unless you and your doctor can come up with a convincing reason why you were charged the higher figure, the most you can claim for the operation is the normal charge. Many plaintiffs become upset, understandably so, when their lawyers give them this kind of bad news, and may suspect the lawyer is wrong or is somehow making a deal with the enemy. He's not. (The reason for this rule, incidentally, is to prevent parties to a suit from conspiring with one another to jack up medical bills and then share the proceeds when the unfortunate defendant is required to pay.)

Frivolous or medically unnecessary bills are also challengeable.

So-called "whiplash" clinics provide one example: Lawyers of a certain ilk are in the habit of instructing their clients to attend these clinics—the lawyer often getting a kickback—where they sit for several hours at a time wearing surgical collars while they watch television or play cards. Bills for this kind of medical "care" rapidly escalate to large figures, and—following artful cross-examination by a defense attorney—juries can become highly suspicious of them. As a result, the jurors refuse to give an award for the clinic's services, and they may decide that the plaintiff in question probably wasn't injured at all. The luckless plaintiff now not only has a bad result from the suit but is faced with having to pay the clinic's bills out of his or her own pocket.

Some challengeable medical bills emanate from a motive more pure. Consider the case of Mr. White, who suffered a fractured leg and a minor concussion in an automobile accident. His alarmed wife insisted he receive round-the-clock private nursing care even though the doctor assured her there was no necessity for it. The jury in his case will almost certainly decide there's no reason to force the defendant to pay for the plaintiff's wife's worry.

Despite these examples, a medical-expense claim cannot be rejected solely on the grounds it proved inadvisable or counterproductive. The issue for the jury to decide, rather, is whether or not the plaintiff or the party ordering the treatment believed, at the time it was undertaken, that it was necessary or likely to prove efficacious.

Based on these rules, therefore, you ordinarily should limit your current medical expenses to those that are both reasonable and susceptible of documentation. Not all lawyers agree with this advice; they believe in tossing everything into the pot in order to build up the highest dollar figure possible. As tempting as this route might be, a number of plaintiff lawyers, rated as outstanding by their colleagues, warned against raising questionable medical expenses, particularly minor ones. In their view, by so doing you not only take on the unnecessary risk of having your credibility challenged by the defense attorney on cross-examination, but you also provide him with an opportunity to divert the jury's thinking from the unchallenged bills by concentrating their attention on the doubtful ones. Opening yourself to such tactics can only harm your case.

As long as you are on solid ground on the medical expenses you have already incurred, testifying about them won't be difficult. Your principal job will be to identify bills as your lawyer shows them to you and affirm that they are accurate. Often the defense will allow the bills to be admitted as evidence without questioning you.

Future medical bills are handled somewhat differently. As a lay person, you are not permitted to testify about the medical likelihood that you will incur them; that's a job for your doctor and other expert witnesses. For instance, your doctor will say that you can be expected to require such-and-such care for so many years and that it will cost approximately so many dollars, or that the percentage likelihood of the treatment is at a certain figure.

However, sometimes future medical care will be elective on your part, and then you will have to testify (and convince the jury) that you intend to have the service performed. In injury cases, the most common elective future medical bill is one for cosmetic (plastic) surgery to remove, or mitigate the effects of, scars.

When the scar is visible and disfiguring, the chances are that the defense attorney won't challenge your assertion that you intend to have the surgery done. As far as he is concerned, the less testimony about disfigurements the better; he's afraid that questioning you about them will increase the jury's sympathy toward you.

However, not all scars are big, disfiguring, or ordinarily visible. For example, assume you were burned, leaving several small scars on your stomach the appearance of which could be improved by cosmetic surgery; however, by the time trial takes place four years have gone by and you have not yet had the operation. Legally, you have every right to assert that you are going to have the surgery, but you open yourself to attack by the defense on the ground that you are trying to collect money for an operation that you probably don't intend to have performed. As before, the danger here is that the defense attorney, by attacking your credibility on this one point, will inferentially cast doubt on your other testimony.

This is not to say that you should never testify that you intend to have minor surgery performed, no matter how long a time has gone by since the injury. You and your lawyer, however, should weigh the possible gains and losses carefully.

Several attorneys who were interviewed said that, in their experience, juries are most likely to give credence to claims of future minor cosmetic surgery when the plaintiff is an unmarried woman —presumably to improve her appearance so she can catch a husband—but less likely to believe her if she is already married. Men are less likely to be believed than women when the scarring is minor—they are supposed to be less vain than women—and blacks less likely to be believed (by white juries, anyway) because, as one lawyer noted, despite medical evidence to the contrary, "the scars don't show as much on blacks." Whatever one may think about this sexist, racist reasoning, the fact is that some jurors are sexist and racist, and if your case might encounter one of these biases, you will want to give consideration to that before raising the assertion that might not be believed.

When developing the medical proof elements of your suit, there is one rule you should never violate: *Always tell your lawyer about any previous medical problems you have had or any new ones that occur at the site of the injury that caused the suit.* (New injuries at old sites are often medically predictable, the first injury weakening your resistance to a second one; a common example is recurrent back problems.)

Based on interviews with attorneys, this is the one piece of information plaintiffs are the least likely to give their lawyers and the one that, if held back, is most likely to harm their cause. Some plaintiffs have simply forgotten an earlier problem—which really means they haven't thought hard enough about their case— but apparently in most instances plaintiffs are silent because they fear that if their lawyer learns they've had a previous or new problem in the injury area, the lawyer will decide their symptoms aren't the result of the wrongful injury and either won't take their case or will drop it because it is now unwinnable.

In one sense, the fear is justified. Whenever the defense can show a prior or new medical problem at the injury site, it is going to try to prove to the jury exactly what the plaintiff fears. But that is also exactly the reason, if you have old or new medical problems at the injury site, you should tell your lawyer about it. If you don't and the defense learns of the other medical problem and introduces it as evidence in your trial, your lawyer, taken by surprise, will have no way to rebut the contention that that's what is causing your symptoms and you could well lose your case. On the contrary, if your lawyer is informed, he can often produce medical testimony to show that the injury that is the subject of the suit aggravated the old problem or caused the new one and you must be compensated precisely for that reason. (In personal injury law, defendants take their victims as they come; thus, if you had a prior heart condition and the defendant's negligence caused you a heart attack, the defendant can't get out of the case by saying his actions wouldn't have caused the attack in someone who was healthy.) Alternatively, your lawyer may be able to produce medical testimony to show that the old and new problems are completely unrelated. In either event, he must know in advance.

In connection with the medical aspects of your case, you should also take the following steps:

Maintain your own medical expense records.

When your lawyer accepts your case, he will obtain from you and from your medical providers copies of all bills already incurred, whether paid or not, whether your responsibility or that of some third party such as Blue Cross. He will also ask you to keep him apprised of any continuing medical expenses. You may intend to do that, but as time goes on—often as years go on—it's likely you won't have given him a complete list. (Have you let him know each time you had a prescription refilled? Probably not, but that's an item that can easily add hundreds of dollars to your medical damages.) Your record, therefore, will usually be more complete than his, at least on minor expenses, and in any event provides a useful cross-check to assure that nothing important has been overlooked.

Whenever possible, pay your medical bills by check.

That includes payment to a pharmacy for drugs. Always note the reason for the check on the memo portion on the bottom of it, and also note the reason on your checkbook stub. By so doing, not only do you create a readily retrievable medical expense record, but also—when no other documentation is available—your canceled checks can be submitted as evidence.

See your doctor when you have symptoms associated with your injury.

After you have been discharged from medical care, it may be wise —especially so when your suit lingers on for several years—to return to your doctor occasionally when pain symptoms recur, even though they may be ones he has told you that you could expect. Always go to him when new symptoms develop near or at the injury site, even though they are not of a severity that would ordinarily cause you to seek medical care. (They may mean the development of new side effects about which little can be done medically but which, when diagnosed, can add substantially to your damage claim.) At trial, a jury may believe your unsupported allegations of continuing or new symptoms, but they will give them much greater credence when backed by evidence that you received treatment for them.

If you do stop seeing a doctor before your suit is resolved, it is usually counterproductive to begin seeing him again immediately prior to trial.

You may have good reason to do so. Several of the former plaintiffs interviewed for this book reported a renewal of their pain symptoms as soon as the trial date was set, quite probably a psychosomatic response but none the less real to them for that. Nevertheless, seeking medical care on the eve of trial after a long abstinence from it is likely to be viewed with suspicion by most juries and will detract from your general credibility as a plaintiff. (We are not considering here the last-minute medical evaluation of your condition by your physician solely for the purpose of the testimony he will give in your behalf. As noted in Chapter Seven, that examination is not part of your medical damages, nor will you be asserting it as such. It is, of course, always possible that, as a result of this examination, the doctor will uncover a previously unsuspected medical problem arguably related to your injury. In that event, a new damage element has been uncovered and can be properly introduced as evidence at your trial.)

If this hasn't been done, ask your lawyer if you should have a full medical evaluation by a specialist.

This can be an important step to take when the treatment of your injury has largely been in the hands of a general practitioner. His diagnosis, while useful as testimony on your behalf, becomes much more authoritative when supported by a specialist, who—it is also quite possible—will discover elements of your condition that have escaped your family doctor and might, once revealed, become significant damage items. Don't assume, because your lawyer hasn't told you to see a specialist, that he has considered doing it and rejected the idea. Lawyers don't always think of everything, and this could be one item yours has forgotten.

When your medical condition warrants it, do not refuse to accept light work.

Your doctor may permit you to return to a job but not allow you, for a short or a lengthy period of time, to engage in strenuous or heavy work that you did prior to the injury. Faced with this order, you may not want to accept the lighter duties for fear that you will lose value in your employer's eyes and be laid off. This is not an unrealistic apprehension in some situations, and one that must be evaluated. However, strictly from the view of the cash value of your suit, returning to heavy work prematurely will often suggest to a jury that you were less seriously injured than you claim, and your entire testimony, therefore, becomes clouded with doubt. On the contrary, testimony by your doctor, backed by your employer, that you were capable of engaging in only light duties provides important corroboration of your claims and makes a large award more likely. (If the lesser duties pay less money or make you ineligible for promotion, then you also have a special-damage claim for loss of income, as noted in Chapter Eight.)

A MEDICAL-DAMAGE CHECKLIST

In making use of the list that follows, remember that you don't need to have paid a bill yourself or even have any intention of reimbursing whoever did pay it, and you can also include bills that haven't been paid. Assuming always that you can meet the necessary proof standards, each item applies to both existent medical costs and those that are reasonably likely to occur in the future.

Cost of care for physical or psychiatric ailments from any licensed health-care provider is a legitimate medical expense item.

"Health-care provider" is defined as any person licensed to practice healing arts, such as: a medical doctor, osteopath, dentist, chiropractor, podiatrist, nurse, and physical therapist. Bills submitted for services by psychologists or any other psychotherapist who is not a medical doctor (but who holds a state license to practice) can be considered part of medical expenses. In some jurisdictions, payments to Christian Science healers have been admitted. Payments to faith healers in general cannot be counted.

Bills resulting from inpatient or outpatient hospital care are compensable.

In addition to regular hospitals, included are cost of services by physical-therapy institutes, convalescent homes, and mental hospitals. In a few cases, judges have ruled that room-and-board charges by hospitals are not compensable medical expenses, while, somewhat more frequently, room charges are allowed but meal charges aren't. In the overwhelming majority of jurisdictions, however, the law recognizes that room-and-board charges incorporate the hospital's medical-services overhead, and both are considered part of one's legitimate medical expenses.

The cost of nursing care provided in the home may be included.

Payments to registered nurses, licensed practical nurses, and nurses' aides, as well as to homemakers hired to do the work of the injured person, including provision of child-care services, are admissible.

The cost of nursing care can also include that of a parent or other member of a family who provides nursing care to the injured party. For that cost to be reimbursed, the one providing it must have been employed and ceased working for the specific purpose of offering the care. The amount of recompense will be based on the average cost of that kind of care in the community, not on the amount of money the person was earning prior to taking on the nursing duties.

Cost of medication, both prescription and nonprescription, is compensable.

For the costs of nonprescription drugs, such as aspirin, to be included, however, they must have been ordered or recommended by a licensed health-care provider who will so testify.

Cost of prosthetic devices is compensable.

This category includes crutches, surgical stockings, surgical collars, artificial limbs, neck braces, eye patches, corsets, orthopedic shoes, and the like. They can include such nonprescription items as Ace bandages and foot and arm pads, as long as their use was ordered by a licensed health-care provider.

The additional cost of a special diet is compensable.

People who ingest harmful products are particularly likely to be placed on restrictive and expensive diets over a short or lengthy period of time. The cost of the diet, less the cost of one's normal diet, provides the net expense.

Transportation costs for the treatment of an injury are compensable.

Included is the cost of ambulance service, taxi service, or other paid transportation to and from the hospital. Included is the cost of transportation and lodging when your injury requires you to obtain medical care outside your own community. Also included would be the same costs for an accompanying spouse, nurse, or other companion when that person's presence on the trip is deemed medically necessary by your doctor. Ordinarily, costs of meals may not be included.

Costs resulting from the need to repeat or correct an unsuccessful medical procedure are compensable.

A defendant who is found liable for an injury must bear the costs not only for successful but unsuccessful modes of treatment. Thus, should a broken leg require resetting, the costs of both the original and the second settings are compensable to you.

When the unsuccessful treatment was caused by medical malpractice, you may choose to sue on that ground separately. You cannot, however, collect from both the defendant in the injury and the defendant in the malpractice case for the same item of cost.

The cost of care for an injury's side effects is compensable.

The side effect can often be more serious than the original injury, such as the fracture of the arm that results in chronic tendonitis or a frozen shoulder. Cost of treatment for a side effect includes that for adverse effects from drugs used in the original treatment.

Treatment for injury-produced psychosomatic pain is compensable.

Although psychosomatic (mind-induced) physical pain is not readily provable, as is evidence of bursitis, a frozen shoulder, and the like, it is a proper item of medical damage, and testimony from your doctor that you complained of such pains and were treated for them is admissible as evidence. (How much credence jurors will give this allegation probably depends on their own experiences and general knowledge of how real a psychosomatic pain can be.)

10

Getting Compensated for Your Pain, Suffering, and Mental Anguish

When a physical injury befalls you, the law generally assumes that it causes you pain and that pain inevitably causes suffering. Presumably, if the blow from the injury knocked you immediately into a coma from which you eventually awoke feeling fine, then you have had no pain and suffering, but with rare exceptions like these, the defense cannot allege you didn't have pain, but it will mightily strive to show that you didn't have as much as you claim.

If your suit is resolved by a settlement, you job is to supply your lawyer with the ammunition he needs to describe your woes in the most horrifying terms possible to the defense in the hope that it—fearing a jury will accept your story—will add money to the pot to prevent a trial.

Should your case go to trial, then your role in proving the amount of your pain and suffering becomes pivotal. Thousands of dollars can depend on how well you tell your story.

As a witness to your injury, you are permitted considerable latitude in describing your pain and suffering to the jury. You are allowed to depict the pain itself, its frequency, its location or locations in your body, and—within limitations—your emotional state as a result of it. You can describe activities that have become painful, such as sitting on a chair, lying on your back, turning your neck, etc. You are not, however, permitted to speculate about whether or not the pain will continue in the future.

Putting pain and suffering into words isn't easy; even the great poets have had trouble doing that. Therefore, don't worry about any lack of fluency on your part. Concern yourself, rather, with being adequately prepared to testify. Some help in this direction will be forthcoming from your lawyer, who, just before trial, will go over this part of your testimony with you, usually in some detail, often suggesting how, generally, you should phrase your statements. However, don't parrot your lawyer's words. If you do, you will sound rehearsed and be ineffective.

The best method of preparation is to maintain a pain diary. In it, note—in as much detail as you can and as soon as you can, while your memory is fresh—both your pain and your mental state, beginning with the date of your injury and continuing throughout the entire litigation period. Jot down descriptions of the pain: "sharp," "dull," "arthritic," and so on. When symptoms begin to appear only sporadically, note the date and length of each recurrence and what you were doing when the pain appeared. Also include in your pain diary, adverse reactions to medication or to physical therapy. The medicine, for example, may have numbed the pain but caused you an upset stomach; that reaction is a form of pain and suffering for which you have a right to be compensated. Similarly, exercises you are required to undergo as therapy for your injury can often be as painful or more painful than the injury itself, and that pain too is compensable.

The day before you are due to testify, study the diary. At trial, you may not read from it, nor will your lawyer permit you to bore the jury with a recountal of every pain you have ever suffered, complete with date and place. However, thanks to the diary, your memory of events will be sharpened and you may discover patterns to the pain of which you had previously been unaware. In this way, the diary will allow you to offer precise descriptions that otherwise would not have been available to you. It is, for instance, much more effective to be able to say, "At least four times this past year the pain became so bad that I had to ask my husband to carry my purse for me," than to have to say, "Sometimes I have difficulty holding on to things." Similarly when you can say, "The pain recurs most sharply during the early spring and late fall, when the weather is changing," you have given the jurors a meaningful fact, but haven't when you can only say, "The pain comes and goes." In describing the pain itself, try to use vivid terms: "The pain was like a continuous toothache" is much more likely to be remembered by the jurors when they are making your award than if you had said "The pain was awful." (Do not, incidentally, be tempted into giving descriptions of pains that haven't occurred; the defense has its medical experts who might be able to prove you couldn't have suffered the pain you claim.)

In describing your pain to the jury, it is also a good idea to point to the places on your body where the pain occurs. Jurors' minds may wander as voices drone on, and while this can be to your advantage when the defense is making some technical point or you're at a weak spot in your own story, when you're talking about your pain, you want their complete attention. The finger-pointing serves that function, directing their eyes to your damaged body and allowing them to imagine for themselves what it would be like to have pain at that place.

Never overstate your case. For example, if you had trouble sleeping after the injury, say that, but if it's no longer a problem, say that, too. By so doing, you impress the jury as someone who is conscientiously trying to tell the truth and nothing but the truth. Even more important, by volunteering the information that some of your problems no longer exist, you deprive the defense attorney of one of his most effective ways of challenging your credibility:

Q. On direct examination, I believe you testified that your pain was so great that you have had trouble sleeping?

A. Yes, sir.

Q. The injury, I believe, occured five years ago. Is that correct?

A. Yes, sir.

Q. And every night since then, because of the pain, you have had trouble sleeping?

A. Well, no.

Q. Oh, it's not a problem now? For how long hasn't it been a problem? One year? Two years? Three years? How long?

By the time he's done with you, the jury may decide you never had trouble sleeping at all. To avoid this kind of damaging confrontation, it is also usually a good idea to omit items that—although they might be true—could seem incredible to the jury. One plaintiff, for instance, in a by-the-way fashion, mentioned that her injury had made her teeth ache. The defense lawyer leaped on this and produced medical testimony to the effect that her injury couldn't have caused that repercussion; undaunted, her lawyer produced medical testimony that her injury could, indeed, have made her teeth ache. All this testimony was to the defense's benefit; because of it, the jury was likely to forget the woman's other, more substantive, testimony about her pain and spend its time, instead, trying to decide if she was telling the truth about her teeth.

Finally, although it sometimes can't be avoided, it is usually a good idea to omit pain-and-suffering testimony that can't be corroborative at least in part by other of your witnesses. (Usually your lawyer will tell you what to include and what to leave out; listen to his advice.)

Ordinarily, your most important corroborative testimony will come from your doctor. Much of what the doctor has to say—along with the testimony of other medical experts you might have—will be focused on the injury you received, its treatment, and its probable future consequences to you. However, a doctor is also permitted to express an expert opinion about the nature and frequency of the pain that an injury such as yours likely will cause. The doctor is also permitted to testify to the pain symptoms you described both at the time of your injury and on subsequent visits while you were recuperating. (This is why, if for no other reason, it is always a good idea to tell your doctor about every pain symptom you have.) The doctor will further be permitted to describe pain-killing medications you were given, their purpose, adverse reactions you had to them, and the time periods over which you were ordered to take them.

In addition to your doctor's record of your treatment, nurses' notes made during your hospitalization can support your pain-and-suffering allegations. These notes are usually made in considerable detail, showing when medication had to be given and your physical condition before and after their administration. They may even contain a helpful passage like "Patient was moaning in her sleep." Such independent evidence of your suffering, at a time you couldn't possibly have been faking it, can be highly effective.

Ordinarily less effective, due to their financial interest in the outcome of your case, is testimony about your pain and discomfort from your spouse and other members of your family, and if this is the only kind of corroborating testimony you have, it may not be worthwhile. (Although not always: Parents' description of the suffering of their child, or a child's of its parent, is often quite powerful.)

To bolster your pain-and-suffering testimony, you should spend some time trying to think of everyone who might have been witness to it. Friends, neighbors, and fellow employees are possibilities. An outsider, such as a policeman who saw you immediately after the injury and before you got aid, could be useful. Or your hospital roommate might be able to help. Did you require physical therapy? The therapist may be able to speak authoritatively about the pain symptoms you exhibited when you were under that treatment.

Do not assume your lawyer will think of these and other possible witnesses on his own. You suggest the names and let him decide who, if any of them, will be helpful.

MENTAL ANGUISH

Unlike suffering, mental anguish can either occur separately from pain or be the result of it. When a woman is harassed by her ex-husband in public, she does not undergo physical pain, but her embarrassment, humiliation, and fear of a repeat performance is mental anguish and a ground for recovery. When the same woman is struck down by a car and as she lies on the ground, feeling pain, she *also* fears she is going to lose her life, that fear is a form of mental anguish, undoubtedly in large measure induced by the pain and suffering the blow caused her, but it has also occurred as a separate response to the peril in which she found herself and therefore is a separate element of her damages.

A mental-anguish claim can sometimes be properly raised by a co-plaintiff in a suit, rather than (or in addition to) the victim. The governing rules for this kind of claim, however, vary from jurisdiction to jurisdiction. In some places, one is not permitted to raise a claim of mental anguish when the fear experienced was solely on behalf of someone else. Under this harsh rule, parents who stand outside a burning house in which their children are trapped have no grounds for suit on mental anguish against the party that caused the fire. However, if they were in the house at the time—in a so-called "zone of peril"—they would have grounds, because then, it can be assumed, they feared for their own safety as well. This dictum, which was once almost uniformly applied in the United States, has undergone a considerable degree of successful challenge in the courts in recent years, and it would now appear that, in most places, an anguish allegation based on fear for the safety of others—usually, however, restricted to members of your own family—need not include personal fears, nor must the person asserting the anguish necessarily even have been on the scene when the injury occurred. (Thus, a mother who sees her seriously injured child after the accident has as good grounds for claiming mental anguish as does the one who sees the injury occur.)

Ordinarily, a mental-anguish claim cannot be made unless there has been some form of physical impact upon the victim. If the woman mentioned above had managed to jump out of the way of the car, she cannot sue on the basis of the fear she experienced during the period she thought the car was going to hit her. This rule, which prevents the courts from being inundated by suits in which plaintiffs claim that certain noninjurious events made them fearful, can have some curious and unjust consequences. In one famous case, a woman saw a dead cockroach embedded in a piece of bread she was about to eat and suffered a nervous collapse; her suit was dismissed because there had been no impact; presumably if her teeth had touched the cockroach, creating impact, the suit would have been permitted. In another case, however, a woman who was defecated upon by a horse while watching a circus did have grounds for her suit; she had suffered impact.

(Physical impact, however, is not required in cases in which the victim was harassed or terrorized; in such suits, the harassment itself becomes an attempt to create an emotional impact on the plaintiff, so that physical touching isn't necessary.)

Either due to the various legal restrictions, or for strategic reasons, you may find that your lawyer won't want to make mental anguish a ground for damage in your case. Don't worry about that. What he will do, instead, is work in evidence of the anguish you felt as a part of your pain and suffering allegations. Only when the mental-anguish evidence is so substantial that it is likely to increase your award meaningfully will it become a separate item, or when—as can happen in many harassment or libel suits—mental anguish is the sole basis for the award.

Assuming you can meet whatever standards for admissibility of evidence are required in your jurisdiction, the following are typical grounds for a mental-anguish allegation:

The injury made you fear for your life or that of a loved one, or caused you terror or shock.

Generally, when there has been impact, the plaintiff can then testify to the fear felt immediately prior to the impact. "Shock," in this sense, refers to the plaintiff's reaction to a frightening or unexpected event; shock is also a medical term for a recognized set of physical symptoms, and when they are present, they become part of the medical damages.

You suffered anxiety about the aftereffects of the injury.

Even when one no longer fears for one's life, the ultimate effects of the injury on one's health may not be known for days or for years; during that period, the anxiety felt is a proper ground for a mental-anguish allegation. Anxiety is often also successfully raised by pregnant women who fear the effect the injury might have on the child they are carrying.

The injury caused you worry about its economic effects on yourself and your family.

However, when this allegation is raised, the defense has the right to introduce evidence (as it ordinarily may not) concerning your financial status and medical-insurance coverage, to indicate that the worry wasn't reasonable. If you have sufficient insurance or are a well-to-do person, introduction of this kind of evidence could lead the jury to reduce the award it might otherwise make.

The injury caused you embarrassment or humiliation.

Although most frequently raised in harassment or libel cases, this allegation sometimes applies to negligence issues as well. Disfiguring injuries provide one illustration. In them, the mental-anguish period begins at the time you knew of the disfigurement and concludes when and if the resultant cosmetic surgery is successful.

The injury caused you to become depressed, neurotic, or psychotic.

Most courts won't entertain testimony to the effect that the injury or the treatment following it merely made you feel "nervous," "upset," "worried," or "not myself." These feelings generally aren't considered to rise to the level of mental anguish.

For such allegations to be admitted, expert testimony is normally required, such as the professional opinion of a psychologist, psychiatrist, or other licensed therapist that the plaintiff's neurosis, depression, etc., was directly caused by the circumstances of the injury. Such testimony, however, is usually given little weight when the therapist has been consulted only long after the injury and close to the eve of trial. In that instance, the plaintiff usually will be suspected of trying to generate evidence for the purpose of the lawsuit.

Testimony about changes the injury wrought emotionally or psychically, however, need not be confined to medical experts. Here you can often be helpful to your case, or if you are bringing the suit on behalf of someone who has become deranged as the result of an injury, helpful to that person. Try to think of people who have known you or the victim for many years. For instance, a neighbor might say: "I have known her for twenty years, and before the injury she was always a warm, outgoing person; now she's withdrawn, introverted, and is suspicious of everyone." The word of one lay person about the emotional condition of someone may not have much weight; each additional lay person, however, adds to the credibility of the others' testimony, and the cumulative effect can be powerful.

The injury caused you loss of life's pleasures.

The law generally recognizes that an important part of life is the ability to enjoy its pleasures: sensual, intellectual, recreational, affectional. Removal of these pleasures, temporarily or permanently, therefore can provide grounds for a mental-anguish allegation. Such situations include injuries that permanently or temporarily cause blindness, deafness, or paralysis. They include injuries that make it impossible for a parent to fondle or care for children, or spouses to touch one another. They include injuries that prevent sexual relations between spouses, *in which event both the injured spouse and the partner usually have grounds for recovery*. The crippled person who used to enjoy hiking has lost one of life's pleasures; the same is true of the amateur pianist who can no longer play, the knitter who can no longer knit, the bowler who can no longer bowl, and so on.

To build this element of your damages, draw up a "loss of life's pleasures" list and give it to your lawyer. Make it as complete as possible. Do not reject an item because you think it trivial. Let your lawyer make that decision, as he well might. (Lawyers generally don't like to overload a jury with complaints by a plaintiff; that can reverse the effect intended.)

Never reject an item because you assume it is unrelated to your injury. One lawyer, for instance, recalled questioning his client about the effects his injury had on his leisure activities. The client couldn't think of anything, mentioning only that if his arthritis didn't improve soon, he'd have to give up his woodworking hobby. Until that moment, almost on the eve of trial, the lawyer hadn't heard of any arthritis complaint. The client said he hadn't mentioned it because the arthritis "obviously" had nothing to do with his injury. The lawyer wasn't so sure. He obtained a delay of trial, ordered a new medical examination of the client, and came up with a diagnosis that arthritis was a predictable—though uncommon—consequence of the kind of injury his client had received. Armed with this diagnosis, the lawyer was able to get a $25,000 settlement of a case in which the previous high offer had been $17,500.

While this kind of enriching development in a suit is undoubtedly rare, it does point up the desirability of telling your lawyer *everything*.

11

Getting What's Due You

Once your case has come to a successful conclusion through a settlement or a trial verdict, you next will want to make sure that you get the correct amount of money due you on the day you and the lawyer divide the proceeds.

When the defendant's check arrives, which both of you must sign before it can be cashed, the lawyer will call you to set up a date to distribute the funds. The meeting will take place at his office. He will provide you—and if he doesn't, you demand that he does—a paper showing where every penny of the award is to go: so much to him for his fee, so much for his expenses, so much to pay any outstanding bills you have, so much to pay off subrogation claimants, with the residue to you.

Assuming you have followed the guidelines given in earlier chapters to help you find a reputable lawyer, the chances are great that the distribution sheet will reflect accurately all the financial aspects of your case. Nevertheless, not all lawyers—not even all lawyers with good reputations—are honest or even good record keepers. Therefore, you should check the distribution sheet in detail, make sure it has accompanying bills or receipts, and that the method the lawyer used to deduct his fee is in accordance with the terms of your contingency agreement, a copy of which you should bring to the meeting with you. Make sure, too, that you are receiving any interest due you on the award. Do not sign the distribution sheet or endorse the check or accept his check in payment to you until you are satisfied you have been properly treated.

While this advice should always be followed—if nothing else, it will help you catch any honest mistakes the lawyer has made—it's not sufficient, by itself, to prevent certain kinds of fraud and contractual violation. For them to succeed, the lawyer is relying on your ignorance, knowing that, no matter how careful you are, if you don't know what to look for, he will be able to take advantage of you.

THE ILLEGAL FEE

One scheme by which you might be victimized is the illegally high contingency fee. While it won't be effectuated until fund-distribution day, it has its origins in the contract you signed at the beginning of the case. This is one time in which the old bromide that ignorance of the law is no excuse does not hold true. If you unwittingly signed an agreement permitting an illegal fee, you have every right to deny the contract and obtain the money that is properly due.

Illegal-fee cases most commonly are associated with Federal Tort Claims Act cases, in which, as we saw in Chapter Four, the maximum fee an attorney is allowed to charge if a claim is settled at a hearing is 20 percent, or 25 percent if it goes to suit. In one case of this kind, a woman was struck down by a U. S. Mail truck; her lawyer got her a good settlement of $60,000 after suit was filed; however, he charged her a 50 percent fee, or $30,000, instead of the legal maximum. The lawyer had succeeded in stealing $15,000 from his client.

Should you find yourself victimized—or about to be victimized—in this fashion, there are steps you can take. First, if you learn you are being overcharged *prior* to the resolution of the case, immediately dismiss the attorney in writing, stating the reason. Next, send a copy of the letter to the Civil Litigation Division of the U.S. attorney's office in the district in which the suit has been filed, with a second copy going to the federal district court judge to whom the case has been assigned. In a cover letter, ask for an extension of time to obtain new counsel. It will be granted. If suit has not yet been filed, meaning the case has yet to be heard by the administrative board of the agency involved, send the cover letter, asking for the extension, to the board. If you don't know how to reach the board, call the agency involved, requesting the information. Should you not hear from the appropriate officials within a week, call them and ask them for advice. In the meanwhile, you should be seeking a new attorney. If you are having difficulty locating one, contact your local bar association, explaining to them what has happened. They will help you find an attorney to protect your legal interests, either as your new attorney or as interim counsel until you can find a lawyer on your own.

Second, should you learn of the violation of the federal fee law *after* the case has been resolved but *before* funds have been distributed, it is too late, for all practical purposes, to dismiss the attorney. Instead, call him and tell him you are now aware of the fee regulation covering your case and inform him you expect him to take for himself no more than the permissible percentage. Follow your phone call with a letter to him repeating your position. He will almost certainly comply. Under the Tort Claims Act, charging an excessive fee to a client is a felony, and the lawyer could be sent to prison for a year and fined $2,000. If, for some reason, he should attempt to brazen it out, send a copy of your letter to him to the U.S. attorney's office, the local bar association, and to the judge or the administrative board that heard the case. At that point, the court will intervene to assure that funds are distributed properly.

Finally, should you learn of the violation only *after* funds have been distributed, you may still be able to recover your money, assuming the statute of limitations governing the fraud has not lapsed. (It probably hasn't; it begins to toll only after you knew *or should have known* of the victimization.) What you should now do is send a letter to the lawyer demanding he reimburse you for the money he has improperly taken. Because he will fear the possibility of criminal or disbarment proceedings being brought against him, he will probably make good at that point.

However, if he ignores your demand, then contact the legal disciplinary committee or tribunal in your county. You can obtain the address and the name of the person to whom you should speak either from your local bar association or from the office of the president judge of your county court. Send the disciplinary-committee attorney a copy of your original contingency-fee agreement and the statement of distribution of funds that the lawyer provided you on the day he gave you the check. The same information should also be sent to the U.S. attorney's office. That should get you your money, one way or another, but there could be situations in which you might have to enter suit.

(Remember that the 25 percent limit on contingency fees relates *only* to actions brought under the Federal Tort Claims Act. Cases heard in federal court for other reasons do not carry that restriction.)

A handful of states also limit the percentage a lawyer may charge, at least for certain kinds of injury cases, most commonly medical malpractice. These laws vary widely in their application and in the penalties they provide. Your case probably carries no such restrictions, or, if it does, your lawyer is obeying them. Should you have any doubt, however, it can be resolved by inquiring of your local bar association; its phone number will be found in the yellow pages of your phone directory, usually immediately prior to listings of individual lawyers.

Should it turn out that your lawyer is overcharging, follow the same advice given for Federal Tort Claims Act violations, except that instead of the U.S. attorney's office, you should, when necessary, file your complaint with your district attorney's office.

In either situation, should you have a co-counsel on your case, contact him. He will often be able to resolve your problem without putting you to the necessity of taking any further steps and will also relieve you of the unpleasant task of confronting the unscrupulous lawyer yourself. Ordinarily, the co-counsel, at that point, will take over the proper distribution of the funds. (As co-counsel, he has a legal responsibility to you to see that you are not cheated.)

FALSIFICATION OF EXPENSES

In your inspection of the summary sheet the lawyer provides you on payment day, be particularly on the alert for expenses of which you had no prior knowledge and any for which there are no receipts. Frequently, when a doubtful item is questioned, the lawyer will excuse himself from the office allegedly to consult with his bookkeeper; when he returns, he will tell you that a mistake was made and that he is glad you caught it. You may be cynical about this explanation, but accept it. Your interest at the moment is not to make accusations but get the money that is due you.

Should you continue to question the expense statement after explanations have been made, or you only begin to suspect you have been cheated after the award is completed, you can take the following steps:

When you have a co-counsel, contact him. If he agrees that your complaint is legitimate, he will contact the offending lawyer and encourage him to "discover" the "clerical errors" that have been made, and you will get your money.

If that fails or you don't have a co-counsel, contact your local bar association's *grievance* committee. The efficacy of this approach varies considerably across the country. Some bar associations take their citizen-complaint duties seriously and make strenuous efforts to resolve the problems; when they do, their persuasive powers can be strong. Other bar associations, however, seem to feel that their main duty is to whitewash lawyers of charges of improper conduct, or else they don't consider such problems as serious and do little or nothing to help the victimized client. Nevertheless, you have everything to gain and nothing to lose by seeking bar-association help.

Should that fail, you may have to hire an attorney on your own. When the amount in dispute is small, and it usually is, this may be an impractical step to take, considering the fee you would have to pay the new lawyer. In that event, you will just have to accept your loss.

Expense cheating can usually be prevented by taking the proper steps at the time you engage the attorney. Inform him then that you want a written estimate of the probable expenses in your case and that you wish to be informed of and approve any additional expenses in advance. The reputable attorney will have no objection to doing this (he may, in fact, suggest the procedure himself), with the disreputable attorney, knowing by your demand that you will be watching expenses, probably deciding that in your case he'd better not try anything.

DOUBLE DIPPING

Double dipping is a practice engaged in by some lawyers by which they "dip" into the plaintiff's award two or more times to obtain a total commission that is in excess of the percentage agreed upon in the contingency-fee contract. The dip can occur so swiftly and with such apparent innocence that the client may never realize it has happened.

The key to the double dip is the subrogation claim. When an insurer (such as Blue Cross) or a government agency (such as a department of welfare) that has subrogation rights learns from court records that you have entered suit or in the case of Blue Cross from hospital records that you have the kind of injury that is likely to lead to suit, it will send you a letter asserting its legal right to be reimbursed for the funds it paid on your behalf. You will be instructed to turn this letter over to your attorney. When the attorney receives the letter, or is otherwise advised by the subrogation claimant, he becomes, in effect, its collection agent and is entitled to a contracted percentage of the money he obtains for it, just as he gets a percentage of your award. The amount he gets paid varies. It could be as low as 25 percent on cases resolved prior to trial, one third on cases that go through trial.

You, however, have your own contract with the lawyer. It states that your award is to be reduced *only* by the mutually agreed contingency percentage, less payment of any suit-related expenses. Those expenses include the subrogation claims. In other words, if your contract calls for you to pay your lawyer a one-third fee, that is the maximum he is entitled to take from your gross award, no matter how he takes it.

To illustrate, assume you have received an award of $54,000, that your attorney is working on a flat one-third fee, that he has $3,000 in suit-related expenses that will be deducted prior to taking commission, and that Blue Cross has a subrogation claim against you of $6,000 and workmen's compensation one of $3,000.

When your attorney is *not* double dipping, the distribution-of-funds sheet he gives you should generally appear in one of the two following ways.

Gross Award	$ 54,000	
Less lawyer's out-of-pocket expenses	− 3,000	
Remainder	51,000	
Less Blue Cross subrogation claim	− 6,000	(lawyer retains $2,000 based on one-third fee)
Remainder	45,000	
Less workmen's-compensation subrogation claim	− 3,000	(lawyer retains $1,000 based on one-third fee)
Remainder	42,000	
Less lawyer's one-third contingency fee	−14,000	
NET TO YOU	$ 28,000	
NET TO LAWYER	$ 17,000	(consisting of $14,000 from you, $2,000 from Blue Cross, $1,000 from workmen's-compensation insurer)

OR

Gross Award	$ 54,000
Less lawyer's out-of-pocket expenses	− 3,000
Remainder	51,000
Less lawyer's one-third contingency fee	−17,000
Remainder	34,000
Less Blue Cross $6,000 subrogation claim *minus* lawyer's one-third share	− 4,000
Remainder	30,000

Less workmen's-compensation subrogation claim *minus* lawyer's one-third share	— 2,000
NET TO YOU	$ 28,000
NET TO LAWYER	$ 17,000

Using either system, the lawyer takes no more than the agreed, one-third fee.

Now let us see what happens to your net award when the lawyer is double dipping:

Gross Award	$ 54,000	
Less lawyer's out-of-pocket expenses	— 3,000	
Remainder	51,000	
Less lawyer's one-third contingency fee	—17,000	
Remainder	34,000	
Less Blue Cross subrogation claim	— 6,000	
Remainder	28,000	
Less workmen's-compensation subrogation claim	— 3,000	
NET TO YOU	$ 25,000	
NET TO LAWYER	$ 20,000	(consisting of $17,000 contingency fee + $2,000 he keeps from Blue Cross payment + $1,000 he keeps from workmen's-compensation payment)

As a result of the lawyer's double dipping into your award, you are $3,000 poorer. By so doing, instead of taking only his one-third fee, he has managed to slice off nearly 40 percent for himself.

Double dipping is probably the most common method employed by lawyers to obtain more than their contracted share of an award. However, unlike Federal Tort Claims Act violations or the expense-account swindle, double dipping is not a crime. The American Bar Association has not taken a forthright stand on the matter, although it seems to consider the practice improper *unless* the lawyer receives a prior consent from the client to take the multiple commissions. This is a tricky matter and you should be wary of it; a lawyer, for instance, might say to you: "Now, you don't mind that I also take a commission from Blue Cross, do you?" If you say you don't mind, you may have agreed to the double dip.

Assuming you haven't made such an agreement, and probably even if you have without possessing an informed awareness of what you were doing, you have grounds—following a double dip executed—for suit against the lawyer for contract violation. Your chances of winning are excellent.

As a plaintiff, however, your goal is not to get involved in new lawsuits at the end of the old one but, rather, to get the right amount of money due you when it is due. You should therefore take steps at the outset of your relationship with the lawyer to prevent the double dip. Consequently, whenever subrogation claims are a factor in your case, make your lawyer aware, prior to signing the contingency agreement, that you know he is eligible for commissions on these claims, and specify to him that you understand that any commissions he takes in that fashion are to be deducted from those he takes from you. You may, if you wish, have this element of your agreement incorporated into the contingency-fee contract. If he refuses to do so, don't hire him.

In the event that, on distribution day, you discover the lawyer is double dipping, attempt first to protect your interest amicably by suggesting to him that his "clerk" must have made a "mistake" in the computations. Given that graceful way out, he is likely to rectify the problem with no dispute. Should this effort fail, refuse to sign the agreement as accurate. Instead, contact your co-counsel, if you have one, or the bar association, or the judge who heard the case. Only when these efforts fail, and they probably won't, will it become necessary to sue.

12

WHEN YOUR LAWYER IS A LEMON

As we have seen in the chapters dealing with the progress of your suit, you will, many times, be faced with making difficult decisions. It is probable that most of them will be made in conjunction with your lawyer in an atmosphere of trust.

Nevertheless, as can happen in all human relationships, the one between you and the lawyer may not always be a smooth one. Problems can arise; mistrust, wrongly or rightly, can grow. Occasionally, the troubles will be overt and serious and require immediate action. One example would be when you learn that the lawyer is trying to cheat you; another, if you discover he is operating a legal assembly line in which he settles cases for less than they are worth in order to generate income quickly.

Most often, however, the problems that develop with the lawyer are ones that are going to be difficult for you, as a lay person, to evaluate. You will have no way of knowing if the situation represents merely a minor annoyance or the onset of a condition that could be inimical to your interests and—as with the cheating lawyer or the assembly-line operator—means you should fire the attorney and locate a new one.

Most of the time, in fact, the annoyances are minor. Live with them. They won't affect the outcome of your case. But there are some signs you could encounter that may mean nothing but *most often* do mean serious trouble.

To begin with, if your lawyer *repeatedly*—not occasionally—

fails to respond to your phone calls or letters, you should seriously consider finding a replacement for him. His silence may mean nothing, but it could also mean your case is unimportant to him, that other, more lucrative ones are getting his attention, and that eventually, just to get rid of yours, he'll try to talk you into settling it for less than it is worth.

Next, you have a right to be concerned if your case is shifted from lawyer to lawyer in the same firm. If this happens once, it may be just one of those internal matters over which nobody has control, but a second change could mean that your case is low rated, and each time it gets shifted, it therefore gets a less experienced and competent lawyer assigned to it. (Do not confuse this situation with the one in which your case is handled by one lawyer in the firm during the negotiation process and then is assigned to another lawyer—who may not even be in the same firm—who is expert in trying cases when negotiations fail. That shift of counsel is usually in your interest.)

Since you have a right to see any legal paper filed in your case, both by your side and the opponent, you should become worried if your lawyer doesn't want to reveal a document to you. His reason may be that he's afraid the paper will prove some incompetent act on his part or his failure to take an action, either of which events could lead to the loss of your case.

A more complex situation occurs when it is increasingly difficult for you to communicate with your lawyer when you are meeting with him, or when it has become obvious to you that he and you have diametrically opposed ideas about how the case should be handled. The possibilities of trouble at this stage of your case, usually a late one, are nearly limitless. However, they include those instances when he wants you to stretch the truth about some factor in the injury and you don't want to (or the opposite could be true); or you feel that one element of the injury is significant and he doesn't seem to understand why you think that and you can't understand why he thinks as he does; or he's pushing you to settle and you want to hold out for more money. When this kind of deterioration in the relationship sets in, it is usually not easily rectified, and as a practical matter, you are going to have to decide either to accept his strategy like a good soldier or else find another attorney.

Should you decide to dismiss your attorney, you do not have to give him a reason, and you can dismiss him at any point prior to the time the case is resolved by a settlement or trial verdict. If you lose at trial or are dissatisfied with the amount of the verdict, you need not use the same lawyer for the appeal as you did for the trial.

Those are your rights. In exercising them, however, you should be careful. Mishandling the dismissal of your lawyer could cost you money and might cost you your case.

The golden rule is this: *Never fire your lawyer until you have obtained a replacement for him.*

By failing to adhere to this dictate, your immediate danger is that you could lose your case through a process known as *nonsuit*. Let us suppose, for instance, that at the time you decide to fire your lawyer, the defense has some kind of motion in your case pending in court. Once you've let your lawyer go, he has no obligation to advise you of this action. As a result, when the day comes to argue it, you will be unrepresented in court and the judge will have no choice but to dismiss your case.

If, on the contrary, you have engaged new counsel prior to dismissing the old one, this lawyer will immediately enter a court appearance on your behalf and notify the defense of his presence in the case. He will ask for a continuance of all pending motions until he has time to familiarize himself with your litigation. The continuance will be granted. You have avoided the risk of nonsuit.

In following this advice, you should be aware that you may not be able to *formally* hire a new attorney until you have dislodged the old one. Many attorneys consider it unethical to intervene in a relationship between a client and existent counsel, with the intervening lawyer possibly opening himself to a charge of malpractice by the removed lawyer. But this is a technical problem for you, not a real one. You and the new lawyer of your choice have every right to discuss the problems you are having with the current lawyer and every right to agree that he will represent you once the dismissal takes place. The new lawyer therefore becomes your lawyer of record immediately after a letter of dismissal is sent to the old one, and no time is lost.

If you have co-counsel on your case, consult with him when

you are having problems with your lawyer. Often the co-counsel will suggest that, before you take any final action, you allow him to discuss the situation with your attorney. Accept the offer. Frequently, difficulties that appear insoluble when limited to you and the lawyer can be rectified by the co-counsel's intervention.

Should the decision be made to fire the lawyer, then the co-counsel can become your new lawyer. You aren't forced to accept him, but he can't reject you at that point, and it is normally a good idea to accept his services, at least until he and you locate a new permanent attorney. (If you don't notify the co-counsel that you have fired the lawyer to whom he sent you, he is relieved of his obligation to protect your legal interests.)

No matter how tempted you are to tell him off, you keep out of the actual act of firing the old attorney. Let the co-counsel or your new attorney do that.

Ordinarily, what will happen is this. The new attorney will dictate a letter of dismissal, which you sign and which is delivered to the old attorney. The letter requests that all records on the case be turned over to the new attorney. The new attorney then meets with the old one. In order to assure his cooperation in the transition, he offers the old attorney one third of any fee he earns on the case. (In the event the dismissal is handled by a co-counsel, this could also occur; in effect, the referring attorney now becomes the attorney of record and the referred attorney becomes the "co-counsel" in the sense only of the mathematical split of the fee. The fee is further split when and if the co-counsel finds a new attorney.) You may be unhappy about an attorney you dislike or mistrust getting any money out of your case, but since none of it comes out of your share of the proceeds, you have no ground for complaint.

On the contrary, you have grounds for rejoicing, because if this deal isn't worked out, the fired lawyer will then almost certainly charge you for the services he has already rendered you. (You almost always open yourself to this financial headache if you try to handle the firing yourself or do it before obtaining a new lawyer.) Depending on the stage of the case at which dismissal occurred, you might owe the old lawyer anywhere from several hundred to many thousands of dollars.

The bill submitted by the old attorney is payable out of your award. You don't have to pay if you don't win or if you drop your suit.

The rules governing a dismissed attorney's right to a fee vary by jurisdiction. Generally, however, he can charge you an hourly rate that is either his standard charge or the one that is standard in the community in which he practices. (Seventy-five to one hundred dollars an hour would be typical.) In most jurisdictions, he can collect for time expended interviewing witnesses, including taking of depositions. He usually cannot charge for the time he alleges was spent negotiating with the defense, and he definitely cannot charge for time he spent meeting with you.

The dismissed attorney is not permitted to hold the records on your case until he has gotten paid. They are your property, not his. This doesn't mean that some attorneys won't try to do just that, and your new attorney will then either have to sue him for the records or else reconstruct them himself from the beginning.

Although you will probably avoid this kind of unpleasant problem if the dismissal of the old lawyer is handled properly, it is always a possibility, suggesting one reason you should always take serious thought before making a change.

You should also be aware that the transition will almost certainly add to your legal expenses. The new lawyer may have to retrace the steps of the old one, spending the same amount of money along the way that the old one did. The old lawyer, for example, may have spent $1,000 obtaining transcripts of sworn statements by witnesses; the new lawyer, dissatisfied with the way the old one handled this procedure, requires new testimony and spends another $1,000. Now you owe $2,000 instead of $1,000 on this single item. (The old lawyer has the same right to reimbursement of his expenses from your winnings as does the new one.)

Since, in engaging the new attorney, it is your expectation he will obtain a better result than the old one, the amount he adds to your expenses may be a price worth paying. It is, nevertheless, a financial consideration, more important in some cases than in others. For instance, let us suppose your original attorney has told you that your case is worth $6,000 and he expects to have $500 in associated expenses. Because he's remiss in returning your phone calls—and this apparently is the single most common reason for client dissatisfaction with an attorney—you decide to dismiss him and ask another attorney to consider taking your case. He also evaluates it at $6,000 and says he will have about $500 in expenses. Your total expense bill has now reached $1,000, representing a significant deduction from the small net return you can expect from your suit. In a case of this size, you probably should not dismiss the first attorney; it's not worth the $500 it's going to cost you.

Changing lawyers is also going to delay the resolution of your case. It might be only a few weeks or a couple months, but when the case is a complex one and the new lawyer must retrace all the steps taken by the old one, your case could age an additional year or more. That time is well worth investing when you are getting a better quality of representation as a result of it, but it is a factor you should weigh when your reservations about your current attorney have nothing to do with his competence and when your need for money from the suit is pressing.

One other risk you incur in changing lawyers—and it can be a substantial one—arises from the inevitable *possibility* that your second lawyer will be no better than the first one and the considerable *probability* that if you change lawyers more than once, the third one will be less competent than the second, the fourth less competent than the third, and so on.

The problem here is that, while few good lawyers have reservations about becoming someone's second attorney, hardly any of them want to become third or fourth in line. Experience has taught them that clients who are constantly changing attorneys are impossible to please, and that trying to serve them is a waste of time. You may not fit that stereotype, but the good lawyer has no way of knowing that and you will be shunned. As a result, by the time you get to the third or fourth attorney, your chance of getting someone of more than minimal qualifications is minimal.

WHEN TO SUE YOUR LAWYER FOR MALPRACTICE

When your case is lost or you receive—either by jury verdict or settlement—much less money than you had originally expected, ordinarily the reason lies in the legal weaknesses of your suit.

Other times, your lawyer will be partly at fault, at least in the sense that he was less competent than your opponent. That your lawyer got beaten by a better lawyer doesn't mean, by itself, that you have grounds to sue him for malpractice. Some lawyers are simply smarter than others, and some are smarter on some cases than on others. Those are the chances you take whenever you hire a lawyer, and when yours falls before the better opponent, that is your misfortune and usually you can do nothing about it legally.

Nevertheless, there can be instances when the quality of the representation you received is so poor that a suit against your lawyer becomes a viable means of retrieving some money from your case.

Legal malpractice can occur many ways, although the malpractice suit won't always be the most efficient remedy available to you. For instance, a lawyer who has cheated you of some of your money has malpracticed against you, but the direct and practical way to make him pay is through a civil-fraud or contract-violation suit, not a malpractice action.

The malpractice suit is best employed when you can show that your case was lost due to some negligence on the part of your attorney.

This most commonly occurs when the lawyer doesn't file a legal paper in a timely fashion. One example is the suit that is dismissed because the lawyer didn't meet the statute-of-limitations deadline.

To bring suit against your lawyer on this ground, you must be able to show he had the opportunity to make the deadline. In one illustrative case, a woman underwent surgery on September 1, 1977. She lived in a state with a one-year statute of limitations. In the second part of September 1978, she began to believe that her continuing medical problems were the result of the surgery, and she contacted a lawyer who filed suit for her, reasoning that the one-year limitation didn't begin until his client was aware of the injury. In a pretrial motion, a judge agreed that the lawyer was right on the law but decided that the woman should have been aware of the cause of her problem sooner than she claimed, and he dismissed the suit on the ground of late filing. Since the woman didn't go to the lawyer until after what was judicially determined to be the passage of the statute, the lawyer couldn't be held responsible for the late filing. However, had she engaged him as late as September 1, 1978 (the day the statute expired in her case), that lawyer would have had the obligation to file suit that day, and if he didn't he was negligent and she could sue him to pay her for the money she probably would have won had he acted in a timely fashion. In other words, your lawyer can't use as an excuse for missing a deadline the fact he had only one or two hours to make it. A lawyer is presumed to know how to act swiftly when it becomes a necessity to protect a client's rights.

Missing the statute-of-limitations deadline is only one of many reasons that your case could be nonsuited at a pretrial stage. Occasionally, the defense will win solely on the merits of its argument. Nevertheless, should you lose your case through *any* pretrial motion, *be suspicious*. The reason may have been your lawyer's negligence.

If you lose for this reason, demand that your attorney explain to you in detail the grounds for the dismissal. Make notes of his explanation; you may need them later should you decide to sue him. Ask him to show you records that prove he responded in time to prevent the defense from obtaining the nonsuit. Even if the attorney's explanation appears reasonable, you may find it wise to check further. Obtain the docket number on your case—it will appear on the legal papers associated with it—and go to the court clerk's office; from the docket number, the clerk will be able to supply you with the folder on your case and also tell you the proper deadline date for filing. The folder may show a reason for the dismissal different from the one your attorney gave you, or it may not include the paper he claims he filed on the date he said it was filed. Alternatively, you could call or write the judge who dismissed the suit and ask him the reason for his action. Should you learn, one way or another, that the suit was dismissed due to your lawyer's negligence, by speedy action, in some instances, a new lawyer will be able to get the case reinstated. Failing that, your only remaining option is to bring a malpractice suit.

Although this happens only rarely, it is also possible to lose your suit not on its merits but because your lawyer filed it in the wrong court. The reasons this can happen are highly technical but usually involve a suit filed in federal court when it should have been entered in state court. Not all cases dismissed on these jurisdictional grounds indicate malpractice, but normally you shouldn't lose a case for this reason, and when you do you should consider discussing your case with a new lawyer, either to see if he can get it reinstated in the proper court or to initiate a malpractice suit against the lawyer who made the mistake.

Failure by your lawyer to pursue your case according to recognized legal practice can also give you grounds for a malpractice claim against him should you lose. As a lay person, you will usually have difficulty recognizing when you have been victimized this way and even more difficulty proving it when you suspect it. The problem here is that, unlike missing a deadline, which is a documentable form of misfeasance, the proper way to pursue a suit is usually a matter of opinion, and no lawyer will accept your malpractice suit if your only evidence is that your lawyer used strategy that, in retrospect, was ill advised. The strategy employed, rather, must have been so improper that other lawyers who are expert in personal-injury law will be willing to testify that your lawyer performed below any acceptable minimal standard of competence.

There are some warning signs for which you should be on the alert. Failure by your lawyer to question important witnesses under oath during the pretrial period could, in some instances, indicate negligence. Failure to raise objections at trial when he should have, failure to bring forth witnesses in your behalf, occasionally failure to research the law properly (with the result that the defense gains a nonsuit before trial or at trial), all are events that may mean nothing in themselves but could establish a pattern of legal misconduct.

A malpractice suit can sometimes also be brought when your attorney doesn't bring suit against the right defendant. Construction-site accidents are typical: was it the owner of the property that was responsible for the accident? or the contractor? or a subcontractor? or a subcontractor to a subcontractor? or the engineering firm? perhaps the architect? The line of responsibility can become inordinately complex to determine, but a lawyer is assumed to have the knowledge to unravel the problem, and when he doesn't and the defendant he does name proves it wasn't responsible, the lawyer may have opened himself to a malpractice claim by his client, particularly if the statute of limitations deadline has passed making it now impossible to sue the right defendant.

Another form of malpractice occurs when a lawyer enters into an arrangement with an insurance company to settle cases for less than they are worth, in order to generate quick income for himself. If you think you have been victimized in this fashion, you will have the Herculean task of amassing evidence of suit after suit to show that the participants regularly settled for suspiciously low amounts, but even if you do that you haven't necessarily proved that happened in your case. This doesn't mean that your efforts won't ever be worthwhile. Once you (or your new lawyer) obtain some evidence, the defendants may offer a good settlement, because they fear the effects of publicity if the case goes to trial.

HOW TO FIND A LAWYER WHO'LL SUE A LAWYER

Traditionally, lawyers have been reluctant to sue other lawyers for malpractice or to testify against other lawyers as expert witnesses in a malpractice suit. To them, the practice smacks of professional cannibalism, and they fear that such suits will lead to scandalous newspaper stories that could cause the public to become more mistrusting—if that is possible—of lawyers than they already are.

However, in recent years many lawyers have begun to rethink their aversion to this kind of litigation. For one thing, the large verdicts that began to be obtainable in medical-malpractice suits during the 1960s and 1970s made attorneys aware there might be analogous fruitful pickings in the legal-malpractice field. Some critics have also asserted that the passage of no-fault insurance laws, by cutting down on the number of automobile accidents on which suits could be brought, encouraged attorneys to look in new directions for ways to drum up business, with legal malpractice cases just one of the ways discovered. Be that as it may, insurance, in another sense, has clearly played a role: By the early 1970s, as the number of suits against them began to inch upward, almost all attorneys had begun to buy professional liability coverage, usually in very large amounts because the rates were cheap. This meant that, by bringing a malpractice suit against a colleague, a lawyer would not be extracting money from that lawyer's pocket but from an insurer, a source that plaintiff lawyers have always considered fair game. In this fashion, because the initial suits encouraged the purchase of insurance, the insurance that was purchased created more suits.

Despite these helpful developments from the plaintiff's point of view, it will still usually be more difficult for you to obtain an attorney to pursue a legal malpractice case than for any other form of litigation. Your problem will be particularly difficult if you live in a rural area or in the southern half of the country.

Should you be having difficulty in obtaining counsel, here are two possible avenues to explore:

Contact your local bar association or that of the largest city near you. Ask for the name of the chairman of its professional responsibility committee or its medical/legal committee. Such individuals almost always know the names of attorneys who litigate legal-malpractice cases for plaintiffs; in some instances, one or the other of the chairmen may be willing to take on your case himself.

Otherwise attempt to obtain, through any lawyer contact you have, the name of a local attorney who specializes in *medical*-malpractice cases. These attorneys are the ones most likely to handle legal ones, and handle them well.

(When contemplating a legal-malpractice case, it is not a good idea to discuss it with a co-counsel. His liability for the malpractice is equal to that of the attorney to whom he referred you, so any advice you might get from him would be too self-interested to be valuable to you.)

HOW TO WIN YOUR MALPRACTICE SUIT

The amount you can win on a malpractice suit—theoretically, anyway—typically depends on the point at which the negligence occurred. If your suit was dismissed at a preliminary stage, the legal issue is *not* whether you would have won, but the probable amount you *could* have won had the negligence not cost you the opportunity to pursue the case. If your case went through to a settlement or a trial verdict, however, in some instances you will have to show both that you would have won and the amount you probably would have won had there not been malpractice. This could mean retrying the original case with the verdict, if any, this time paid not by the original defendant but by your old lawyer or his insurance company.

Legal malpractice suits hardly ever go to trial. For his part, the lawyer you are suing will almost always want to avoid trial and its attendant publicity and will urge his insurer to settle. The insurer won't need much urging. It considers any lawyer sued for malpractice a prime target for jury bias.

All that sounds to the good for you, and occasionally it will be. Unfortunately, there's another side to it. If you reject a settlement and take the case to trial, you may be able to win it, but you may not be able to keep it won. In the average personal-injury case, unless a very large award or controversial legal issues are involved, the losing defendant won't appeal, and if there is an appeal, there is rarely more than one. Not so when a lawyer loses a legal-malpractice trial. With his reputation at stake, he has only begun to fight. He will make a series of appeals on the most imaginative points, and the chances are excellent that somewhere along the line he'll find a sympathetic ear from appeals judges, who, after all, are fellow lawyers. As a result, a new trial is ordered, opening the way for a whole new host of appeals in its wake. By the time such cases are resolved, if they ever are (one notorious New York suit begun in 1963 was still kicking up and down the court system as recently as 1979), the trial-related expenses accumulated by the plaintiff can exceed any possible verdict, with the plaintiff's lawyer, who knew what the road ahead was going to be like, almost certainly having required the plaintiff to pay most or all of those expenses in advance.

Due to the unpleasant prospects that trial presents both sides, the hardest-fought courtroom battles in a legal-malpractice case will be those in which the defense seeks a motion to dismiss the charge on the ground that the plaintiff hasn't presented enough evidence in the suit to allow the case to proceed. Such losses on pretrial motion are most frequent when the allegation is poor legal strategy by the accused lawyer; they are rare when the case is based on failure to meet a deadline.

Assuming you get past the pretrial motions, the defense is almost certain to try to settle, but the offer is going to be a low one in relation to what you could probably have won had there been no malpractice. Although your lawyer will almost always be able to bargain this figure upward, a point will occur at which the insurer backs off and dares you to go to trial. In so doing, it knows that, as much as it doesn't want the expense of trial, it is better equipped to go ahead than you are. You recognize that too, and so you settle. The insurer has saved itself money.

But you have won too. By calling your old lawyer to task for his bungling or misbehavior, you have retrieved some money from what appeared to have been a lost cause.

Therefore, when an attorney agrees you have grounds for a malpractice suit against your former attorney, initiating that action is usually a sensible step for you to take. Never, however, go ahead with it if the lawyer asks for a fee in advance. If he's not willing to work on a contingency basis, you can assume you are about to be milked for money on top of the money you have already lost.

13

The Defendant in Trouble

Until now, we have been concerned with how you can protect and further your legal interests when you are the victim of an apparently wrongfully inflicted injury. Since you can also, rightly or wrongly, be accused of causing such an injury, in this chapter we will consider what can happen to you and how you can protect your interests when you are named a defendant.

The great likelihood is that any injury you are accused of causing will be one for which you are insured.

Personal-injury insurance is widely available—and widely purchased—in the United States. Almost everywhere, automobile drivers are required to carry it by state law in one form or another, and often in specified amounts. Homeowner policies often include coverage for injury to others as part of the total insurance package, and when they don't, this kind of policy can be purchased separately. Moreover, almost all businessmen and private institutions that deal with the public carry insurance to cover the costs of injuries that occur on their property or are caused by their employees. In addition, most manufacturers carry product liability insurance, with doctors, lawyers, and other professionals protecting themselves through the purchase of professional-liability (malpractice) insurance.

No matter how it was obtained, a liability policy guarantees that the carrier will, in return for premiums received, pay the costs of a claim or suit of the type and in the circumstances described in the wording of the policy. The costs the insurer undertakes to pay include those associated with defending the claim, including legal fees (the insurer almost invariably has the right to choose the lawyer), as well as any settlement or jury award up to the face value of the policy, less any deductible. In other words, if you carry a personal-injury policy with a face value of $50,000 per claim and a $500 deductible, and a suit against you costs the company $50,000 to settle plus $5,000 in legal fees and other costs, the company pays $54,500.

If you should have a claim filed against you for which you are insured, you will probably find that the carrier responds properly and efficiently to the allegation, with a minimum of inconvenience to you. You may have to do nothing more than fill out a report on the accident and answer questions posed by the company's claims adjuster. Sometimes you will be required to respond to a plaintiff's interrogatory—though the actual work will probably be done by the insurer—and answer questions at a deposition. Taken together, these activities will rarely cost you more than four to eight hours. Only if the case goes to trial does your time involvement become substantial. Unless a deductible is involved, there's about a 98 percent chance your suit will cost you nothing out of pocket.

What usually happens, however, doesn't always happen. Not only is it conceivable that the suit could cost you money, but it is somewhat more probable that your insurer may refuse to defend you. To see how these problems can arise—and learn what you can do to avoid or confront them—a study of the catechism that follows should prove helpful.

DANGER: NONNOTIFICATION OF A CLAIM

Question: How will I know a claim has been made against me?

Answer: Usually you will receive a letter from the plaintiff's attorney asserting that you wrongfully caused an injury to his client and that you are responsible for paying all resulting costs. Sometimes, however, the letter will go directly to the insurer, in which event the insurer will notify you.

Question: What should I do when I get such a letter from the plaintiff's lawyer?

Answer: Immediately advise your insurer, either by contacting the company itself or through your insurance agent. The initial contact can be made by phone. But do not rely on the phone notification. *Always* send the letter or a copy of it, along with a dated covering letter from yourself by registered mail to the company or the agent, making sure to include your policy number and date. Retain a copy of the correspondence. Retain a copy of the plaintiff's letter. Retain the registered-mail receipt. These items are your proof that you advised the company of the claim, should it subsequently attempt to refuse to defend you on nonnotification grounds.

Question: Does that mean that if I don't notify the company of a claim, it doesn't have to defend me?

Answer: Not necessarily, but it provides the company with an excuse that it may be seeking and that could be upheld in court. The company will assert that the nonnotification—or the delay—caused it to lose its ability to defend the claim properly. Should this problem arise, you will probably require the services of an attorney to fight the company. That could mean money out of your pocket.

Question: What is the permissible delay period?

Answer: There's no set rule. A few weeks might be too long; delays over ninety days have frequently been ruled excessive.

Question: Does an insurer have other grounds for refusal to defend on nonnotification?

Answer: Yes. Failure or delay in filing an incident report could have the same result.

Question: What is an incident report?

Answer: Many personal-liability policies require the customer to notify the company of *any* incident involving an injury to another, regardless of who the policyholder thinks is at fault and regardless of whether or not the injured party has threatened legal action.

Customers are often reluctant to file incident reports. They believe, not always without justification, that the company will use the report to raise their premiums or—when it suits the company interest—to cancel the policy.

When the incident-report requirement is violated and the company does not otherwise receive notification of pending litigation, it may have a legal excuse not to defend. While it is rare for an insurer to adopt this posture, and most judges are reluctant to permit one to do so, you should be aware that the possibility exists.

DANGER: DENIAL OF COVERAGE

Question: What is the meaning of denial of coverage?

Answer: The insurer claims that the policy doesn't require it to defend, because the circumstance of the injury-causing incident is outside the scope of the policy. Frequently customers think they are covered for a certain kind of accident, but under the fine print of the policy they are not. So-called umbrella insurance policies often contain such loopholes. Suppose, for example, you carry an umbrella policy which, among its other provisions, covers all members of your household against personal-injury suits. Visiting you one summer is your eighteen-year-old nephew, who causes an injury to someone. Is your nephew covered?

The insurance company will probably argue that he is not, because the policy, it will insist, is intended to cover only permanent members of the household. You, on the contrary, will say that since the nephew, a close blood relative, was living with you, he was a member of your family and should be defended by the company. There is no governing law. Faced with this kind of problem, courts have come to opposing conclusions.

Next, suppose that your family has an umbrella-type policy that you believe covers the cost of suits caused by the actions of any family members. You have an eighteen-year-old son who lives with you but owns and drives his own car. In this situation, if your son injures someone while driving the family car, the insurer will have to defend. The policy, however, may not cover the son when the injury occurs while driving his own car. If he doesn't carry separate insurance for it, he may not be covered even though the only reason he didn't buy insurance was your and his assumption that he was covered by the family policy.

(As these examples illustrate, not all family or inclusive automobile-insurance policies necessarily have the umbrella effect you might have thought when you bought them. Before purchasing any policy, be sure you understand precisely *whom* it covers and *when* it covers them. Don't accept verbal assurances from the agent. He could be misleading you to make a sale. Get the assurances in writing, and if you don't understand the terminology, obtain a memo or a rider from the company that explains the coverage in clear language.)

In addition to denial of coverage due to escape clauses in the policy itself, the insurer is *never* obligated to defend or pay when the injury was caused by an intentional act.

Question: But can an insurer always prove that an injury was intentionally caused?

Answer: No, and then it has its problems, but so do you. For instance, suppose there are two men, Mr. Brown and Mr. Jones, who are bitter enemies. One night, Brown, driving at an excessive rate of speed, ran down Jones as he was crossing a street. If Brown hit Jones deliberately, then he committed an intentional tort, which is not covered by insurance. If, however, it was simply an unfortunate coincidence that his enemy was the victim of his careless driving, then Brown's insurer is obligated to defend him and pay for the costs of the injury.

In this case, rather than investigating the plaintiff, the insurance company will expend its greatest effort investigating its customer, Brown, hoping to find evidence to prove he acted deliberately. But perhaps it won't succeed. The evidence may be ambiguous. In that event, the company will probably send Brown a *reservation-of-rights* letter, in which it tells him that it tentatively accepts his story that the injury to Jones was an accident and will defend him on that basis, but further informing him that if evidence develops to show an intentional injury, it will then withdraw its defense and refuse to pay any award.

Brown is now faced with the realization that his insurance company is going to continue to try to prove him a liar but is simultaneously providing him with an attorney who is supposedly going to help him prove he is telling the truth. In that situation, Brown, like anyone else who receives a reservation-of-rights letter, is going to wonder how zealous will be any defense he is going to get from the insurance company. Occasionally, faced with this kind of conflict of interest, the insurance company will permit someone like Brown to hire his own attorney, whose fee the company pays, but it is under no obligation to do so, and the likelihood is that a customer like Brown will find himself defended by a lawyer he neither wants nor trusts.

What will finally happen in Brown's case is uncertain, but his position is far from as difficult as it might seem. The chances are that he is about to gain an important new ally: his old enemy, Jones.

Although Jones may be mortally convinced that the hated Brown ran him down deliberately, his lawyer will have told him that the only way he can get insurance money for his injury is to accept Brown's version. If Jones agrees to do that, as he almost certainly will, it is now the insurance company that is in the difficult position. With negligence as the only charge Jones is making, it also becomes the only one to which the insurer can respond. (Because Jones refuses to raise the intentional-tort issue, there's no way the insurance-company lawyer can; to do so would be to accuse his own client of a criminal act, a fundamental breach of ethics that could bring about the lawyer's disbarment.) Therefore, the only way open to the insurance company to get out of the case is to try to prove that Brown wasn't at fault or that Jones somehow was, arguments the insurance company probably knows are false but that it may make anyway. The suit, in this fashion, has become a sham. Should it get to trial, the jury never learns the salient fact of the nature of the relationship between Jones and Brown—it probably won't even be told they knew each other—and makes its decision solely on the negligence issue. If

Brown is found liable, the insurer now has to pay. Assuming he did deliberately injure Jones, Brown has beaten the system.

But defendants who deny intentional torts don't always make out that well. In these suits, the defense is often based on the allegation that the wrongful event never occurred, although it is undeniable that, if it did, it was intentional.

One of the more sensational cases on this theme involved a psychiatrist we'll call Dr. Green. He was accused by a patient of forcing her to have sex relations with him, allegedly as part of her therapy. He denied the episodes ever took place. His insurer therefore had no choice but to defend him. A jury believed the plaintiff and awarded her $250,000.

Once the verdict came in, the insurer was out of the case. Not only did it not have to pay the verdict, but—an appeals court subsequently ruled—it didn't have to pay the doctor's legal fees either.

Question: Are there any other grounds for denial of coverage?

Answer: Yes; the insurer can refuse to defend by alleging customer fraud.

This most commonly occurs when a company believes its customer and the plaintiff have conspired to fabricate an injury in order to collect from the company. Fraud, however, can also be alleged when the company learns that a customer provided false information when applying for a policy.

A customer who is wrongfully accused of fraud by an insurer has grounds for a defamation-of-character suit against the company.

WHAT TO DO WHEN COVERAGE IS DENIED

Question: When my insurer refuses to defend me, for whatever reason, what steps can I take?

Answer: Any of the following four courses of action are open to you:

You can hire an attorney yourself to defend the case and hope you win.

Or you can hire an attorney to take the insurance company to court to force it to defend you. Should you prove successful, the judge will not only order the company to perform its duty but will also *probably* require it to pay your attorney's fee.

Or you can do nothing. If you refuse to defend yourself, the plaintiff will then have judgment entered against you for the maximum amount of damage that can be shown. Assuming you can't pay the judgment or can pay only part of it, the plaintiff will then sue the insurance company to try to force it to pay, on the ground that its refusal to defend you was illegal. Should the insurance company lose that suit, it will then be required to pay the judgment, including any amount that is in excess of the face value of your policy. (Because it never contested the personal-injury action, the insurer cannot, at that point, argue that the award was too high.)

Alternatively, as soon as you are informed by the insurer that it won't defend you, send a letter advising the company that you have no intentions of paying to defend yourself. This may force the company to rethink its position. It knows that, even if it is proceeding from viable legal grounds, there's a good chance its denial of coverage won't be upheld when the plaintiff sues it to pay the award. (Juries are notoriously unsympathetic to insurers who try to get out of defending their customers.) Consequently, the company may decide to take up the cudgels on your behalf because that way it has an opportunity to negotiate a settlement that will almost certainly be less costly than any uncontested judgment it might eventually have to pay.

Since each case of denial of coverage has its own nuances, and since defendants will have varying degrees of vulnerability to a judgment against them, no general advice can be offered as to which of these choices is the preferable one. When in doubt, and if you can possibly afford it, seek a consultation meeting with a lawyer. Take along a copy of your policy and all correspondence on the case from the insurance company. The lawyer will be able to outline to you the strengths and weaknesses of each of your options, and in some instances, realizing the insurance company is bluffing, will be able to bring it quickly into line without recourse to a suit and at only a minimal fee to you.

Question: What effect does a deductible clause in my policy have on the insurer's obligation to defend?

Answer: None. The only effect is on the award. Let's suppose you have a $2,000 deductible on your policy. In that event, if a case is settled against you for $2,000 or less, you pay the entire award. However, the cost of investigating and defending the claim is still borne by the insurer.

WHEN THE JURY AWARD IS GREATER THAN YOUR INSURANCE COVERAGE

Question: What happens when the award in a case exceeds the face value of my insurance?

Answer: Legally, you are required to pay the additional amount *unless* you can show an absence of good-faith bargaining by the insurer. If you can, the insurer must then pay the full amount.

Question: What is the meaning of "good faith" in that sense?

Answer: An insurer has the legal obligation to attempt to settle claims against its customers within the limits of their policies. This does not mean that a company is required to settle every claim for that amount, nor does it mean that, any time the plaintiff offers to settle the case for the face amount, the company must agree.

However, when a company refuses to accept a plaintiff's offer to settle for the face value and the award is in excess of that value, the company opens itself to the charge that it failed to bargain in good faith and can—when a court decides that the circumstances warrant it—be required to pay the entire amount.

Question: How can I find out if my insurer bargained in good faith?

Answer: Most of the time, you don't have to do anything. The plaintiff's attorney knows he made an offer to settle for the face value and has a record of that offer. Having gotten an award over that amount, he can try to collect the excess either from you or from the insurer. He will almost invariably choose the insurer, since he knows it has the ability to pay. You therefore will be contacted by the plaintiff's attorney and asked to become a plaintiff against the insurance company along with the person who sued you, with the attorney representing both of you (but at no cost to you). If the insurance company loses, any judgment that has been placed against you is removed and you are out of the case free and clear.

Question: But what if the original plaintiff doesn't go after the insurer for the excess amount?

Answer: This can happen. If you are a person with significant assets—perhaps you were sued in your capacity as owner of a thriving business—the plaintiff may decide to proceed against you, rather than spend the time and effort trying to force the insurer to pay the additional amount.

Therefore, whenever you are faced with having to pay the additional money yourself, and the plaintiff doesn't act against the insurer, you should explore the possibility of doing so yourself. If the plaintiff's attorney has evidence that bad-faith bargaining has occurred, he will probably be cooperative; after all, he doesn't care from whom he collects, just so he collects from somebody. Ordinarily, however, you will have to hire your own attorney for this purpose; if you win, the court will direct that the insurance company reimburse you for the fee your lawyer charged you. If you lose, you still owe the excess amount and have to pay your lawyer's fee as well. That's the gamble you take.

Question: Can my insurer and the plaintiff reach a settlement agreement in excess of my policy limits?

Answer: No. You have to be consulted and your agreement obtained. Should this situation arise, never take the insurance company's word that it is a wise decision for you to agree to pay the additional amount. After all, they don't care how much the settlement costs you; they are interested only in getting out of the case for themselves as cheaply as possible. Therefore, at this point, you have the right to engage an attorney on your own, and you should do so. Often, he will be able to negotiate the plaintiff's demands downward so that you don't have to pay anything extra.

In the event you do finally agree to pay the additional amount, you must pay your share at the time the insurer pays its, or else the agreement becomes void and the case goes to trial. At the time the payment is made, be sure that you obtain a release from the plaintiff's attorney from further legal action against you. If you don't, you might find yourself sued separately. Your personal attorney will know how to protect you from this problem.

Question: If the settlement agreement is *within* the policy limits but I think the claim against me is nonmeritorious, what can I do?

Answer: Maybe nothing. Most insurance policies carry a clause giving the carrier the right to settle a case within the limits without the customer's approval. Where that clause does not exist, you can refuse to agree and force the case to trial.

Question: If I do that, will the insurer defend me properly?

Answer: That's not a problem. Once it finds itself at trial, the insurer will want to win regardless of how it feels about your recalcitrance.

Question: Then, if I think I'm right on a suit and I don't have to agree to a settlement, should I demand a trial?

Answer: As a practical matter, this is usually an unwise decision to make. You will then be required to spend many hours with the lawyer preparing the case and anywhere from several days to several weeks in a courtroom. That can be an expensive experience for you. Moreover, if you lose, the verdict could be in excess of your insurance and you'll lose money that way. Finally, by forcing the insurer to trial when it wants to settle, you are requiring it to pay additional money in legal fees and court costs, an expenditure you may soon find reflected in a premium increase or in a cancellation of your policy.

Question: How otherwise might my experience as a defendant affect my standing with my insurance company?

Answer: There is no certain answer to this, but any claim against you—whether meritorious or not, whether resolved by trial or by settlement—may cause you to become a bad risk in the insurer's eyes and lead to a cancellation of your policy or a substantial increase in your premium. Defendants in automobile injury cases appear particularly vulnerable here. Due to a single claim, they can find themselves dumped into a so-called "high risk" pool of drivers, who pay far greater premiums than the norm.

WHEN YOU ARE SUED AS AN EMPLOYEE

Question: As an employee, are there any circumstances in which I may be held responsible for injuries I cause by my negligence in a job-related situation?

Answer: Yes. Although under the doctrine of *respondeat superior* an employer is usually responsible for the accidental—not deliberate—injuries caused by an employee to a nonemployee, there are some exceptions to the rule, of which you should be aware.

First, when the employer is a government agency or charity that is immune from suit, then you, as an employee, can be sued.

However, many government agencies holding sovereign immunity and some institutions covered by charitable immunity will, despite their exemption, as a matter of good employee relations or by union contract, agree to defend and pay for injuries caused by workers. If your employer has immunity, therefore, you should ascertain its practices toward sued employees before considering purchase of insurance yourself for this purpose.

Secondly, when your employer lacks the ability to pay a judgment, a plaintiff may be able to try to collect from you.

This can happen when your employer goes bankrupt, disappears, or lacks the assets (or insurance) to pay for the verdict in full or in part. However, for collection to be attempted against an employee, the employee must have been found liable as a result of a trial verdict. When only the employer is named as a defendant or only the employer is found liable, collection may not be levied against the employee who actually caused the injury.

Next, an employer may sometimes attempt to prove that the injury you caused wasn't job-related. The law here is by no means uniformly applied. However, you will probably be held responsible for injuries you cause while on your way to work, on your way home from work, and while on your lunch hour. Accidents that occur at these times, however, typically come about while driving, and in that event your automobile insurance should provide you the necessary coverage.

Finally, your employer may be able to deny that you are an employee. Commission salespeople who represent more than one employer, such as manufacturers' representatives, are particularly vulnerable. Under the law, these individuals are usually considered self-employed, even though they may be working on a draw against commission. The *respondeat superior* protection conceivably could be invoked when the salesperson, at the time of the injury, was exclusively—even if only temporarily—representing one employer. The specific nature of the contractual relationship between the parties will determine whether or not an employer/employee relationship existed.

PROTECTING YOURSELF FROM SUIT WHEN YOU ARE UNINSURED

Question: Whichever way it happens, what choices are open to me when I am sued in a situation in which I am uninsured?

Answer: When you are sued as an employee, and your employer (or his insurer) is going to pay for the defense and any award, you need do nothing. When the suit is against you as an uninsured individual, you can either hire an attorney and fight, or you can do nothing and allow the plaintiff to enter a judgment against you and try to collect from you.

Should you decide to fight, your attorney will charge you on either an hourly or a flat-rate basis. Invariably, he will require a substantial portion of the fee in advance. Failure to pay additional amounts as they become due releases the attorney from further obligation to you, and you have no right to demand a refund of the money already paid. If you win, the judge might order the plaintiff to pay your legal fees, but this happens only rarely.

When you elect not to fight, the amount you owe will be based on the plaintiff's statement of the damages he incurred. The judgment gives the plaintiff the right to collect from any assets you own personally, including bank accounts and property. The latter could be sold at auction to satisfy the debt.

The plaintiff cannot collect from assets owned jointly with a spouse, child, or any other party. However, when jointly owned property is sold, should the plaintiff learn of it your share of the proceeds can be attached to satisfy the judgment.

An unsatisfied judgment affects your credit. While it is in existence, you may find you will be unable to purchase or sell property.

Faced with a suit when uninsured, you may receive advice that you should transfer title of your assets to your spouse's name, that of another family member, or a friend. Before contemplating this course, you should be aware of the possible adverse consequences:

First, once you have transferred assets, they no longer belong to you; thus, if you are a man who has put his funds in his wife's name to avoid collection, and your wife leaves you, you have no right to any property, including bank accounts; everything in her name is hers.

Second, transferring assets to avoid collection is a fraud, civil and criminal. It can be set aside by court order, and you could be sent to jail.

Other schemes (false declaration of bankruptcy; conversion of assets into cash, which is then kept in a safe-deposit box; etc.) open you to similar legal peril.

Although it doesn't answer all the problems that could arise, if you are a person who doesn't carry liability insurance and you want to take preventive steps to avoid the financial consequences of a suit, you should consider placing all your property—monetary and real—in joint title. However, *you must do this before anyone sues you,* so that you cannot be accused of fraud.

14

You and the Law

When people first formed governments, they did so, at least in part, out of the realization that unless rules of conduct were created for the citizenry and someone was given the right to enforce them, chaos would result. Not only would the people, unorganized, be prey to their enemies from without but also to the depredations of malefactors within the group. Lacking an established means of punishment of internal wrongdoers, victims would have no choice but to try to exact personal vengeance and, by so doing, sunder the very security the society was formed to provide.

By granting to the government the right to punish those who violated a society's laws, the assumption was made that the primary purpose of punishment was to promote the common good, not to serve individual interests. It followed, therefore, that penalties exacted against transgressors should be carried out publicly. That way, the law-abiding knew that the government was fulfilling its mandate and the nonlaw-abiding could take warning.

From this reasoning sprang, in ancient times, the doctrine of *lex talionis*. Its essence was enunciated in the Old Testament Book of Leviticus: "When a man causes disfigurement in his neighbor," it is written there, "as he has done it shall be done to him, fracture for fracture, eye for eye, tooth for tooth; as he has disfigured a man, he shall be disfigured."

Stated by the author of Leviticus (brutally perhaps but completely) is the judicial philosophy of deterrence. Not only is the wrongdoer punished so that he is discouraged from repeating his offense, but he is punished in such a way that—as he walks the streets of the town absent eye or limb—all who see him will shudder and fear to do what he has done.

Although the punishments have changed—with the public executions and mutilations of olden times replaced by private executions, imprisonments, and systems of probation—the belief that one person can be deterred from committing an offense by knowing the punishments that have been inflicted on others remains today at the heart of all modern thinking about justice, the American system no less than any other.

YOUR RIGHT TO SUE

However, even if it can be argued that fear of punishment will deter wrongdoing—a proposition that has long been debated to no certain conclusion—it is apparent that neither *lex talionis* nor any of its modern equivalents provides redress for the person victimized by the transgressor. (Will the victim be comforted to see his enemy lacking a leg when he himself is starving because his own loss makes it impossible for him to work?) Although the problems of the victim do not seem to have impressed the author of Leviticus, they were given some attention by the great lawgiver Hammurabi, king of the Babylonians. In his Code, promulgated in the eighteenth century B.C., Hammurabi accepted the wisdom of his time by providing *lex talionis* as his principal mode of punishment but in Rule 198 went one crucial step further; there he stated: "If the eye of a nobleman he has destroyed, or the limb of a nobleman he has broken, one mina of silver shall he pay."

While Hammurabi's Code is the earliest known body of laws that gives some people the right of compensation for their injuries, other societies of the pre-Christian era, including those of Greece and Rome, also enforced, in one manner or another, their own injury-payment rules. It was not, however, until the sixth century A.D. that the groundwork for our present personal-injury justice system was established.

The progenitors were a group of Anglo-Saxon monarchs (of whom one, legend has it, was King Arthur) who set out to enforce uniform national law in a land that, until then, had known only the varying legal impact of tribal custom. The last and greatest of these kings was Ethelbert, who, around A.D. 600, proclaimed a list of injuries for which victims, regardless of their station in life, were to receive money from those who wrongfully harmed them.

To make sure the grievances were justified, special tribunals were established throughout England; they became known as *civil* courts. (*Civil* law, in this sense, means law for the use of citizens, i.e., *civil*ians, as contrasted to the state-controlled criminal law.)

The judges who presided over the civil courts soon enough developed general rules to be followed in determining verdicts to be given in the cases the *suitors* brought before them. (*Suitor* is a Middle English word with a Latin origin which, like *suit* and *sue*, basically means to prosecute or chase, i.e., pur*sue*; the word *suit*, in its meaning as an article of clothing, derives from the garb the civil-court officers wore.)

Each succeeding generation of judges accepted the basic precepts of its predecessor, modifying or interpreting them afresh as new issues arose. As a result, over the centuries a vast body of judge-created law came into existence, although none of it, unlike the acts of king or parliament, could be found in a book of statutes. These judge-created rules of civil governance are what is meant whenever the term *common* (from the Latin *communis*, i.e., community) law is used.

An inheritance from our British past, in the United States the common law has always been used to decide most civil disputes. Its power, however, is not absolute. The Constitution is its superior, and its rules can be modified, expanded, even obliterated by legislative enactment. But this hasn't happened often; for the most part, the common law as it is applied in the American courtroom of today does not differ significantly from that of medieval England.

As this brief history suggests, the criminal and civil justice systems are alike in that each seeks to deter wrongdoing—the one through threat of loss of freedom, the other through threat of loss of money—yet in one important regard they differ from each other: Government, in every society, has seen that it has a positive duty to deter and prosecute crime; the prosecution of civil trespasses against one individual by another, however, is perceived as a voluntary act in which the government provides the means of enforcement but nothing more. Only when the private dispute threatens the public peace and welfare does government intervene.

Therefore, if you are injured in such a way that you have absolutely certain grounds for a successful suit, but you don't sue because you don't understand your right to do so, no judge is going to step forward and tell you what to do. Similarly, should you knowledgeably elect not to pursue your claim, that is no one's concern but your own.

When, however, you do recognize your legal right and want to enforce it, then the justice system, with its courtrooms and its judges and its juries, is there for your use.

But, even after you have begun suit, you remain a free agent. At any point in the proceeding, you can drop your claim and walk away with nothing. At any point, even while the trial is in progress, or after it is over and while appeals are pending, you can agree to a private settlement by accepting money from the defendant and bring the case to a conclusion that way. Except in rare circumstances (usually involving protection of minors), neither the judge nor anyone else in the justice system can or will try to stop you or your opponent from reaching that private arrangement.

PROPERTY INJURY AND PERSONAL INJURY

Whenever your person or your property has been wrongfully harmed by the actions of another, you are said—except in the case of a contract violation—to have suffered a *tort,* with the wrongdoer being known as the *tortfeasor.* (Tort, like "distort" and "retort," comes from a Latin word meaning "to twist.")

Although, in this book, we have been concerned only with those torts involving personal injury, quite often a single action can cause several torts, and when that happens, each alleged wrongdoing will be incorporated in a single suit.

For example, suppose you have been peacefully demonstrating in front of a government building, and a police officer, without cause, hits you with a nightstick and arrests you for disorderly conduct. You can sue the officer (and usually the employing government agency) for two kinds of harm to yourself: the tort of wrongful imprisonment brought about by the arrest, and the tort of personal injury rising from the blow of the nightstick.

Or, much more commonly, if less dramatically, suppose that as you are driving, you are sideswiped by a car, causing injury to yourself and damage to your automobile. In that event, your suit will allege the torts of personal injury and property damage.

Suits based on multiple torts don't have to be joined permanently. For instance, after the automobile-collision suit is entered, it is quite possible that the insurer of the car that sideswiped you will agree to pay for your property damage but refuse to pay for the physical injuries, perhaps because it thinks you are exaggerating their seriousness or demanding too much money for them. You can accept the property-damage payment as a separate item. However, in signing a release form to settle a property-damage claim, *always make sure the opponent hasn't sneaked into it a release on the injury claim as well*. If you sign the release without striking that clause, you lose your right to sue separately for the injury.

WHO CAN SUE AND WHO CANNOT BE SUED

A personal-injury suit can be brought by any person, adult or minor, a rule that includes actions involving injuries inflicted prior to birth. Suits initiated by survivors of people killed as a result of an injury are also permitted.

However, as was observed in Chapter One, there are limitations to the right to sue, some of them applied universally, others holding true only in certain jurisdictions. Since it is possible that the suit you are contemplating might run into one or more of these problems, you should know what they are, why they are, and what alternative means of compensation, if any, may be available to you. The discussion that follows is necessarily generalized; when in doubt consult an attorney.

Suits involving members of the same family are sometimes not permitted.

Most of the time, spouses may not sue each other. There appear to be two reasons for this common-law dictum. First, since husbands and wives are considered one person legally, suit becomes a logical impossibility, since one cannot sue oneself. Second, permitting such suits has been perceived, as one commentator put it, as tending "to disrupt marital harmony," a role the law traditionally is not supposed to play (hence the often illogical roadblocks laid down by the judiciary over the centuries to impede divorce in England and the United States). Whatever the historic foundations for this rule, its practical purpose appears to be to prevent spouses from conspiring with one another to falsify injuries in order to collect from an insurance company.

In recent years, the rule against interspousal suits has undergone challenge, with some limited success. At present, in most jurisdictions, *legally separated* spouses can sue one another when the injury was a violent one, as when a husband beats a wife. The same right is usually not extended when the violently injured spouse is still living with the one who commits the act. Suits for injuries to one spouse caused by the other due to carelessness or negligence are not permitted even when the spouses are legally separated. A divorced person, however, can bring suit against an ex-spouse, apparently even when the injury occurred while they were still married.

Family members other than spouses are permitted to bring personal-injury suits against one another. However, the same fear of collusion that has strengthened the courts' resolve not to permit suits between spouses hangs over these cases as well, making them difficult for the plaintiff to win.

Ordinarily, parents cannot be sued for injuries caused by their very young children.

A child under the age of ten or twelve will usually be considered too immature to realize the consequences of its acts, and the parents—since they can't be held responsible for teaching a child something it is incapable of understanding—cannot be sued in their role as the child's legal guardians. Nevertheless, if you can show that a parent was present at the time you were wrongfully injured—for example, the child threw a stone and hit you—and you can further show that the parent could have taken action to prevent the injury but didn't, then suit can be brought against the parent.

When a child has reached whatever a court determines to be the age of reason—and that clearly includes all children over the age of twelve—both the child and its parents can be sued. (Generally, a retarded person of any age is judged by the same standards as a minor in determining whether or not suit is permitted.)

Injuries that occur by the commission of an illegal act are not subject to suit.

Basically, this means that a burglar can't sue you when he breaks his leg while ransacking your house.

The illegal-act rule for many years also protected doctors from being sued by a woman injured during the course of an abortion. (The doctor in those days, of course, could be arrested for the crime of abortion and so could the woman.) With the legalization of abortion, not only did these suits become permitted, but they also opened the way for wrongful-birth suits. In them, typically the doctor is alleged to have negligently failed to diagnose a condition in the mother (such as German measles) that made the pregnancy dangerous and that resulted in the delivery of a brain-damaged or otherwise-injured infant. In the suit, the mother will argue that had she been informed of the condition, she would have had the pregnancy terminated. Suits of this kind are frequently successful, with awards in the upper hundreds of thousands of dollars not unknown.

A wrongful-birth suit also becomes possible when the doctor has failed to perform competently a requested sterilization of either parent or failed to diagnose a pregnancy in time to permit abortion. To allow suit, the child need not have been born with injuries. The parents of a healthy child, wrongfully born, can still allege injury to themselves in the form of unnecessary medical bills and the cost of rearing the child. These suits, however, tend to be less likely of success than when the child was born injured.

Ordinarily, an employee who is injured by the negligence of an employer or fellow employee may not bring suit.

Payment for employment injury is provided by workmen's-compensation legislation in every state, and federal employees have similar coverage. Although the provisions of these statutes vary widely, they all require payment for: *part* of loss of wages (usually no more than two thirds of the gross wage—the loss of net income that results, however, is largely balanced by the fact that workmen's-compensation payments are not subject to income tax); part or all of medical bills incurred; and when the employee is killed by the injury, death benefits to surviving immediate family (spouse and/or minor/dependent children). Payment is made by the insurance company from whom the employer has purchased the workmen's-compensation insurance policy.

If your injury falls into this category and the insurer refuses to pay, you are permitted to appeal the ruling to a state-administered workmen's-compensation board, which will either require the insurance company to pay or else set a hearing to listen to the facts of the case and then make a ruling. If either side is dissatisfied with the result of the hearing, the case then goes to a regular court on appeal.

You may also appeal when the compensation offer appears inadequate under the law or when payments are cut off prematurely, in your judgment.

Employees may represent themselves before the board or a court, and—in some jurisdictions—unionized employees are permitted representation by a shop steward or other union official. However, due to the complexity of the statutes involved, if you are an employee having problems with a workmen's-compensation insurer, you will usually fare best with the services of a lawyer, and particularly so when the insurer has cut off payments before you believe you are capable of returning to work.

The lawyer is paid a percentage of the amount you receive. He gets no fee if he loses. The maximum percentage he can charge is regulated by statute in many states. (20 percent to 25 percent is typical.) A staff member of the workmen's-compensation board can advise you of any fee regulations that apply to your case. When there is a maximum, let your lawyer know that you know what it is; that will remove from him any possible temptation to overcharge you.

The lawyer is not permitted to earn a fee on benefits you are already receiving. For instance, if you were getting $100 a week and the lawyer succeeds in raising that to $150, his percentage is based on the additional $50 only, which he receives for as long as that payment lasts. (You don't pay him directly; the check you receive is minus his fee; the insurer sends him his share.) Should payments have been stopped and the lawyer gets them reinstated, he is then entitled to his percentage of the entire check.

Not all injuries covered by workmen's compensation need occur at the work site. Payments have been made in cases involving injuries occurring while going to and from work, and for injuries (such as heart attacks) that can be shown to have been caused by the stressful conditions of the job.

For some workplace injuries, lawsuits are permitted.

First, railroad workers and seamen, under the provisions of the Federal Employees Liability Act and the Jones Act, respectively, can bring suit against their employers for causing them wrongful injury.

Second, an employee who is injured because of a defect in a product or a piece of machinery used in the course of work is permitted to sue the manufacturer of the item and is also usually permitted to receive workmen's-compensation payments.

Third, an employee injured by a nonemployee while carrying out the duties of the job—such as a salesman injured while driving—can sue the injuring party and will also be able to collect workmen's-compensation payments.

However, if you are receiving workmen's compensation and win a suit in one of these situations, you probably will have to reimburse the workmen's-compensation insurer for the payments it made, under subrogation law. When you are injured by a fellow employee for reasons that are not work-related (as when one employee attacks another), that injury is not covered by workmen's compensation, and your only recourse for payment is to bring suit just as you would for any nonworkplace injury.

Not all employers are required to carry workmen's-compensation insurance. The various state laws define who is an "employer" for this purpose. Generally, employers of household help and those who hire transient labor (such as the householder who pays a boy to shovel snow from the sidewalk) are not required to carry workmen's compensation insurance. Employees injured in this situation must sue the employer to recover.

Ordinarily, if your employer is liable under the law to pay workmen's compensation insurance but has not done so, you have not forfeited the right to collect. Special emergency insurance funds cover this contingency.

To learn more about the workmen's compensation law in your state, contact the Workmen's Compensation Bureau; its number will either be listed separately or under the Labor Department heading of the state government listings in the white pages of your phone book; or phone your state capital. Many states offer brochures to the public describing how and when to make a claim and how to file an appeal.

In states with no-fault insurance laws, the victim of an automobile accident may not sue the driver alleged to be responsible, unless the injury is such that, under the state law, suit is permitted.

As with workmen's compensation, the provisions of no-fault laws vary. The system, presently in force in twenty-three states, however, invariably provides that payment is made, regardless of who, if anyone, was at fault, by the injured party's insurer. In the event a passenger is injured, the insurer of the car in which the passenger was riding pays. If the driver isn't insured, then the insurer of any other driver in the accident pays. Pedestrians are paid by the insurer of the car that struck them. If none of the parties are insured, your only alternative, as a victim, is to sue the party you believe to be at fault, *unless* you were driving and carried uninsured-motorist coverage, in which event your insurer pays you but only if the other party, in fact, was at fault.

No-fault benefits are always limited to economic damage, i.e., compensation for medical bills, lost wages, and in some states, funeral expenses, cost of hiring replacement labor (such as a housekeeper), and physical rehabilitation or job retraining courses. This means that *payments for pain and suffering and other noncash expenses are not covered by no-fault*.

Sometimes the insurer will refuse to pay benefits or cut them off prematurely, in the victim's judgment. Should that happen to you, you may have to hire an attorney to gain or regain the benefits.

In most states, the no-fault insurer pays the injured party's medical bills up to the statutory maximum. (The amount in no-fault payments permitted is regulated by each state's law as explained in Appendix I.) Payments by Blue Cross/Blue Shield or similar private medical insurance plans begin only after the maximum has been reached. However, residents of Connecticut, Georgia, Kentucky, Pennsylvania, South Carolina, and South Dakota are permitted to collect both from the no-fault insurer and from the private medical plan for the same item of medical expense.

If you live in one of these states, do not make a dual assignment of benefits at the outset of medical care. This happens when a hospital or doctor asks you to provide both the no-fault insurance-policy number and the medical-plan number. When you give the medical provider both numbers, it can collect twice, and it's possible you won't get any money back. Therefore, provide only the medical-plan number. That way, you can still collect from the no-fault insurer for most of the expenses covered by the medical plan. If anybody is going to take advantage of this loophole in the law, it might as well be you, not your doctor or the hospital.

In one way or another, the right to sue is retained in every no-fault state. In most states, however, the victim may sue only when his or her medical expenses exceed a so-called "threshold" limit. A typical figure is $750, but in a number of states there is no limit, while in still others you must prove certain specified "serious" injuries, a definition that usually includes death, before suit is permitted. (See Appendix I.)

Certain individuals have official immunity from suit.

Included are elected officials who hold policy-making positions (the President, a governor, legislators), but immunity is ordinarily limited to times when they are carrying out the duties of their office. A citizen of a foreign country holding a diplomatic passport may not be sued, but any other foreigner (including foreign-owned companies) may be.

As a rule, officials carrying out administrative duties (including policemen and most other government employees) may be sued for causing a wrongful injury, although the applicable statute may require that only the agency for whom the person works be named as defendant.

Units of government may not be sued if the state provides for sovereign immunity.

In these states, suit may be brought only against the employee who is alleged to have caused the injury, not against the employing agency.

Sovereign immunity is an anachronistic carry-over from the days when it was believed "the king can do no wrong." In recent years, many states have abolished their sovereign-immunity statutes in whole or in part, and it seems likely that eventually all of them will do so.

Although negligence suits against the United States Government are permitted under the Federal Tort Claims Act, members of the armed forces may not sue the Government for injuries suffered while carrying out their duties. It is for this reason that soldiers who were exposed to radiation during nuclear-bomb tests and subsequently developed cancer have not been permitted to gain redress from the federal government for causing their often fatal illnesses. Veterans, however, may bring injury suits against Veterans Administration hospitals. (For a description of sovereign-immunity statutes, see Appendix I.)

Institutions enjoying charitable immunity may not be sued.

Employees of the institution, however, may be sued. When a state provides charitable immunity, the exemption usually does not cover noncharitable activities by the institution. Thus, a hospital operated by a church can be sued for injuries it causes to patients or visitors. In a few states, however, charity patients may not sue.

As with sovereign immunity, charitable exemptions from suit appear to be on their way out in the United States. (For a state-by-state analysis, see Appendix I.)

Suit may not be filed after the passage of the statute of limitations.

All fifty states, as well as the federal government, enforce laws limiting the time period during which a suit may be brought. The period can vary depending on the kind of injury alleged.

In the vast majority of cases, the statute begins to toll from the day the injury occurred. Thus, if you are injured on December 1, 1980, and live in a state with a two-year statute of limitations, you have until December 1, 1982, to file suit.

The law, however, recognizes that for some injuries—most typically medical malpractice cases and those caused by inhalation of noxious fumes—the plaintiff may not know of the injury on the date of its occurrence. When this happens, the limitation period begins when the plaintiff first knew or should have known of the injury.

As an example, assume you live in a state with a one-year statute of limitations and you suffered a broken leg on January 15, 1980. At the hospital, the doctor put the leg in a cast which was removed six weeks later. Because the doctor didn't set the leg properly, you are left with a permanent limp. Since there is no way you could have known that that fate was about to befall you on January 15, the earliest date the one-year limit on filing suit could begin would be the date the cast was removed, and it might be later than that, depending on when you first had reason to suspect that the setting of the fracture was performed negligently and that you were to be handicapped as a result.

In cases involving minors, the time limit for discovery of the injury can become quite lengthy. In one instance, a six-year-old girl underwent an operation that left her deaf. Her parents, who could have brought suit on her behalf if they thought the deafness was caused by medical negligence, were convinced by the doctor that the girl's injury was an unfortunate but predictable risk of the surgery. When the girl reached the age of twenty-one, she brought suit against the doctor. It was permitted, and she won.

She was fortunate, because in her state the statute of limitations did not begin to toll until the minor reached her majority. In other states, she would not have been allowed to sue at that late date. Therefore, if your case involves late discovery of the injury, whether it's a matter of weeks or of years, only a lawyer can tell you if you still have time to file suit, and the interpretation of the laws can get so complicated that even he may not be sure.

For a description of the statute of limitations in your state as it applies to *most* suits, see Appendix I.

Although wrongful-death suits can be filed in every state, there may be restrictions in bringing them and limits on the amounts that can be won.

Wrongful-death suits present a different situation from other injury suits, because they are forbidden under the common law. The reasoning behind this rule was encapsuled in a question posed by an eighteenth-century judge: How, he asked, does one pay money to someone who is dead?

While the common-law dictum may have the charm of logic, it violates the principle of deterrence that the civil courts are supposed to help enforce. In effect, it means that if A injures B wrongfully, then A must pay B, but if A is lucky enough to kill B, then A doesn't have to pay anything.

The common-law rule also places the families of people who died from a wrongful injury in an inferior position to the families of those who survived. The latter can use the money from their award to help support their dependents until they recover, but the families of dead victims—who may have lost the sole source of their financial support—are allowed nothing.

Recognizing the injustices prompted by the common-law rule, the United States Congress and the individual states, over the years, have passed laws that permit the survivors of a wrongfully killed person to bring suit. ("Person," in this sense, has usually been interpreted to include a fetus killed as the result of an injury.)

Because they are the handiwork of legislators working separately from one another, the various American wrongful-death statutes lack uniformity. Some put a limit on the amount a survivor can recover—as little as $10,000 in a few places—while others have no limit. Some statutes permit only a surviving spouse or minor children to enter the suit; others allow family members less directly related to become plaintiffs. Some permit a cash recovery for loss of the deceased person's companionship; others don't. If the dead person was a child, some statutes limit the amount the parents can recover to the probable amount of support the child would have given them, but this figure may have to be reduced by the amount the parents spent to support the child; the result typically is a zero verdict.

Whatever the restrictions placed on them, awards in wrongful-death suits are based on the damage the death caused the survivors, not that caused the victim. Ordinarily, therefore, the largest single item of recovery will be loss of future income to the family, as when the deceased was the breadwinner, or cost of replacement of services to the family, as when the deceased was a fulltime housewife and mother.

In addition to wrongful-death actions, in most states the family may also file a *survival* action. In these, the plaintiffs receive an award for the dead person's pain and suffering, as well as expenses incurred and paid by the victim prior to death. Usually the courts require that survival and wrongful-death actions be joined in a single suit.

If a member of a family has begun a personal-injury suit and dies of an *unrelated* cause before that suit is resolved, in some jurisdictions the survivors may continue the suit and receive for themselves the award the plaintiff would have gotten had he or she lived. The attorney who was handling the litigation will know what steps must be taken to preserve the suit.

WHERE SUIT CAN BE FILED

Some suits must be filed in state court (or county court, as it is sometimes called). Others must be filed in the local federal district court. Still others may be filed in either court; for these, the decision is the plaintiff's.

As a rule, federal-court cases come to trial much more rapidly than those filed in state court, a national average of one year compared to four. Thus, if you are desperately in need of money as a plaintiff and you have a choice between the two systems, you might want to ask your lawyer to enter your suit in federal court.

However, there can be other considerations. In some parts of the country, the federal courts are administered by highly conservative judges, who are pro-business in their orientation, many of them coming from law firms that represent corporations, and that is not the kind of judge you want when a business firm or an insurance company is involved in your case.

Moreover, if you live in a large city, the jury you get if you filed suit in the local court will probably have a sizable number of low-income people on it, and they, as a group, tend to be pro-plaintiff. This isn't likely to occur in federal court, where jurors are chosen from the entire district the court covers—an area almost always larger than your city—and you are therefore likely to get much more well-to-do jurors, who, as a group, tend to be pro-defense. On the other side, if you live in a small town and the party you are suing is prominent and powerful there, you may well want to try to get into federal court if you possibly can, in that way obtaining a jury that's less likely to be impressed by the stature of your opponent.

As these illustrations suggest, when there is a choice between the two courts, the question of where to file suit is open to many strategic considerations. Although you have the right to make the final decision, give your lawyer's opinion great weight; he will be more conversant than you can possible be with the odds in choosing the one court over the other.

In any event, as a party to a suit, you have a right to know how the court system works. Since many lawyers are remiss or inadequate in making explanations to their clients, the following description of the rules governing court jurisdiction is offered to provide you with a general understanding.

To begin with, suits brought under the Federal Tort Claims Act must be brought in federal court even if the injury didn't occur on United States property. For instance, if you are a resident of Chicago and injured when struck down on a city street by a U. S. Mail truck, your suit is filed in the Chicago federal district court.

When both the plaintiff and the defendant are residents of the state in which the accident occurred and the federal government isn't involved, then suit must be filed in a court of that state and ordinarily in the county in which the injury occurred. The fact that the defendant may be a business firm with corporate headquarters in a different state has no bearing. As long as it does business in your state, it is considered a resident of that state for purposes of suit.

However, when the plaintiff lives in one state and the defendant in another, then suit may be filed in federal court. Suits of this kind are known as *diversity of citizenship* cases. They originated in the early days of American history, when the citizen of one state often didn't get fair treatment in the courts of another state. To relieve this inequity, the more-impartial federal courts were given jurisdiction. In these cases, the federal judge applies the rules of the state in which the accident occurred, not federal law.

When diversity of citizenship exists, the plaintiff may, however, if he so chooses, file in state court, rather than federal.

(For some years, the federal courts have been contemplating a repeal of the diversity-of-citizenship rule. Should this change be made, diversity cases—though apparently with some exceptions—will always have to be filed in state court.)

Next, when the plaintiff and the defendant don't live in the same state and the injury occurs in a third state, ordinarily the case is heard under the rules of the state in which the accident occurred, but the suit need not actually be tried in that state.

In a mobile society, such suits are not infrequent.

For instance, suppose that Mr. Bell, a resident of Ohio, is visiting in California when he is injured by a car driven by a resident of New Jersey. Bell can file suit in California, as the state in which the accident took place, or in New Jersey, as the residence of the person who caused the injury. (He may not file suit in Ohio.) He further has a choice—under the diversity-of-citizenship rule—between filing in state court in California or New Jersey or in the federal district court in either state. Whatever he does, the defense may dispute him. Cases like this can lead to lengthy courtroom battles over jurisdiction and which state's laws should be applied in which court, since the laws of the one may be more favorable to the plaintiff than the other. The presence of no-fault automobile-insurance laws in one state but not another can be one factor; while, in wrongful-death suits, the defense may want the case heard in a state that allows only a minimal award, while the plaintiff will want it heard in the state that has the more generous system, and so on.

Injuries occurring to American citizens outside state boundaries are heard in federal court. The category includes, but is not limited to, most injuries that occur on the sea or in the air. For example, Ms. Allen is injured while a passenger on a Bahamas cruise ship owned by an Italian company. Ms. Allen does not have to go to Italy to file suit; she files it in federal court, usually the one nearest her home.

Another example: A jet airliner, owned by a New York company, explodes in midair and crashes to the ground in Florida, killing one hundred passengers from thirty states. Initially, all the wrongful-death suits resulting from the crash will be amalgamated into one large suit. The Federal Judicial Panel on Multi-District Disputes will then decide which federal court will hear the case. Ordinarily, it will be one that is in proximity to the majority of the litigants and also one that, at the time the litigation is begun, has a light caseload.

The case will first be tried solely on the question of who, if any, of the defendants was responsible for the accident. Assuming a liability finding is made, it is next necessary to determine how much money should be awarded to each family. (Even though all the people on the airplane died the same way, the financial impact of their deaths on their families will vary; the financial loss of a family whose breadwinner died will be more substantial than that of the family in which the victim was a retired person, and so on.) The judge who heard the case originally may retain all the cases, hearing each one separately on the issue of damages; or he may assign each case, for that purpose, over to the federal jurisdiction in which the victim lived.

15

NEGLIGENCE

One evening as you are driving your car, you pass a woman jogging by herself in a dangerous neighborhood. You turn to your companion and say, "Doesn't she care what happens to her?" or "How careless of their own safety can a person be?" And then you drive on, thinking no more about it. However, suppose you learn that the same woman, in order to enjoy her jogging, each evening leaves her two-year-old child alone at home. Now you are likely to say: "What kind of mother is she? How can she leave her child that way?" You are angry and want something done about her, a reaction you didn't have when you saw her carelessness as affecting only her own welfare.

The law, as the organ society has developed to codify its ideas of right and wrong, will perceive the woman just as you did. A police officer, the enforcing agent of the law, will not arrest her because she's jogging in a dangerous neighborhood; careless she might be, but that's her own affair; she has no legal duty not to be there. She does, however, have a duty, which you have recognized and the courts will enforce, not to leave her small child unprotected; therefore, the same officer who pays no attention to her jogging might come to her house and arrest her on charges of child neglect, and a court could order the child taken from her.

As this illustration suggests, both the popular and the legal meanings of negligence carry with them a connotation of failed duty that isn't always present in mere carelessness. Thus, if you walk into the street without looking where you are going and are hit by a car as a result, not only have you acted carelessly but you have also negligently failed in any duty you might have to yourself and your family to be careful, and more important, failed in your duty toward the driver, who may also be injured as a result of hitting you.

For an act to be negligent, however, it need not always originate in carelessness. The owner of a public building who doesn't replace faulty wiring may be careless, but his omission could have also been the result of his lack of awareness that wiring should be checked, or perhaps occurred because he didn't want to spend the money to have repairs made. Whatever his reason, the law will hold that the owner should have known he had a duty to maintain the safety of his building; when he didn't, he was negligent and could be fined or imprisoned. Similarly, a public official who fails to carry out the duties of his office may have been careless, but he could also have been dishonest, incompetent, or ignorant; whatever his reason, the law says that by accepting the office he should have known its duties and performed them properly, and when he didn't, he was subject to dismissal, and under some circumstances to criminal prosecution as well.

In personal-injury suits based on negligence, the same theory of duty prevails. If the defendant had no duty not to cause the injury, there has been no negligence. One illustration of this principle was observed in the previous chapter in the case of small children who, because they are incapable of understanding duty, cannot be held liable for actions that, if committed by others, would be negligent.

Those of us who are considered legally responsible citizens have our duties prescribed for us by two sets of laws, statutory and common. A speeding driver may be charged by police with statutory negligence even if he harms no one, not so much because he was driving carelessly (although that may have been the reason he was speeding) as because he violated a law he was presumed to have known when he obtained his license. If he does injure someone due to his speeding, then, under the common law, the victim can charge him separately with negligence. But if there's no injury there can be no suit, regardless of the statutory negligence.

To illustrate, assume that we have a man, Mr. Jordan, who starts across the street and as he does, a car comes speeding toward him; with great presence of mind, Jordan jumps out of the car's path and is unharmed. By speeding, the driver violated a statutory law and can be punished for that, but Jordan has no grounds for suit, because the driver's negligent conduct did not cause him injury. However, assume that immediately after Jordan leaped out of the car's way, he was felled by a heart attack. Now he has grounds for suit, based on the driver's statutory negligence, since he will be able to claim that either his acrobatic leap to safety or the fear engendered by the near miss, or both, caused the heart attack.

Not every violation of a statutory law that results in an injury, however, makes the violator subject to suit. For instance, suppose you drive through a stop sign—a statutory violation—and nearly hit Mr. Jordan, who lands against a passerby. The passerby, who has his judgment befuddled by narcotics, thinks Jordan deliberately hit him and takes a knife from his belt and plunges it into Jordan's stomach. Even though your statutory violation set into motion the events that led to Jordan's stabbing, he does not have grounds for suit against you, because the addict's actions were beyond your legally *foreseeable orbit of duty*. In other words, as a driver, you had the duty not to go through the stop sign and could be held responsible for any injury to Jordan or, for that matter, any injury to someone else as a *direct* result of Jordan's trying to get out of your way, but you cannot be expected to foresee that the act of going through a stop sign would cause a drug addict to misunderstand what was going on and attack Jordan criminally with a knife.

Despite unusual cases like this one, ordinarily when a plaintiff has evidence of statutory violence—such as a police report pinpointing driver negligence as the cause of the accident—the case against the defendant is measurably strengthened. Many negligence suits, however, perhaps the majority of them, don't involve statutory violations. For instance, a town may not have an ordinance requiring that householders clear their sidewalks following a storm, but if a householder doesn't and someone is injured as a result, under the common law the victim may have grounds for suit.

Unlike statutory law, which specifies, in writing, which acts are wrongful, the common law, as we have seen, is a distillation of the results of centuries of lawsuits, leading to no single written code, with the predictable result that not all judges have agreed on its meaning. Consequently, it is quite possible that your lawyer will be able to find an old decision on a case like yours that favors your point of view, and the defense lawyer will be able to find one that favors his. These old decisions are called *precedents,* and the judge will select among them—or perhaps do his own research—and then inform the jury what he believes the law to be. The jurors are required to accept his version of the law as true and apply its tests to the facts of the case in reaching their verdict. Many suits involving fine points of negligence common law, therefore, will be determined by which side wins the battle of the precedents.

Another test for negligence under the common law, more practical if more subjective, is the so-called *reasonable-man* doctrine. Although the law recognizes that not all reasonable people agree on what is reasonable, it ignores this insight, because it is looking not for a philosophy of life but for a consensus view of what is reasonable in the case at hand. Therefore, when addressing a jury in a negligence case, a judge may say something like this: "In your deliberations, members of the jury, ask yourselves what a reasonably prudent person would have done in a situation like the one you have before you. If you decide that such a person, acting with due care, could have avoided inflicting the injury that occurred here, then it is your duty to find for the plaintiff. On the contrary, if you believe the defendant has been shown to have acted with the diligence and care you would expect to have exercised toward you in similar circumstances, then you must find for the defendant." The same reasoning applies to the plaintiff. If a reasonably careful plaintiff would have acted differently from the way this one did, then the jury may find that, even though the defendant was partly at fault, the plaintiff's negligence was such that the defendant must be exonerated. (See also "Contributory Negligence" later in this chapter.)

The reasonable-man doctrine represents a judicial genuflection to the world of reality. Even were a judge not to make these comments to the jury, the jurors themselves, in the privacy of their deliberations, would be likely to do so. They will weigh the evidence presented to them in terms of trying to decide what *really* happened and what *should* have happened if the various parties had acted with proper regard for their own safety and that of others. These considerations, more than legal doctrines a judge might burden them with, probably are the most important determining factors in negligence verdicts.

Considering the impact of the reasonable-man doctrine and the idea of duty, we might therefore say that a negligent act, in a personal-injury sense, is one that occurs when a party who has an obligation to do so fails to act in prudent or careful regard for the safety and well-being of others.

While this definition is accurate as far as it goes, there's a bit more to it than that.

To begin with, our duty to protect the safety of others does not mean we have to endanger or fail to protect ourselves in the process. For example, suppose you are accosted by a mugger but manage to break away and run from him; as you do, you bump into a pedestrian, causing that person to fall and break an ankle. Although running about the streets and knocking people down is almost always negligence, in this case it isn't, because you were acting in reasonable protection of your own safety. The only party who can be sued by the person whose ankle you broke is the mugger, on the theory that if he hadn't attacked you, then you wouldn't have been running from him and the injury would never have occurred.

(In cases like this one, lawyers love to use the phrase *proximate cause*. By it, all they mean is that the party who precipitated the injury is responsible for it, not necessarily the one who actually perpetrated it. Proximate cause is also used to describe situations in which the injury was not the direct result of an impact, as in the case of Jordan's heart attack following the near miss by the car.)

Defendants will also sometimes be excused from an apparent act of negligence when—although not fleeing from an obvious danger—they, even so, lacked a reasonable opportunity to prevent an accident-causing situation.

For example, suppose the unfortunate Mr. Jordan is walking home on a winter's evening and that twenty-four hours earlier a snow had fallen and frozen over, causing slippery footing in places. Jordan falls and breaks his leg on the icy sidewalk in front of Mr. Green's house.

Jordan, it would seem, under the common law, has grounds for a successful suit against Green. Green had ample opportunity (twenty-four hours) to perform a known duty (free his sidewalk of a hazard) but failed to do so. Green, however, may be able to win the suit if he can show he was ill or housebound or hospitalized while the hazard was forming and could not have, by himself or through the agency of others, cleared the walk. Green's chances are significantly poorer if his only excuse for leaving his sidewalk icy was that he was out of town at the time of the accident; under those circumstances, as a prudent person, he may be expected to have made arrangements to have his walk cleared in the event of snow.

Alternatively, suppose Jordan had fallen on the icy sidewalk within an hour of the conclusion of the storm. In that event, Green probably didn't have sufficient time to clear the walk, and Jordan has no grounds for suit. Cases such as these are good examples of ones that can usually be decided only by resort to the reasonable-man doctrine. Thus, following a blizzard, seventy-two hours might not be enough time to clear a sidewalk, but following a lesser storm, you might be found liable by a jury if you didn't clear it within a couple hours.

When the opportunity to prevent the injury exists, a defendant can be found negligent even though he or she was aware of the possibility of causing the injury and made a conscientious effort to avoid doing so. Consider the following examples:

First, we have Mr. Jordan driving at a legal rate of speed when a child runs in front of his car. He sees the child and tries to avoid hitting it. In the process, however, he inadvertently turns the steering wheel the wrong way and the child is struck and injured.

Next, Mr. Jordan is digging a drainage ditch on his property. Because the trench is to exit at the curb, he must also dig up the sidewalk. When that part of the task is completed, evening has come and he decides to stop for the day. Aware that the ditch is a hazard to pedestrians, he goes to his garage and brings out a lanterned barrier he has purchased as a warning device. During the few minutes he is gone to fetch the barrier, a pedestrian comes along, falls into the ditch, and breaks a leg.

In the first example, Jordan, as a licensed driver, is presumed by the law to have the necessary skills to turn his wheel in a direction that would avoid, not cause, injury. Therefore, though not careless in any usual sense of the word, he did act incompetently, and—like an incompetent public official—is negligent.

In the second case, Jordan's purchase of the barrier showed he was a careful person, who recognized his duty to avoid situations that might be dangerous to others. However, as in the first example, he acted incompetently. The law will say that a competent—i.e., a reasonably prudent—person in Jordan's position would have had the barrier at hand when it got dark or else would have posted someone to warn passersby of the hazard while he fetched the barrier. Had he taken either step, he would not have been responsible for the passerby's fall. Because he didn't, he was negligent.

From this discussion, we can say that for a defendant to be negligent he must have had the legal *duty,* the presumed *ability,* and a reasonable *opportunity* to avoid the injury caused by his actions.

A NEGLIGENCE QUIZ

Assume you were involved in the following injuries, each of them representing situations that could occur to almost anyone.

1. You are digging a hole in your back yard. Even though you know that neighbors' children frequently use your yard as a shortcut, you leave the hole unguarded at night. A child falls into it, breaking his leg.

Do the child's parents have grounds for suit against you?

2. An employee of the electric company arrives at your home to read the meter in your basement. You accompany him to the stairs, warning him to be careful because the fifth step down is broken. Even so, he missteps, falls down the rest of the stairs, and breaks his leg.

Does the meter reader have grounds to sue you?

3. You are driving in excess of the speed limit; a pedestrian steps out in your path, sees you coming, dives out of the way to

safety, but falls on a second person, who is injured by the impact. The second pedestrian is helped up by a third one, who, in the process, steps off the curb and is hit by another car.

Who, if anybody, can sue you?

4. As you are driving, inadvertently you go through a stop sign, and as you do so a small child runs out into the street in front of you. With great agility, you manage to avoid hitting the child. Standing on the sidewalk is the child's mother; frightened by what she has been witnessing, she faints, falls, and fractures her skull when she hits the pavement.

Does the mother have grounds for suit against you?

5. You are driving on a foggy, rainy night. As you round a curve, your car skids to the left into oncoming traffic. To avoid injury to yourself and the people in the cars approaching you, you swing your steering wheel sharply to the right, causing your car to run up on a sidewalk and strike and injure a pedestrian.

Does the pedestrian have grounds for suit against you?

6. You are employed as a chemist, but you are quite handy with all things mechanical. A neighbor who has been having trouble with the brakes on his car asks if you can fix them. You agree to try, and after making some adjustments, you tell him the brakes are now safe. He thanks you, drives off, and in a few moments has wrapped himself around a tree when the brakes fail.

Does the man have grounds for suit against you?

The answers:

1. The parents have grounds for suit for their child's fall into your back-yard drainage ditch. Because you knew that children used your yard as a shortcut, you had as much legal obligation to protect them from that ditch as you would one you had dug through your front sidewalk. To defend this suit, you would have to show that you had regularly warned neighbors to keep their children out of your yard and probably that you had taken reasonable steps—such as erecting a fence or gate—to keep them out. You cannot, however, take unreasonable steps against improper use of your property. Were you to electrify the fence or build a wall with jagged glass coming out the top, the law would consider that such protections were taken in careless disregard for the safety of others, and a child injured by the fence or cut by the glass would have grounds for suit against you. An adult intruder who used your yard for a shortcut would ordinarily not have the

same protection as a child, but you might, even so, be sued in this situation if the adult could show that use of your property as a thoroughfare was well established, known to you, and accepted by you.

2. As a householder, when you told the meter reader to watch out for the broken step, you performed a legal duty properly, just as you would have had you put up the barrier in front of the ditch. The meter reader, however, may sue you anyway, claiming you didn't warn him, and a jury might believe him, rather than you. So the answer is that legally you are in the clear, but as a practical matter you might not be; the safest course is to get the step repaired before anyone falls.

3. The first pedestrian has no grounds to sue you, since he wasn't injured. The pedestrian who was knocked down by the first one can sue you as the person who was the precipitating cause of the injury. The Good Samaritan third pedestrian, who helps the second one and is injured for his efforts, probably doesn't have grounds for suit against you for the same reason that Jordan couldn't sue you when he got stabbed by the drug addict.

4. On the surface, this case appears similar to the one in Question 3, the mother having the same grounds to sue you as did the second pedestrian; that is, if you hadn't run the stop sign and nearly hit her child, she never would have fainted and fractured her skull. However, there is a crucial difference. The pedestrian was in the immediate area of the accident, or, as it is known in the law, the *zone of danger*. The mother, who was never in danger of being hit by your car, wasn't in that zone and therefore cannot bring suit against you. At least, she can't in most places. In recent years, some jurisdictions have rejected this narrow concept of the zone of danger, and suit will be permitted with the judge instructing the jury that it must decide how far the danger zone extended. If they decide it extended as far as the mother, you lose. The best answer to Question 4, consequently, is that the mother's right to sue depends largely on where you and she live. (This kind of case—and it's far from an uncommon one—points up the unequal way in which negligence law can sometimes be applied from jurisdiction to jurisdiction.)

5. The pedestrian has sufficient grounds to sue, but your chances of winning are good. As we have seen, legally you always have a right to protect yourself from injury, a step you took when

you swerved the car to the right. You did not, therefore, act out of carelessness when you hit the pedestrian, so the only remaining question is: Did you act competently? That is, could you have changed the car's direction in such a way that you would not only have avoided injury to yourself and other drivers but also avoided the pedestrian? Given the rainy, slippery conditions of the road, probably you couldn't, but juries, in cases similar to this one, occasionally have been known to find against the defendant.

6. The man can sue you on the grounds that, by offering to repair his car, you assumed the responsibility of doing it properly, and that you unnecessarily caused him harm by attempting a task you should have known you weren't competent to perform. In your defense, you will allege that he should have known better than to ask a person who wasn't a licensed mechanic to repair his car, and he, therefore, not you, assumed the responsibility for his own injury. You will probably win, but the case points up the exposure to suit you can sometimes incur when you volunteer to perform services for others.

SUING THE EXPERTS

Question 6 leads us to a major feature of the laws governing negligence. By it, people who are licensed or who hold themselves out as capable of performing expert services are held to a *standard of care* common to others who perform the same services. In practical terms, this means that, as a member of the public, you have a legal right to expect expert service from people you have reason to believe—by their licensure or advertising—can perform expertly. Thus, if the man in Question 6 had taken his car to a licensed mechanic to have the brakes repaired and they failed immediately afterward, he cannot be accused of having assumed the risk for his own injury, as he could when he asked someone he should have known was a nonexpert to repair them.

Based on this reasoning, if you hold a driver's license, you are presumed by the law to be expert in driving, but *not* presumed to be an expert mechanic (since the training to become a driver does not require passing a course in automotive repair). Bus and taxi companies, however, and all other licensed public carriers are expected to be expert in maintenance and repair of their vehicles, since, under their charter, they are supposed to buy equipment that is safe and hire experts to keep it that way. Their drivers are also held to a higher standard of performance than are private drivers, under the same public-charter theory. This means that you can often bring suit against a public carrier when you couldn't bring it against a private driver.

Practitioners of the following *occupations* are also among those who are held to an expert standard of care when named as defendants in a personal-injury suit: doctors (medical doctors, osteopaths, dentists, chiropractors, podiatrists, etc.), registered nurses, pharmacists, engineers and architects (when buildings they construct collapse and injure people), chemists, various licensed mechanics, beauticians. Lawyers and certified public accountants also are required to perform to a professional standard of competence and can be sued for monetary losses when they don't, although, in the exercise of their work, they can hardly cause anyone a personal injury.

When a licensed expert is accused of causing an injury, both the plaintiff and the defendant can present expert witnesses from within the occupation to testify to its recognized standards of competency. In medical cases, experts will normally be in the same field of specialty as the defendant, i.e., a neurosurgeon will testify about the appropriate standard of care in neurosurgery, a psychiatrist in psychiatry, and so on.

The standard of care is also determined other ways legally. A medical textbook will help establish what a doctor should know, an architectural text what an architect should know, and so on. In addition, precedents and the reasonable-man doctrine can play important determining roles.

Whenever an expert is found not to have met an acceptable standard of performance, he has *malpracticed* (i.e., mis-practiced) in the licensed area of expertise. Although, in common usage, the term malpractice is nearly exclusively applied to doctors and other professionals, a negligent motorist, beautician, or mechanic has also malpracticed.

A STANDARD-OF-CARE QUIZ

Consider the application of the standard-of-care principle in the following situations:

1. A friend has bought a new car and takes you out for a spin

in it. As you are driving, he comments that the steering wheel feels "stiff." A few moments later, he can no longer control the wheel, the car ends in a ditch, and you have a fractured skull.

Do you have grounds for suit against your friend?

2. You are riding in a subway train and almost miss your stop. You rush to the door, which is about to close, and push it open to get out. As you do, the train starts up and you are flung forward, in your fall suffering fractures and internal injuries.

Do you have grounds for suit against the subway company?

3. Your husband goes to a doctor for treatment of a pain in his lower back. The doctor diagnoses a pulled muscle and prescribes medication and exercise. Over the next six months, your husband's pain intensifies, but the doctor does not change his diagnosis or treatment. Finally, you and your husband seek out a new doctor, who orders X rays. Only then is it discovered that your husband is suffering from a cancer that is inoperable, and a year later he dies.

Do you have grounds for a malpractice suit against the first doctor?

The answers:

1. You do not have grounds for suit against the driver. The law does not expect him to have the mechanical expertise to know that a "stiff" steering wheel might mean a faulty steering wheel. You (and your friend), however, could have grounds for suit against the dealer that sold him the car and the company that manufactured it.

2. The subway company, as a public carrier, had a duty to maintain its equipment so that the train could not start into motion when a door was open; therefore, it doesn't matter that you were the one that forced the door open; you can't be held responsible for something that shouldn't have been possible. Consequently, you have the basis for a winnable suit, either against the subway company or the company that provided the defective equipment, or both. However, if you were a passenger in a private car and pushed open a door and fell out while it was in motion, you don't have grounds for suit against the driver, since drivers are not required, as is the public carrier, to maintain their doors so that they can't be opened while the vehicle is moving. You might, however, have grounds for suit against the car's man-

ufacturer if you can prove the door was faulty when the car was sold.

3. You probably have sufficient grounds to bring a malpractice suit against the doctor. You will not win the suit, however, just because you can prove the doctor made a mistaken diagnosis. Error, by itself, is not negligence. Back pains of the kind your husband suffered normally mean nothing more than this doctor thought they did; a pulled muscle or some other minor problem. The legal question to be resolved, rather, is, did this doctor *persist* in his error after other doctors would have recognized the initial diagnosis was wrong? If so, the doctor didn't meet an acceptable standard of care, i.e., was negligent. But, even so, he may still not have been responsible for your husband's death. Perhaps your husband's cancer was past the treatment stage when he first consulted the doctor; in that event, the negligent treatment did not affect the medical outcome. Therefore, to win the suit, you must show that the doctor was negligent by holding to his wrong diagnosis when competent doctors wouldn't have, and that, because of his negligence, your husband did not receive treatment that might have saved or prolonged his life.

CONTRIBUTORY NEGLIGENCE

Despite all the circumstances that provide you with grounds for a suit based on negligence, traditionally, under the common law, if you helped cause the injury by your own negligence, the defendant is supposed to win.

For example, Ms. Shultz, who is not watching where she is going, breaks her leg when she trips over a box carelessly left in an aisle by a storekeeper. Or, Ms. Corcoran, not thinking what she is doing, starts across the street in the middle of the block and has her leg fractured when she is hit by a speeding car. Neither woman has grounds—under the doctrine of contributory negligence—to bring suit, the one because she negligently failed to observe where she was going and the other because she negligently jaywalked.

As a result, the storekeeper in Shultz's case walks away free and clear, even though had it not been for his carelessness, Shultz's inattention would have caused her no harm. The same is true of the driver in Corcoran's case, even though his speeding was obviously a much more dangerous and negligent action than jaywalking.

Recognizing that the contributory-negligence doctrine can often lead to these inequitable results, over the past several decades, many states have adopted so-called *comparative* negligence laws. As the name suggests, in these jurisdictions the degrees of negligence by both plaintiff and defendant are considered, with the plaintiff's award reduced by the percentage of his or her fault. To illustrate, in Shultz's case, the jury might decide her injury was worth $10,000 but also determine she was 25 percent at fault; therefore, it awards her $7,500. In some states, however, if the jury rules the plaintiff was 50 percent or more at fault, the defendant wins. Because the defense can no longer win by attributing some particle of fault to the plaintiff, suits filed in comparative-negligence jurisdictions are somewhat more likely to result in pretrial settlements than are those filed in contributory-negligence jurisdictions. (To learn the law in your state, see Appendix I, *"Contributory and Comparative Negligence."*)

But what happens if you live in a state that still adheres to the contributory-negligence doctrine and you recognize that you have had a minor degree of blame in causing the injury? Does that mean you should give up on your suit?

Often, you should not. To begin with, in most contributory-negligence jurisdictions, if you are slightly at fault but can show that the defendant acted in a "wanton and grossly negligent" manner—such as a hit-and-run driver or a drunken driver speeding at ninety miles an hour who sends you flying while you are jaywalking—the court can rule that your trivial negligence need not be considered by the jury. But even when the defendant's conduct doesn't rise to some terrible degree of infamy, you shouldn't automatically decide you can't win a suit due to minor negligence on your part. Take Corcoran's case as an example. Jurors live in the real world and tend to be reasonable people; they know, from their own experience, that they frequently cross streets in the middle of the block, and they also know that such crossings can sometimes be safer than those undertaken at a busy intersection, no matter what the law says. Consequently, depending on the particular circumstances in Corcoran's case, the jury—after politely listening to the judge's description of the meaning of contributory negligence—may well agree that Corcoran was indeed legally negligent and then proceed to ignore that conclusion and find in her favor anyway.

If your case is analogous to Corcoran's, therefore, your major problem may not be with the decision the jury will reach but how you can manage to get the case to a jury. The defense will be certain to try to get your suit dismissed if you have admitted to your negligence either at deposition or at trial, and if a judge agrees, you have lost. In a case like Corcoran's, the call is a close one: it could go either way.

Aware of the danger of a judge's dismissing a suit on contributory-negligence grounds, plaintiffs often find themselves tempted to lie about what happened. Thus, Ms. Shultz, rather than risk an adverse decision from a judge, may decide to testify she was watching where she was going while in the store, and Ms. Corcoran may deny she was jaywalking, asserting instead that the car flung her to the midway point at which she was found.

The perjury that is encouraged by the contributory-negligence doctrine is hardly limited to plaintiffs. A defendant, knowing he was at fault in an accident but also knowing he can win if he fabricates a story that makes the plaintiff partly at fault, has a strong motive to do so.

This inclination can be present even if the person who caused the accident is an employee who will not have to pay for its costs or lose his insurance as a result of being a losing defendant in a suit. The employee may well fear that his carelessness, if he tells the truth about it, could cost him his job. His employer and the employer's insurance company won't closely question his self-serving statement, since it promotes their interest too. In some instances, the employee will be encouraged, even ordered, to fabricate a defense, and knowing his job could be at stake, he will feel he has no choice but to do so.

This doesn't mean that perjury doesn't occur in courts applying a comparative-negligence rule. The plaintiff may want to deny all fault, because to admit it will reduce the size of the verdict. The defendant will similarly prevaricate to prevent a big verdict, and the motive for perjury by an employee who fears loss of job is in no way diminished. Nevertheless, the impulse toward perjury is not as pervasive in a comparative-negligence jurisdiction as it is in a contributory one, because plaintiffs know they can tell the truth—or much of the truth—about their own negligence and not risk a dismissal, and defendants know they can no longer win solely by falsely implicating the plaintiff to some minor degree.

RISKS IN COMMITTING PERJURY

Perjury is never a risk-free venture, because jurors, spying a falsehood, may conclude from it that the utterer is falsifying the entire story. They may reach this decision on their own, but they also could be encouraged to do so by the lawyer who has caught out the falsehood, and by the judge, both of whom will explain to them the doctrine of *falsus in uno, falsus in omnibus,* meaning that if the jurors decide a party has lied about a material fact, they then have the right to disbelieve all of that person's testimony.

A plaintiff or defendant in a personal-injury case, however, almost never need fear arrest as a result of false swearing. There are a number of reasons why this is so. To begin with, perjured testimony in a criminal case is viewed by the justice system as endangering the safety of the society and is therefore treated as a serious matter, while in the civil case—where its ill effects will be limited to the disputants—it is not. But even if this were not so, an indictment will not result, because there is no one to urge it. The judge is hardly likely to turn evidence of perjury over to a prosecutor, even if he felt it was his duty to do so, because he knows that the prosecutor, facing criminal-court dockets that are already overcrowded, will not want to add indictments arising from private disputes. Neither will the plaintiff or the defendant have any purpose served by filing a private criminal complaint charging perjury. Their goal is either to make money or to save it, and for that purpose their interest is served by the appeals process. Thus, if you were to lose your suit and subsequently learn that a witness for the other side gave false testimony—and you can prove it, which won't be easy—you have grounds for a reversal of the verdict. That, not any criminal prosecution, is what you want.

This discussion of the impact of perjury in negligence cases applies equally to the intentional-harm and strict-liability suits discussed in the next two chapters.

16

Intentional Injuries

You can bring a personal-injury suit on grounds of assault against anyone who deliberately attempts to injure you. If someone takes a swing at you and misses, that person has assaulted you, just as if the blow had connected. When you are hit, you have been the victim of both an assault and a battery. (Battery—i.e., a "battering"—describes any unpermitted touching of your body and need not necessarily result in an injury, any more than an assault, for you to have grounds for suit.) Should the assault result in the death of the victim, the surviving family can bring suit.

That the person who committed the assault is arrested and charged with a crime doesn't affect your right to bring suit against that person. The criminal and civil cases are tried separately, and ordinarily it is to your interest to delay your civil case until the criminal one is ended, because, if the defendant is found guilty, you can introduce that verdict as evidence against him at the civil trial. It doesn't work the other way; if the defendant's found not guilty of the crime, he can't use that verdict in his favor at the civil trial. (The reason lies in the different proof standards. In a criminal case, a defendant's guilt must be established beyond a reasonable doubt, while in a civil case, the defendant loses—except in contributory negligence cases—when only the majority of the evidence is against him. Therefore, jurors in a civil case are permitted to learn of the guilty verdict, since it was reached under higher proof standards than they are to employ, but can't learn of the not-guilty verdict, since it does not indicate there isn't sufficient evidence against the defendant to find him liable under civil rules.)

Not all assaults are physical in nature. Someone who threatens you is verbally assaulting you, and you have grounds for suit on that basis.

PROBLEMS IN BRINGING AN INTENTIONAL-INJURY SUIT

In thinking about filing suit following a deliberate injury, you should always consider that any money you win must be collected from the defendant personally, because insurance companies don't write policies to cover intentional torts. Sometimes, as in the case described in Chapter Thirteen, of the man who ran down his enemy with his car, the evidence can be interpreted as proving either an intentional or a negligent injury; when that happens, you should always charge the defendant solely with negligence in order to bring and keep the insurer in the case.

Most of the time, however, the injury will be undeniably intentional in nature, and when that's so, if the defendant doesn't have assets you can seize upon winning, your chances of ever seeing a penny from your award range from minimal to nonexistent. Remember, too, in making your decision that some apparently well-to-do defendants can't be touched financially because they hold their assets in joint title.

Unless the defendant is one that can be forced to pay—and we shall look at some such instances later in this chapter—you should also be aware that in intentional-tort suits you will find it impossible to hire a lawyer to represent you on a contingency basis. No lawyer wants to litigate a suit unless he knows he can collect the winnings and take his percentage from them; for this reason, if you insist on suing someone without readily seizable assets, your lawyer will require you to pay a fee in advance. The amount will hardly ever be less than a thousand dollars and could be a great deal more than that.

If paying a lawyer a fee is no problem to you, then you may find that a suit against a nonpaying defendant is not without its satisfactions. The irate neighbor who punched you in the jaw may never pay you the verdict you win, but because of the judgment against him, he is—at the least—going to have trouble obtaining credit in buying property and great difficulty selling it. Nevertheless, before you take the step, you should know that some intentional-injury suits can have boomeranging effects financially. For instance, you may be able to win the suit against the neighbor who took a swing at you and didn't hit you, but you will probably win no more than nominal damages, usually one dollar, and there's a very real possibility that the judge, angry at you for clogging the courts with a trivial case, will require you to pay the trial costs and possibly even the defendant's legal fee.

The financial aspects to one side, intentional-injury suits can sometimes cause an additional problem. Unlike someone who has injured you through mere carelessness, the person who has injured you intentionally bears you ill will. A suit against such a person, therefore, has the potential of making a bad situation worse, and that's a possibility you should consider before you bring it. Although the ill effects can happen in many ways, not untypical was the experience of a woman we'll call Mary Jones. Shortly after she began divorce proceedings, her husband, John, instituted a campaign of harassment against her that he would later defend as "proof that I still loved her and wanted her back." He began, mildly enough, with long haranguing and pleading phone calls; when they didn't work, he followed her on the streets, intercepting her and demanding in loud tones that she return to him. Then, within a week after the divorce became final, he showed up at her place of work and—in front of several of her fellow employees—accused her of "sleeping with any man who would have you." Not long after, she started receiving phone calls late at night from him demanding she tell him whom she was sleeping with at the moment. During this time, he would also sometimes station himself outside her apartment building with binoculars trained on her window, allegedly to discover evidence of her promiscuity. One day, about six months after the divorce, he accosted her in a restaurant when she was with a male friend and told her that if he couldn't have her he would "fix her" so that no other man would want her. With that, he took a vial of liquid from his pocket and threw it in her face. It turned out to be water. As he left, he informed her that the next time it would be acid.

During this period, Ms. Jones had several times gone to the

police for help; it was refused on the grounds that John hadn't yet done anything to harm her. As the harassment escalated, she tried to bring him to court to impose a so-called "peace bond" on him; the first time, he showed up and signed the bond, and it was within a month after that that he began to spy on her apartment. The second time, he didn't appear in court; a bench warrant was issued for his arrest, but nothing came of that. Eventually, following the water-throwing episode, the now terrified Ms. Jones imposed on a lawyer friend who, without charging a fee, entered a personal-injury suit against John on the grounds of both his verbal assaults and his physical one (the throwing of the vial of water). The lawyer told her she could not expect the suit to be heard for at least three or four years, but perhaps it would frighten John into peacefulness. It didn't. A month after the injury suit was entered, he managed to get into her apartment, struck her, and threatened to kill her unless she stopped "persecuting" him. After that episode, Mary Jones dropped the suit, quit her job, and moved several hundred miles away; when interviewed a year later, she was still living in fear that her ex-husband would discover her whereabouts.

As Mary Jones's case shows, the law provides all kinds of alleged remedies for people who are harassed and assaulted, but none of them are necessarily effective, and some—including, in her case, the lawsuit—might escalate the probability of violence. People like Ms. Jones are the true outcasts of the American justice system.

WHEN THE INTENTIONAL-INJURY SUIT WORKS

Despite the majority of instances in which, for one reason or another, filing an intentional-injury suit is inadvisable, there are also times when, with the right defendant, these suits can produce sizable and collectible verdicts.

Assault by police or company private detectives.

False imprisonment—any wrongful stoppage of your freedom of action—is a tort and grounds for suit by itself. Almost invariably, a false arrest is accompanied by force and therefore also provides grounds for bringing an intentional-injury suit. The force need not always be a blow from a policeman's nightstick. For instance, suppose you are shopping in a department store and a detective comes over to you, tells you to come with him, and taking you by the arm, leads you to an office of the store, where you are wrongfully accused of shoplifting. You have now been the victim both of a false arrest and of an assault and battery (the unpermitted taking of your arm by the detective). You have excellent grounds for suit, and you have, in the department store, a defendant that will be able to pay any judgment against it. In this kind of case, you will also usually be able to find a lawyer who will represent you on a contingency-fee basis.

Assault suits against the police can be somewhat more difficult to win. A police officer is permitted to use "necessary force" to effect an arrest, with courts varying in their interpretation of the meaning of the word "necessary." Clearly, however, any resistance on your part to the arrest—even if you aren't guilty of the offense with which you are charged—will substantially weaken your chances of winning the suit. The police officer nevertheless cannot win the suit solely because the plaintiff committed the offense that led to the incident. For instance, you might be demonstrating against a nuclear power plant and enter the plant's property without permission; that makes you guilty of the charge of trespass, but that guilt has no legal bearing on the officer's beating you, assuming you offered no resistance to the arrest.

In police-brutality suits, both the officer and the government agency that employs him will be named as defendants, with the government providing you with an able-to-pay defendant, thereby making the case attractive to a lawyer on a contingency-fee basis. When the government enjoys immunity from suit, the case is ordinarily worth bringing against the officer individually only when the government has the policy—and most do—of paying for all verdicts in civil suits brought against its police force.

Wrongful-death actions against government.

Intentional-injury suits of this kind almost always involve killings of civilians by policemen. The same general rules apply to them as to police assault cases, and occasionally they will result in a fairly substantial award. In one notorious case in Philadelphia several years ago, an American Indian ironworker was gunned down by a member of its constabulary and then left to lie in his own blood surrounded by about a dozen other policemen until he obliged them by dying. His family received an award of $135,000.

Slander, libel, and invasion of privacy.

Defamatory utterances and unwarranted intrusions into one's personal life are grounds for a personal-injury suit. These torts are frequently motivated by malice—hence the discussion of them in this chapter—but they can also be solely or partly the consequence of negligence. Awards in these actions are based on the mental anguish the wrongful action caused, with punitive-damage awards not uncommon.

A slander is any statement made in conversation, by one person about another, that is both false and designed to (or reasonably likely to) cause damage to that person's reputation. Thus, when John Jones accused his ex-wife of sexual promiscuity, he slandered her, assuming she can show that what he said was untrue. This means that if you think you have been slandered, you could have the burden of proving the falsity of the accusation, a task that may be both difficult and humiliating when the alleged slanderer's lawyer is done with you on cross-examination. ("At what time did Mr. X leave your apartment, Ms. Jones? Oh, 2 A.M.? And what were the two of you doing until that hour?" and on and on, sometimes through your whole life history.)

Another practical difficulty in bringing a slander suit is the ease with which the offending remark can often be denied. You probably weren't there when it was said, and even if you were, it might still be your word against the defendant's, and so you will have to rely on the testimony of people you believe heard the remark made, and their memories (even if they want to help you) can be attacked as unreliable, self-interested, and so on.

There's still one other barrier you will have to overcome in pursuing a slander case, and that is the constitutionally protected guarantee of free speech. For example, Mr. Roberts is asked about the quality of work done by a certain mechanic. He says, "Don't take your car there. That SOB overcharged me and the car still wasn't fixed right."

Roberts has not slandered the mechanic. He is expressing his opinion, and his right to do so is absolutely protected by the courts. His use of the phrase "SOB" might technically be construed as a slander of the mechanic's mother, but the phrase is so commonly used to express criticism of the individual involved, not his mother, that it is hard to imagine a jury that would make an award on that basis, or a judge who would permit such a suit to get to a jury. In order to slander, rather, Roberts must express a malicious and reckless disregard for the provable facts: "The mechanic buys his parts from a car-theft ring" might well be slanderous if untrue, since that is a specific allegation of criminal conduct calculated to cause the mechanic to lose reputation and inflict on him mental anguish.

Due to all these problems, slander suits are rarely brought, and when they are, the plaintiff's chances of winning are no better than poor to fair.

Libel is somewhat less difficult to prove than slander, because libel involves written or published utterances, and they usually can be documented, as oral ones cannot be. (Remarks made on radio or television or in motion pictures are considered a form of publication, and therefore, when they are defamatory, grounds for a libel—not a slander—suit, even though they are spoken.)

Just as is true of oral remarks, people have a constitutionally protected right to state their opinion of others in writing as long as their comments are not both false and defamatory. For example, if in response to a request to provide a reference about one of your former employees, you write, "Ms. X had proficient skills as a secretary, but she was often late in arriving at work, spent too much time talking to her co-workers, and was late in completing assigned work," you have probably effectively caused Ms. X not to get the job she has applied for, but you have not defamed her personally and she doesn't have grounds for a libel suit against you, even though she might claim she was rarely late for work, didn't spend too much time talking to her fellow employees, and so on. All that is a matter of opinion, not of libel. However, should you add to your letter that "she is sexually promiscuous," then you have attacked and defamed her, and she could have grounds for suit against you if you can't prove your allegation.

To take this example one step further, suppose you are Ms. X and you have quit your job because your superior made sexual advances toward you. Angered at your rejection of him, he places in your personnel file derogatory and false statements about you. When a prospective employer asks for a reference concerning you, these statements are provided to him, and you don't get the job. Now you have grounds for a libel suit both against your former superior based on his malicious libel of you and against the company for negligently allowing those kinds of comments in its file and forwarding them to the prospective employer. You may not be able to collect any part of the award made against your former superior, but you should be able to collect from the company for its role, and this kind of suit can therefore be well worth bringing.

Although cases like Ms. X's occur occasionally, the large majority of libel suits filed each year are against reporters or authors and their publishers, and broadcasters and their employers.

The laws governing libel by the media are highly complex and —thanks to a series of United States Supreme Court decisions of the late 1970s—are in a state of transition, one that is generally moving in favor of plaintiffs. Whether that trend will continue, however, is far from certain.

In any event, the law is well-enough defined to say that a newspaper or any other public medium of information has a positive duty to make a reasonable effort to check the accuracy of the material it publishes. In other words, a publication cannot act as the conduit for the malice of others. Thus, if your boss tells the press that you were fired because you were caught embezzling funds, the newspaper can publish that accusation, but it has a duty to make sure it doesn't give the public the impression that *it* believes you are an embezzler, and it has the further duty to make a reasonable effort to get your side of the story.

Despite these basic restrictions, because we have always believed, in this country, that a free press is our best guarantee to prevent the imposition of a tyrannous form of government, the news media are allowed wide latitude in reportage and commentary, with widest scope given to discussion of persons, companies, and groups whose activities could affect the public interest.

People who belong to this category include those who seek, serve, or have served in public office, and it doesn't matter whether or not a person was paid for his or her services. For instance, if you are a member of a school board, a newspaper has the right to find out how you got your post, how often you come to meetings, and why you vote as you do, and to publish information about any enrichment you or your family or business associates might have received as a result of your position, and so on. That the stories aren't accurate and may be defamatory is usually not sufficient grounds for suit; to sue and win, rather, you must show a conscious, malicious, or reckless disregard for the truth on the part of the publication. That's a hard standard of proof to meet.

Invasion-of-privacy suits are almost invariably brought against the news media, and as with libel suits, large elements of the governing law appear unresolved.

Generally, however, you have the right to be let alone in your personal life as long as you proceed in a lawful and private manner. When publicity is directed toward you, without your seeking it, and appears in the form of a published story, a photograph, or some form of broadcast, your privacy may have been invaded even though the publicity received was intended as favorable.

For example, in 1975 a man helped prevent an attack on the life of President Gerald Ford. In a laudatory newspaper account, the man was described as a homosexual. He sued the publication, asserting that his sexual preferences were a private matter, and since they had no bearing on the role he played in saving the President from assassination, they should not have been included in the story. He won the suit. The decision in this case would seem to indicate that when you have been involved in a matter that a newspaper deems to be of public interest, your actions can be reported without permission from you, but other information about you that is irrelevant to the story may not be published without your permission. The issue of what is or isn't newsworthy, to say nothing of what is or isn't relevant to a newsworthy story, can lead, as might be imagined, to legal arguments of the most dazzling complexity.

Your privacy cannot be invaded when a published story is based on a public document. Thus, should you file for divorce or —for that matter—file a personal-injury suit, your action becomes part of a court record, making it a public document, and no one need request your permission prior to publishing a story about it. However, should that story also contain private information, then you might have grounds for suit. For example, if you begin divorce proceedings against your spouse and the story adds that you are a member of Alcoholics Anonymous and that statement wasn't part of the divorce allegations on either side and wasn't information you gave the reporter, then, even though the information is true, your privacy probably has been invaded and you have grounds for suit.

In bringing suit against a publisher or a broadcasting company, you have the comfort of knowing—assuming the prime defendant is a corporation with substantial assets—that you will be able to collect your winnings. But before entering into this kind of litigation, be cognizant of some of the difficulties you face. An invasion-of-privacy suit may be theoretically winnable, but if the story was favorable to you or otherwise not of the kind that would cause most people mental anguish, a jury may decide your allegation is groundless or else make a nominal award of one dollar. Moreover, because both publishers and broadcasters perceive libel and invasion-of-privacy suits as attacks against the freedom of the press, you had best assume your suit will be hard-fought by the defendant and that any victory you might achieve at trial will be subjected to long rounds of appeals, causing you heavy legal expenses.

Suits against employers alleging "outrageous conduct" by employees.

For conduct to be outrageous, it must go beyond that which is merely rude or offensive. (If suits were permitted to victims of rudeness, the courts of the land would have no time to try any other kind of case.) Although outrageous conduct has never been precisely defined, it clearly includes actions that were intended, or could have reasonably been expected, to inflict emotional and mental harm upon the victim.

One case involved a patient who had undergone a miscarriage in the sixth month of her pregnancy. While she was resting groggy in the hospital recovery room, a hospital staff member informed her that the hospital would be willing to take care of the burial of the fetus. Unable to bear the thought of seeing it, the patient agreed. As time went on, however, she worried increasingly about the rightness of her decision and decided she would feel better if she could view the interment site. With that in mind, she returned to the hospital for information. Annoyed at her request, an administrator, without preparing her for what she would witness, directed an orderly to show her the way. He led her to a room in which was a large refrigerator. From it, he took a bottle in which the woman saw the well-formed fetus floating, pickled in formaldehyde. She suffered a nervous breakdown. The administrator's conduct was ruled legally outrageous, and the hospital that employed him was required to pay the woman $175,000.

By contrast, consider the following case: Two women, one thin and the other overweight, were having lunch together, with the stout one shoveling away her food with abandon, leading the thin woman to say to her: "No wonder you look like a hippopotamus; you eat like one." The stout woman, who was sensitive about her weight, brooded over the hippopotamus remark to the extent that she eventually could no longer work and required psychiatric care and hospitalization. Although the thin woman's malicious comment had the same effect on the stout woman as did the hospital administrator's conduct toward the woman who had the miscarriage, the thin woman's words were not legally outrageous. The difference in the two cases lay in the predictability of the consequences. The thin woman, as an average citizen, could not be expected to know that her remark could possibly lead to the stout woman's nervous breakdown, but a hospital administrator would be expected to know, particularly after his institution had deliberately misled the woman about the nature of the "burial," that to show her the fetus she had carried for six months floating in formaldehyde was likely to have the devastating effect it did.

If you were the victim of an incident that approaches in seriousness that involving the fetus, both in its circumstances and its results, you should consult a lawyer. You may have grounds for suit and one in which the award is collectible if the defendant was acting in the capacity of an employee.

Intentional medical injuries.

A doctor who performs an operation upon you knowing it was medically unnecessary has assaulted you just as if he were a mugger who stuck a knife into you on the street. When you hire one surgeon to perform an operation, but it is performed by a second surgeon without your permission, the second surgeon has assaulted you and the first one is equally responsible as a conspirator to the assault. Further, when you agree to a course of medical treatment and are injured as a result of it, and the doctor has knowingly failed to warn you of the possible adverse consequences, you may also have grounds for an intentional-injury suit. And when a doctor, under the guise of providing therapy, induces you to have sexual relations, that, too, is a form of assault, giving you grounds for suit.

As a practical matter, whenever it is possible to interpret one of these injurious actions as a result of negligence (which will usually be the case when the doctor failed to warn you of adverse consequences to the treatment), rather than intent, you should always assert negligence in order to bring the doctor's insurance company into the case. When that is not possible, you may have substantial difficulty collecting your award; doctors, as educated people, are quite sophisticated about placing their assets so that they can't be touched by a judgment against them. However, in many intentional-injury cases involving doctors, and particularly those involving surgery, it will be possible also to name the hospital as a defendant, and any judgment brought against it will be collectible.

17

Strict Liability

Most of the dangers that could confront us at any time in our everyday lives are ones over which we have some measure of control. We know, for instance, that in crossing a street it's always possible that a driver will run us down, but we also know that if we observe the approaching traffic diligently before setting out, the odds of that happening to us are minimized. We further know that, in venturing into the streets at all, we face the possibility that we could get mugged, but we also know that if we stay away from dark and deserted sectors, we have improved the chances that won't happen to us. We know, too, that snowstorms create hazardous walking conditions, but we also know that if we pick our way carefully and try to stay on snowy, rather than icy, patches, our chances of falling and hurting ourselves are lessened. And so on.

But there are other dangers, of which we can have no foreknowledge, no means of avoidance. For instance, as we walk down the aisle of a grocery store, a soft-drink bottle explodes and a shard of glass enters our eye, partly blinding us. We could not predict, much less prevent, that danger. Or, we live peacefully in a little town in Utah and have no way of realizing that the government has poisoned our air and land and water and shortened our lives with its atomic testing twenty years earlier. Or, we are proud of the athletic ability of our sixteen-year-old son, a bright lad, and (though we know there's some predictable danger to it) we encourage him when he wants to play football, not suspecting —having no way of suspecting—that, as happened in one case, the helmet he wore to protect him from injury could, if jarred against the base of his skull at just the wrong angle, leave him for the rest of his life with the mind of an eight-year-old.

When harm derives from unavoidable dangers such as these, the law sometimes will allow the injuring party to be held to a standard of *strict* liability. Under this doctrine, a defendant is held liable for an injury solely because it owned or was responsible for the distribution of the cause of the injury. Today, strict liability is most commonly applied to product injury cases, but the rules are old ones, coming into existence in the Middle Ages, when it was recognized that owners of dangerous animals had a special duty to protect people from harm from them.

DANGEROUS ANIMAL ACTS

For example, a farmer owns a bull, which he attempts to keep penned at all times. One day, however, the bull gets loose when a bolt of lightning strikes down part of the fence that encloses it. Many hours later, the storm over, the bull wanders into a glen, where it comes upon a picnicking group consisting of a mother and her two small children. The frightened mother orders the children to run off while she distracts the bull from them by waving the picnic cloth in its face. Enraged, the bull charges her, knocks her down, and injures her.

If this case were tried under negligence law, the owner of the bull would probably win. He could argue that the bull got loose through no fault of his, that he made every effort to recapture it, and that it was simply unfortunate that, before he could do so, it happened upon the picnickers. Moreover, he would point out that the mother contributed to the causation of her injury by waving the cloth in the bull's face, an action she knew or should have known was likely to make it charge her.

But negligence law doesn't apply to this case. Strict liability does. Under the so-called Dangerous Animal Acts, a bull is an animal "of known dangerous propensities," and owners of them are responsible for the injuries they cause *even though the owner may not have been negligent and the victim was*. Thus, although the farmer wasn't responsible for the bull's getting out of its pen, he was responsible for its actions, and the picnicking mother, once confronted with the danger posed by the presence of the bull, could not have acted in a legally negligent fashion as she attempted, wisely or not, to protect herself and others from it.

Owners, however, aren't always responsible when their dangerous animals cause an injury. For example, assume you are out on a day's hike and come across a wooden fence inside which you see a bull grazing. The bull looks peaceful to you, and so you climb the fence and start across the pasture. The bull sees you, charges you, knocks you down, and injures you. By deliberately entering the pasture with the bull, you put yourself in danger and assumed the risk of injury, and you have no grounds on which to sue the farmer.

The difference in liability between the two bull examples, therefore, is one of voluntariness. Both you and the picnicking woman may have acted negligently, she by waving the cloth in the bull's face and you by climbing the fence in careless disregard for your own safety, but her negligence doesn't count, because she was confronted with a peril not of her own making, while yours does count, because you voluntarily prompted the events leading to your injury.

To assume legally the responsibility for your own injury, you need not necessarily have acted negligently. For instance, if you are at a baseball game and a foul ball hits you in the face, breaking your jaw, you certainly weren't negligent in any way, yet you have no grounds for suit against anyone on either intentional, negligence, or strict-liability grounds. The law, instead, will say that you knew or should have known that getting hit by a ball was a normal risk in attending the game. However, if you were poisoned by food you bought at the game, then you do have grounds for suit, since food poisoning is not the kind of risk you legally assume by attending an athletic event. In other words, to assume the risk (responsibility) for your injury, the risk must have been inherent and knowable in a situation you voluntarily entered, regardless of negligence on anybody's part. Getting injured by a tackle in a football game thus is inherent and knowable; getting injured by a defective football helmet is not. Reaching out your hand to stroke a dog that is snarling at you probably means voluntarily assuming the risk for the bite that follows; reaching out your hand in the same way to protect yourself from an attacking dog does not assume the risk, even though your gesture might not have been the smartest thing you could have done under the circumstances.

PETS AS DANGEROUS ANIMALS

No master list exists to define which animals are inherently dangerous to humans. These matters are decided on a case-by-case basis, with common knowledge the criterion usually applied. In this way, it has become possible to decide that a bull is an animal of known dangerous propensities, but that a cow is not; a boar is, but a pig isn't, save that a nursing sow might be, and so on, with the ruling reached in one case becoming the determinant for later ones. Wild animals are a category unto themselves. They are always considered to have dangerous proclivities, and you should be aware of that if you are tempted to purchase one as a pet. Animals recognized as domestic pets, such as dogs and cats, are a somewhat different matter.

For example, suppose you keep both a jaguar and a poodle as pets. One day, they both get out of the house and go their separate ways. The jaguar comes upon a woman standing at a street corner and does not attempt to harm her. Even so, upon seeing the beast, the woman becomes frightened and runs out into the street without looking for traffic and is struck down by a car. No matter how docile your jaguar might be, under the law it is a wild animal and you are strictly liable for the injuries it causes by its actions, even when they aren't threatening ones. Therefore, just as with the owner of the bull that escaped its paddock, you cannot defend yourself on the grounds that it wasn't your fault the animal got out of your house, nor can you charge the woman with contributory negligence by not watching where she was going when, perceiving herself to be in peril, she fled from it. You are going to have to pay for her injuries. (The fact that your wild-animal pet is not as overtly threatening-looking as a jaguar makes no difference; your sweet ocelot, your charming monkey, your gentle-natured python are still wild animals under the law, and you can be held strictly liable for injuries they cause either directly or indirectly.)

Meanwhile, as your jaguar is approaching the woman, your poodle comes upon a man who happens to be one of those people who have a morbid fear of dogs. Responding to that fear, he, too, runs out into the street without looking for traffic and is struck down by a passing car. Since a poodle, despite the man's dread of it, is not legally considered an animal of known dangerous propensities, the man cannot sue you on strict-liability grounds. He can only charge you with negligence in allowing the dog on the street without a leash, where it might terrorize people like himself. Now, however, unlike with your wild-animal pet, you have grounds to defend yourself. Perhaps you will be able to show that the poodle got out of your house when someone broke into it and left the door open upon fleeing (probably as a result of seeing that jaguar); in that event, if anyone's to blame for the man's accident, it is the burglar, not you. Or, even if the poodle got loose through your carelessness, you can still argue (as you can't with your jaguar) that since the poodle didn't attack the man, he, no matter how frightened he was, still had a duty to himself to watch for traffic as he ran, and when he didn't, he was contributorially negligent. The chances are you will win that suit.

There are times, however, when a dog—or, theoretically, even a cat—could become legally an animal of known dangerous propensities, and when that happens, you can be sued on strict-liability grounds if the pet injures someone.

For example, assume you allow your dog—which has never bitten anybody—to wander freely on your property. One day, a boy chases a ball into your yard and your dog runs up and bites him on the ankle. The boy was intruding, no matter how innocently, on your land, and your dog, in attacking him, was acting on its territorial protective instinct, and there is apparently no ground for suit against you. Now, however, you could have a problem. Your pet has taken the one free bite that dogs traditionally are allowed, and has shown by this incident a proclivity to be dangerous, making it possible that you could be held strictly liable for the dog's future bites. You would be wise to make sure the dog is no longer allowed the freedom of your premises, or else you should post a prominent warning so that others who might think of entering do so at their own risk. Even then, you might be held strictly liable if the victim of the second bite were a child who could not read the warning sign or understand its import.

Not all dogs are allowed even one free bite. If the canine guardian of your property is attack-trained, legally it will probably be considered to have dangerous propensities and you will be held strictly liable for any bites it inflicts on innocent parties.

INJURIES CAUSED BY EXCEPTIONALLY DANGEROUS CONDITIONS

Just as there are animals of known dangerous propensities, so are there lines of business that have been legally determined to create "ultrahazardous" conditions. While there is no master list of them, any more than there is of dangerous animals, the category clearly includes manufacturers and transporters of explosives, dangerous chemicals, inflammable materials, and poisons, and probably includes businesses engaged in the disposal of those items.

Therefore, if you were burned when a truck carrying chemicals exploded or you became ill from inhaling the noxious fumes emitted, you have grounds for suit against either the manufacturer or the trucker or both, and you do not have to prove that the accident was caused by anyone's negligence. This right to sue, however, does not extend to you if you are an employee of the ultrahazardous business; as with accidents caused by negligence, your only financial recourse is through workmen's-compensation insurance. Situations in which an employer such as a chemical firm knowingly keeps its workers unaware of a hazardous condition could possibly provide grounds for an intentional-tort suit, although the law here is very complex. It is also conceivable that if you have been injured in this kind of situation, you might have grounds for a strict-liability suit, if not against your employer, then against some other party, perhaps a supplier involved in creating the ultrahazardous condition; seek out an attorney who is expert in this field of the law.

No matter how hazardous a condition it creates, the United

States Government may not be sued on strict-liability grounds. Therefore, the residents of Utah who were apparently injured by the atomic testing in order to sue must allege that the government acted negligently, presenting a much harder standard of proof to meet under the circumstances than would be strict liability.

FAULTY PRODUCTS

Until a series of major decisions changed the law, in the late 1950s and early 1960s, it was impossible to bring suit against the seller of a damaging product on strict-liability grounds. This meant that if you were injured by a product, you would have to pinpoint specific acts of negligence by some party within the manufacturing or distribution process before you could sue. Considering the multitudinous stages an item can go through from raw material to its final, packaged appearance on a shelf for sale, the law as it stood placed an extraordinary and often insuperable burden on plaintiffs, and product injury suits were, as a result, relatively rare. To make suit even more difficult, in many places, if the victim of the injury wasn't also the purchaser of the product, suit wasn't permitted. As the courts finally became cognizant of the unfairness of these rules to plaintiffs, they turned to the Dangerous Animal Acts for guidance. From them, it could be seen that the relationship between seller and product was analogous to that of farmer and bull. Just as the farmer is supposed to know that a bull is dangerous and see to it that it never gets into a position in which it can do harm, so can the seller of a product be assumed to know when it is dangerous and should not let it out of its pen either while it remains in that condition. By adapting the Dangerous Animal Acts to products, the door was opened to the filing of thousands of suits each year that previously would have been unwinnable.

In current product injury law, the term "seller" is broadly defined. It can be the retailer who sold the product to the customer. It can be the wholesaler who sold it to the retailer, the supplier who sold it to the wholesaler, the manufacturer who sold it to the supplier, or the factory that sold parts of the product to the manufacturer. The key "selling" party, however, normally is the one that put the product on the market, because it can be presumed to have had the greatest measure of control over it. For this reason, whoever else is or isn't named as a defendant in a product-liability suit, the manufacturer almost invariably is.

There is no requirement, however, that a product injury suit be based on a strict-liability allegation. The grounds can be strict liability, can be negligence, and typically are both.

For example, the ABC Company places a liquid cleaner on the market that it knows contains ingredients that are harmful if swallowed. Even so, neither in its advertising nor on the bottle does it make mention of this danger. A child drinks the contents of one of the bottles and suffers internal injuries.

By failing to put a warning on the label, the manufacturer acted negligently, and the child's parents were not contributorially negligent (as they would have been had the product been properly labeled and they then failed to keep it out of reach of their child). The manufacturer, however, was also strictly liable for having placed a dangerous product on the market without a warning, and suit could be brought on either or both grounds.

While the strict-liability allegation makes it easier for you to win a product injury suit than when negligence was the only ground, a defendant, nevertheless, is not without resources. To begin with, the defendant may be able to win if it can prove that you altered or damaged the product in a material way, that is, in such a fashion that injury was the result of the alteration and would not have occurred had the product remained in its pristine condition.

However, the number of owners a product has had is legally irrelevant, as is the amount of nonmaterial alteration it has undergone, as is (in most jurisdictions) the age of the product. For this reason, automobile manufacturers have been held liable for intrinsic defects (such as a faulty steering wheel) even though a car has been on the road for many years and been frequently repaired (though not for steering-wheel problems).

The following case provides an example of this rule: At her doctor's suggestion, a mother bought a portable room humidifier to alleviate asthma attacks to which her six-year-old son was prone. Shortly after the purchase, an attack occurred; the mother plugged in the humidifier, which emitted scalding steam, burning the child.

By placing a defective product on the market, the manufacturer of the humidifier would appear to be strictly liable for the injury it caused. However, the manufacturer might argue that none of its other humidifiers had malfunctioned in the way this one did, and therefore the mother must have dropped or otherwise damaged this particular humidifier before using it. In that event, she assumed the responsibility for the injury.

But even if the manufacturer is able to prove this charge, the mother may respond that the manufacturer was negligent in failing to construct its humidifiers in such a way that they wouldn't become dangerous instruments simply by dropping them, and she could win her suit on that basis. As this case shows, while alteration of a product can defeat a strict-liability suit, it doesn't necessarily rule out victory on negligence, pointing up one good reason why many of these cases are brought on both grounds.

Your suit could also be defeated if the defendant can show that your injury was caused by an unpredictable misuse of the product.

For example, a man purchases a pair of electric hedge clippers. On the box are instructions for the proper use of the clippers, but there is no mention of uses to avoid. Having completed the trimming of his hedge, the man sees that crabgrass is growing between the stones of his patio, and he applies the clippers. As he does, the friction caused by the electricity shreds a patio stone and a sliver flies up and enters his eye, partially blinding him.

In this case, the plaintiff cannot argue that the product was dangerous when used for its advertised purpose. On the contrary, while the man was using it as it was meant to be used, the product did the job it was supposed to do. The strict-liability issue here, therefore, is foreseeability of misuse; that is, could the manufacturer have predicted that a person using electric clippers on a hedge might also improperly use them to snip off crabgrass growing between stones in a patio? In the suit on which this case is based, a jury decided that the manufacturer should have been aware that such a misuse was predictable, should have warned against it in its package instructions, and was therefore liable.

To the extent that any rule about foreseeability of use is decipherable, the defendant will be liable when the misuse that caused the injury was one associated at least indirectly with a normal use of the product. That's what happened in this case. If, however, the owner of the electric clippers had used them to trim his son's hair and lopped off one of his ears in the process, that would be a use of the product totally disassociated from any conceivable purpose for which it was sold, and the manufacturer would not be liable. (At least, that's probably so; there have been some strange verdicts, going both ways, in suits on this issue.)

Turning the circumstances around, it would seem to follow that when a company specifically warns against an improper use or an inherent danger associated with a product, it is then free of liability, and so it usually is. Cigarette manufacturers, for instance, cannot be sued when one of their customers develops lung cancer, solely due to the warnings of the hazards of cigarette smoking that the federal government has forced them to put on all their advertising.

A manufacturer, nevertheless, will not be free of liability when the proper-use warning has not been stated in readily understandable language by the people who are the most likely prospective users. Should they be children, then any warnings or instructions on use must be stated in a vocabulary children could be expected to understand. Warnings on all products must be placed prominently on the product or its packaging. A warning published in tiny type or hidden in a lengthy compendium of instruction may not be considered legally adequate, with the manufacturer liable for ensuing injuries.

You may also lose your suit if the manufacturer can prove its product wasn't "unreasonably" dangerous. A knife, for instance, to be useful must be sharp, and consequently it is dangerous but not unreasonably so. However, suppose it is a carving knife manufactured with a slippery material on its handle; in that event, the knife becomes unreasonably dangerous, and you have grounds for suit if the slippery material causes you to lose your grip on it and you are cut as a result. As with knives, alcoholic beverages have the potential for danger for everyone but are not considered unreasonably dangerous when prudently used; however, were a distiller accidentally to use wood, rather than grain, alcohol in preparing a batch, then the product has become unreasonably dangerous.

The meaning of "unreasonably" dangerous is often not as clear-cut as in these examples. For instance, if one manufacturer's car is constructed in such a way that it is more difficult to exit in time of danger than is another's, does that make the exit defect in the first car unreasonably dangerous? If so, would it still be unreasonably dangerous or defective if the safer model were not on the market?

On questions like these, various courts have come to differing conclusions. Only in two states, California and Pennsylvania, has it been decided that *any* defect in a product that causes an injury makes that product, by its nature, unreasonably dangerous. Were this view to be adopted by other jurisdictions, the way of the plaintiff would be made easier.

Nevertheless, as a general rule, whether a product is naturally dangerous or not, you will be able to get past the unreasonable-danger hurdle when you can show that the product has defective parts or an unsafe design, and sometimes when it might not be unreasonably dangerous for some people to use but would be for those whose use the product was marketed.

In one case that illustrates this general rule, a mother bought a cotton flannelette nightgown for her four-year-old daughter. One evening before bedtime, while wearing it, the little girl climbed onto the kitchen counter to get herself a cookie. As she did, the hem of the gown touched a hot coil on the electric range next to the counter. Within seconds, the child was enveloped from head to foot in flames. Her baby-sitter managed to put out the fire, but the child suffered second- and third-degree burns over nearly two thirds of her body. Although burns of this severity are usually fatal, excellent medical care saved the child's life. Over the next fifteen years, however, constant operations would be required both for cosmetic purposes and to remove scar tissue so that the skin could expand as the child grew.

The parents in this case brought their suit on both strict-liability and negligence grounds. In his pretrial memorandum on the law, their attorney argued that a garment that could suddenly envelop its wearer in flames was unreasonably dangerous and defective by nature, and those responsible for its presence on the market must be held strictly liable for the injuries they caused. The liability was intensified, he noted, by the fact that the dangerous garments were sold for wear by small children, who, it was predictable, would not be as careful as adults in avoiding situations that could result in an ignition. (It is, for that matter, questionable how many adults would realize that cotton flannelette could become a flaming shroud merely by the touch of a hot coil.) Those who manufactured the garment also acted negligently, the attorney argued, by selling the nightgowns when they knew, from testing within the textile industry, that untreated cotton flannelette is highly hazardous. By its negligence, the attorney added, the manufacturer had virtually guaranteed injuries of the kind the child received. The child won an award of $2.9 million.

A FOOTNOTE ON THE PUBLIC INTEREST

Although personal-injury suits usually have as their sole purpose to serve the interest of the individual plaintiff, and even though the workings of the system that administers the litigation is frequently cumbersome, with its final judgments based on factors that may have little or nothing to do with any objective ideas of justice, occasionally the system does fulfill its deterrent purpose, and when it does the public as a whole is the better for it.

Medical-malpractice suits, as one example, have led to meaningful reforms in hospital and medical procedures. During the 1970s, large verdicts in a number of cases involving surgical instruments left in patients' bodies forced many hospitals to adopt a counting system to avoid such accidents (and such expensive suits) in the future. Suits based on falls from hospital beds have also made it more likely that side railings will now be kept raised than was true in the past. Drugs, although still too often carelessly prescribed, are somewhat more carefully monitored now than they were even a few years ago, largely due to malpractice litigation. Also, largely thanks to the law developed by these suits, doctors are now required to explain the risks of procedures carefully to their patients and obtain their informed consent before going ahead, thereby making inroads on the number of unnecessary and unnecessarily risky operations that are performed each year.

But it is probably the product injury cases, which less than a generation ago were thwarted by the courts but are now permitted, that have in recent years served the public best. These suits have forced businessmen to assume a virtue they apparently don't always have. Now knowing that their dangerous products can cost them millions of dollars from one suit alone (only a portion of it covered by insurance), they have grown more careful, become more likely than once they were to remove a dangerous product from the market or to redesign it so that it will be safe. Although too many dangerous products—ranging from ill-engineered automobiles to toys with sharp points—still clutter the marketplace, adding to the hazards of living, it is also true that the football-helmet injury mentioned at the beginning of this chapter won't happen again, because a suit forced its manufacturer to remove that dangerous item from the shelves; similarly the flaming-nightgown suit has made it highly probable that little children of the future will never again be horribly injured and disfigured as this one child was. In these kinds of cases, when the plaintiffs win, so does society.

APPENDIX I

No-Fault Automobile-Insurance Laws

NO-FAULT PAYMENTS

Between 1971 and 1976, twenty-five states passed no-fault laws to provide payment of benefits to people injured in automobile accidents. The law in Illinois was subsequently declared unconstitutional by its supreme court, and that of Nevada was repealed by its legislature. Since 1976, efforts to pass new no-fault laws at the state level have virtually ceased; however, legislation to establish a national no-fault system was introduced in each session of the United States Congress during the second half of the 1970s, and it would appear that if any further expansion of the system is to take place, it will be at the federal level.

The table below, based on a 1978 study, describes the major provisions of no-fault laws by state. The following terms are used:

Under the category INSURANCE—
No-fault yes means that all drivers licensed by the state must purchase no-fault insurance.
No-fault optional means that drivers are not required to purchase no-fault insurance.
Liability yes means that all licensed drivers are required to purchase personal liability insurance to provide coverage in the event they are sued as a result of an automobile accident.
Liability optional means there is no requirement in the state law that drivers buy liability insurance.

Under the category BENEFITS—
PIP stands for Personal Injury Protection. The PIP figure is the

maximum amount the no-fault insurer is required to pay to an accident victim. In some states, individual cost items also have ceilings and they are shown, but the total of all these payments cannot exceed the PIP maximum.

Medical refers to the maximum reimbursement you are allowed for medical expenses.

Wages refers to the maximum reimbursement you are allowed for any injury-related loss of income or reduction of your earning capacity.

Death refers to the maximum payment allowed, if any, to survivors when the injury results in death. If the no-fault law in your state doesn't permit death benefits, your only method of recovery is through a wrongful-death suit.

Funeral refers to payments allowed, if any, for funeral expenses.

Rehab. refers to payments allowed, if any, to provide training in new job skills for persons whose injuries make it impossible for them to resume previous employment.

Other refers to all miscellaneous payments that the state's no-fault law permits. Almost always, they are limited to the costs of hiring a housekeeper and child-care service during the recuperation period.

Under the category SUIT—

Unrestricted means the state's no-fault law has no prohibitions on bringing suit against a driver who causes a wrongful injury. However, any benefits you have received under the no-fault system are deducted from the award you receive from the suit.

Limited means that suit is not permitted against a driver who wrongfully injured you unless you can meet the enumerated requirements. When you can't, the total recovery for your injury is that permitted under the PIP benefits. In *limited* states, as well as in *unrestricted* ones, when suit is brought, you may not be paid for the same item of damage by both the no-fault insurer and a defendant in the suit.

In both *unrestricted* and *limited* states, no-fault benefits never cover your pain and suffering or mental anguish; these damages are recoverable only through suit. (For a general discussion of no-fault laws, see Chapter Fourteen, pp. 194–95.)

In using this table, bear in mind that it is possible that changes have been made in your state's law since the study was completed. However, if your no-fault insurer refuses to pay you the benefits outlined here, you should contact your state insurance department for clarification; the refusal may be improper. In some instances, it will then be necessary to hire a lawyer to obtain the money due you. If the problem is merely a matter of processing a form, the lawyer should not charge you for that service. In studying the SUIT requirements above, note that if your medical expenses can be shown to exceed the maximum the state has ordained, you can bring suit even if your injury doesn't meet the other requirements.

ARKANSAS—INSURANCE: *No-fault optional,* but motorist must reject in writing any or all parts of coverage offered; *liability optional*/BENEFITS: *PIP* payments dependent on amount of insurance purchased; *medical*—$2,000 maximum; *wages*—up to $140 weekly for 52 weeks; *death*—$5,000 maximum; *funeral* —none; *rehab.*—none; *other*—up to $70 weekly for 52 weeks/ SUIT: *Unrestricted.*

COLORADO—INSURANCE: *No-fault yes; liability yes*/ BENEFITS: *PIP* payments dependent on amount of insurance purchased; *medical*—$25,000 maximum; *wages*—up to $125 weekly for 52 weeks; *death*—$1,000 maximum; *funeral*—none; *rehab.*—up to $25,000 within five years; *other*—up to $15 per day for 52 weeks/SUIT: *Limited* to injuries in which medical expenses exceed $500, or those causing death, disfigurement, dismemberment, or uncompensated earnings beyond 52 weeks.

CONNECTICUT—INSURANCE: *No-fault yes; liability yes*/ BENEFITS: *PIP* maximum $5,000; *medical*—included in PIP maximum; *wages*—included in PIP maximum but in any case never more than $200 weekly; *death*—included in PIP maximum; *funeral*—$2,000 maximum; *rehab.*—included in PIP maximum; *other*—included in PIP maximum/SUIT: *Limited* to injuries in which medical expenses exceed $400, and certain specified serious injuries regardless of medical expenses.

DELAWARE—INSURANCE: *No-fault yes; liability yes*/ BENEFITS: *PIP* maximum $10,000 per injury, $20,000 per year if more than one injury; *medical*—included in PIP maximum; *wages*—100% up to PIP maximum; *death*—none; *funeral*—$2,000 maximum; *rehab.*—none; *other*—100% up to PIP maximum/ SUIT: *Unrestricted.*

FLORIDA—INSURANCE: *No-fault yes; liability yes*/BENEFITS: *PIP* $5,000 maximum; *medical*—80% of total but only up to PIP maximum; *wages*—80% of gross income if declared for federal income-tax purposes, otherwise 60%, up to PIP limit; *death*—none; *funeral*—$1,000; *rehab.*—included in medical expenses; *other*—included in PIP limit/SUIT: *Limited,* may be brought only when injury is included as "serious," or for specified periods of disability; wrongful-death suits apparently permitted.

GEORGIA—INSURANCE: *No-fault yes; liability yes*/BENEFITS: *PIP* $5,000 maximum; *medical*—$2,500; *wages*—up to $200 within PIP limit; *death*—payable up to PIP limit as if deceased were alive but totally disabled; *funeral*—$1,500 maximum; *rehab.*—included in medical expenses; *other*—up to $20 per day within PIP limit/SUIT: *Limited* to cases in which medical expenses exceed $500 or any disability lasting more than ten days, or any number of "serious" injuries (including death) regardless of medical expenses.

HAWAII—INSURANCE: *No-fault yes; liability yes*/BENEFITS: *PIP* $15,000 maximum; *medical*—up to PIP limit for medical expenses occurring first year; additional payments determined annually thereafter; *wages*—up to $800 monthly within PIP limit; *death*—up to $800 monthly payment to survivors up to PIP limit; *funeral*—$1,500 maximum; *rehab.*—included in medical; *other*—up to $500 per month within PIP limit/ SUIT: *Limited* to cases in which medical expenses exceed PIP limit, or any "serious" injury or permanent injury (including death) regardless of medical expenses.

KANSAS—INSURANCE: *No-fault yes; liability yes*/BENEFITS: *PIP* payments dependent on amount of insurance purchased; *medical*—$2,000 maximum; *wages*—100% up to PIP maximum if recipient declares as taxable income; otherwise maximum of $650 per month for one year; *death*—payment to survivors based on same formula as wage loss; *funeral*—$1,000 maximum; *rehab.*—$2,000 maximum; *other*—up to $12 per day for 365 days within PIP limit/SUIT: *Limited* to cases in which medical expenses exceed $500 or death or various enumerated "serious" injuries regardless of medical expenses.

KENTUCKY—INSURANCE: *No-fault optional,* but rejection must be in writing; *liability yes*/BENEFITS: *PIP* $10,000 maximum; *medical*—included in PIP limit; *wages*—maximum of $200 weekly up to PIP limit; *death*—payments to survivors same as for wages; *funeral*—$1,000 maximum; *rehab.*—included in medical; *other*—up to $200 weekly to PIP limit/SUIT: *Limited* to cases in which medical expenses exceed $1,000 or for death, fractures, or other serious or disfiguring injuries regardless of medical costs.

MARYLAND—INSURANCE: *No-fault yes; liability yes*/BENEFITS: *PIP* maximum $2,500; *medical*—included in PIP maximum; *wages*—100% within PIP limit; *death*—none; *funeral*—up to PIP limit; *rehab.*—up to PIP limit; *other*—up to PIP limit/SUIT: *Unrestricted.*

MASSACHUSETTS—INSURANCE: *No-fault yes; liability yes*/BENEFITS: *PIP* maximum $2,000; *medical*—included in PIP limit; *wages*—up to 75% of loss but only when combined with other loss benefits and only up to PIP limit; *death*—paid to survivors up to PIP limit; *funeral*—up to PIP limit; *rehab.*—none; *other*—up to PIP limit/SUIT: *Limited* to cases in which medical expenses exceed $500 or for other "serious" injuries regardless of medical expenses.

MICHIGAN—INSURANCE: *No-fault yes; liability yes*/BENEFITS: *PIP* payments dependent on amount of insurance purchased; *medical*—no limit up to coverage purchased; *wages*—maximum of $1,000 per 30-day period up to three years; *death*—payments to survivors same as for wages; *funeral*—$1,000 maximum; *rehab.*—no limit up to coverage purchased; *other*—$20 per day maximum for three years/SUIT: *Limited* to cases in which damages exceed PIP limits of economic loss or for death, serious impairment of bodily functions, or serious disfigurement, regardless of economic limits.

MINNESOTA—INSURANCE: *No-fault yes; liability yes/* BENEFITS: *PIP* maximum $30,000; *medical*—up to $20,000; *wages*—maximum of $200 weekly but no more than $10,000 in total; *death*—up to $200 weekly to survivors for loss of deceased's contributions to family, and up to $200 weekly to replace services provided by deceased, but maximum of $10,000; *funeral*—maximum of $1,250; *rehab.*—included in medical; *other*—$15 per day up to $10,000/SUIT: *Limited* to cases in which medical expenses exceed $2,000 or for disability of more than 60 days, regardless of medical expenses, or for permanent or disfiguring injuries regardless of medical costs.

NEW JERSEY—INSURANCE: *No-fault yes; liability yes/* BENEFITS: *PIP* payments dependent on amount of insurance purchased; *medical*—up to PIP limit; *wages*—maximum of $100 weekly for no more than 52 weeks; *death*—$5,200 for wage earner, and $4,380 for nonwage earner; *funeral*—up to $1,000; *rehab.*—up to PIP limit/SUIT: *Limited* to certain serious injuries, and soft-tissue injuries in which medical costs exceed $200 exclusive of the hospital or diagnostic expenses.

NEW YORK—INSURANCE: *No-fault yes; liability yes/* BENEFITS: *PIP* maximum $50,000; *medical*—up to PIP limit; *wages*—maximum of $1,000 per month for no more than three years within PIP limit; *death*—$2,000 in addition to PIP maximum; *funeral*—none; *rehab.*—included in medical; *other*—$25 per day up to one year within PIP limit/SUIT: *Limited* to cases in which medical expenses exceed $500, or death, disfigurement, dismemberment, some fractures, and permanent loss of use of body parts when medical expenses don't exceed $500.

NORTH DAKOTA—INSURANCE: *No-fault yes; liability yes/* BENEFITS: *PIP* maximum $15,000; *medical*—up to PIP limit; *wages*—maximum of $150 per week within PIP limit; *death*—same as wages plus $15 per day for replacement of deceased's services, both subject to PIP limit; *funeral*—up to $1,000; *rehab.*—up to PIP limit; *other*—$15 per day up to PIP limit/SUIT: *Limited* to cases in which medical expenses exceed $1,000 or disability of more than 60 days, or death, dismemberment, or disfigurement regardless of medical expenses.

OREGON—INSURANCE: *No-fault yes; liability yes*/BENEFITS: *PIP* payments dependent on amount of insurance purchased; *medical*—maximum of $5,000; *wages*—maximum of $750 per month for one year within PIP limit; *death*—none; *funeral*—up to $1,000; *rehab.*—none; *other*—$18 per day up to one year within PIP limit/SUIT: *Unrestricted*.

PENNSYLVANIA—INSURANCE: *No-fault yes; liability yes*/ BENEFITS: *PIP* payments dependent on amount of insurance purchased; *medical*—no limit within amount of coverage purchased; *wages*—up to $1,000 per month applied to a per capita earnings formula with a maximum of $15,000; *death*—up to $5,000; *funeral*—up to $5,000; *rehab.*—up to PIP limit; *other*—up to $25 per day for one year/SUIT: *Limited* generally to medical expenses exceeding $750, or death, permanent injury, permanent disfigurement, or total disability for more than 60 consecutive days regardless of medical expenses.

SOUTH CAROLINA—INSURANCE: *No-fault yes; liability yes*/BENEFITS: *PIP* maximum $1,000; *medical*—up to PIP limit; *wages*—up to PIP limit; *death*—none; *funeral*—up to PIP limit; *rehab.*—none; *other*—up to PIP limit/SUIT—*Unrestricted*.

SOUTH DAKOTA—INSURANCE: *No-fault optional; liability optional*/BENEFITS: *PIP* payments dependent on amount of insurance purchased; *medical*—maximum of $2,000; *wages*—maximum of $60 weekly for 52 weeks; *death*—up to $10,000 but only if death occurs within 90 days of accident; *funeral*—none; *rehab.*—none; *other*—none/SUIT: *Unrestricted*.

TEXAS—INSURANCE: *No-fault optional; liability optional*/ BENEFITS: *PIP* maximum $2,500; *medical*—up to PIP limit; *wages*—up to PIP limit; *death*—none; *funeral*—none; *other*—"reasonable" expenses within PIP limit/SUIT: *Unrestricted*.

UTAH—INSURANCE: *No-fault yes; liability yes*/BENEFITS: *PIP* payments dependent on amount of insurance purchased; *medical*—maximum of $2,000; *wages*—maximum of $150 weekly up to 52 weeks; *death*—up to $2,000; *funeral*—$1,000; *rehab.*—included in medical payments; *other*—up to $12 per day for one year/SUIT: *Limited* to cases in which medical bills exceed $500, or death, disfigurement, dismemberment, fracture, or permanent disability regardless of medical cost.

VIRGINIA—INSURANCE: *No-fault optional; liability optional*/BENEFITS: *PIP* payments dependent on amount of insurance purchased; *medical*—maximum of $2,000; *wages*—maximum of $100 per week for 52 weeks; *death*—none; *funeral*—none; *rehab.*—none; *other*—none/SUIT: *Unrestricted.*

STATUTES OF LIMITATIONS BY JURISDICTION

The table that follows is intended primarily for the use of the vast majority of plaintiffs who knew of their injury on the date it occurred. For them, the deadline for filing suit expires on the date of the injury at the end of the statutory period, i.e., suit on an injury occurring on September 1, 1980, must be filed by September 1, 1981, in a state with a one-year deadline.

If you discovered your injury only subsequent to its occurrence (see also Chapter Fourteen, pp. 197–98), the statutory period typically begins from the first day you knew, or a court determines you should have known, of the injury. There are, however, many variations, and while the table lists the principal ones, in late-discovery injuries you should always consult an attorney as quickly as possible in order to protect your rights.

In many states, deadline for filing suit depends on the grounds alleged or on who is named as defendant. In the table, the general rule for filing *most* personal-injury suits in which the victim survived is shown first, with principal exceptions, if any, listed next. Following that, the deadline for filing a wrongful-death suit is given, with exceptions to that rule also noted.

In the listings of exceptions, the word *intentional* refers to a variation in filing suit for intentional torts; *libel,* to a variation in filing suit for libel, slander, or (usually) invasion of privacy; *med. mal.,* to a variation in filing suit for medical malpractice. Other exceptions listed are self-explanatory.

One important variation in deadlines can occur in actions brought against a government. In some states, it is necessary to file a *claim,* asserting your injury and making a demand for payment, in a much briefer time than is permitted for the actual filing of suit. Ninety to 120 days is a commonly used period. Consequently, if you don't file a claim within that time period, you lose your right to file suit subsequently. Because of the extraordinary variety and complexity of these laws, no attempt is made to list all of them in the table, although, where the law appears clear, parenthetical mention is made. *Do not, however, assume that if no time limit for filing a claim against a government is listed, that one does not exist.* Therefore, should a unit of government be a prospective defendant in your case, your safest course always is to obtain a lawyer as soon after the accident as possible.

The table is intended to be accurate as of 1979. Use the table only for personal-injury cases. Other types of civil suits may, and often do, have different deadlines.

ALABAMA—*Personal injury,* 1 year. Exception: med. mal., 2 years, maximum of 4 years on late discovery./*Wrongful death,* 2 years.

ALASKA—*Personal injury,* 2 years./*Wrongful death,* 2 years.

ARIZONA—*Personal injury,* 2 years. Exception: med. mal., 3 years./*Wrongful death,* 2 years. Exception: med. mal., 3 years.

ARKANSAS—*Personal injury,* 3 years. Exceptions: intentional, 1 year; libel, 1 year; med. mal., 2 years./*Wrongful death,* 3 years.

CALIFORNIA—*Personal injury,* 1 year. Exception: med. mal., 3 years, or one year after discovery of injury, whichever is less./*Wrongful death,* 1 year. Exception: med. mal., same as if injury didn't result in death.

COLORADO—*Personal injury,* 6 years. Exceptions: intentional, 1 year; med. mal., 2 years, maximum of 5 years on late discovery./*Wrongful death,* 6 years. (Claim against municipal government must be filed within 90 days.)

CONNECTICUT—*Personal injury,* 2 years. Exception: late discovery to maximum of 3 years./*Wrongful death,* 2 years. Exception: on late discovery, ordinarily to maximum of 3 years.

DELAWARE—*Personal injury,* 2 years./*Wrongful death,* 2 years.

APPENDIX I

DISTRICT OF COLUMBIA—*Personal injury*, 3 years. Exceptions: intentional, 1 year; libel, 1 year./*Wrongful death*, 1 year.

FLORIDA—*Personal injury*, 4 years. Exception: med. mal., 2 years./*Wrongful death*, 2 years.

GEORGIA—*Personal injury*, 2 years./*Wrongful death*, 2 years.

HAWAII—*Personal injury*, 2 years. Exception: med. mal., maximum of 6 years on late discovery./*Wrongful death*, 2 years.

IDAHO—*Personal injury*, 2 years./*Wrongful death*, 2 years. (Claim against a municipal government must be filed within 120 days.)

ILLINOIS—*Personal injury*, 2 years. Exceptions: libel, 1 year; med. mal., maximum of 4 years on late discovery; suits against state and Chicago Transit Authority, 1 year./*Wrongful death*, 2 years.

INDIANA—*Personal injury*, 2 years./*Wrongful death*, 2 years.

IOWA—*Personal injury*, 2 years./*Wrongful death*, 2 years.

KANSAS—*Personal injury*, 2 years. Exceptions: intentional, 1 year; libel, 1 year./*Wrongful death*, 2 years.

KENTUCKY—*Personal injury*, 1 year./*Wrongful death*, 1 year.

LOUISIANA—*Personal injury*, 1 year./*Wrongful death*, 1 year.

MAINE—*Personal injury*, 6 years. Exception: med. mal., 2 years./*Wrongful death*, 2 years.

MARYLAND—*Personal injury*, 3 years. Exceptions: intentional, 1 year; libel, 1 year./*Wrongful death*, 3 years.

MASSACHUSETTS—*Personal injury*, 3 years. Exception: injuries resulting from defects in a right-of-way, 2 years./*Wrongful death*, 2 years.

MICHIGAN—*Personal injury*, 3 years. Exceptions: intentional, 2 years; libel, 1 year; med. mal., 2 years; government as defendant, 2 years./*Wrongful death*, 3 years. Exception: med. mal., 2 years.

APPENDIX I

MINNESOTA—*Personal injury,* 6 years. Exceptions: libel, 2 years; med. mal., 2 years; intentional, 1 year./*Wrongful death,* 6 years. (Claim against a municipal government must be filed in 60 days.)

MISSISSIPPI—*Personal injury,* 6 years. Exceptions: intentional, 1 year; libel, 1 year; med. mal., 2 years./*Wrongful death,* 6 years.

MISSOURI—*Personal injury,* 5 years. Exceptions: intentional, 2 years; libel, 2 years; med. mal., 2 years./*Wrongful death,* 2 years.

MONTANA—*Personal injury,* 3 years. Exceptions: intentional, 2 years; libel, 2 years; med. mal., 5 years; government as defendant, 2 years./*Wrongful death,* 3 years. (Claim against a municipal government must be filed within 120 days.)

NEBRASKA—*Personal injury,* 4 years. Exceptions: intentional, 1 year; libel, 1 year; med. mal., 2 years; claims against government units, 2 years./*Wrongful death,* 2 years.

NEVADA—*Personal injury,* 2 years./*Wrongful death,* 2 years.

NEW HAMPSHIRE—*Personal injury,* 6 years. Exception: product-liability suits, 3 years; libel, 2 years./*Wrongful death,* 2 years.

NEW JERSEY—*Personal injury,* 2 years. Exception: libel, 1 year./*Wrongful death,* 2 years.

NEW MEXICO—*Personal injury,* 3 years. Exception: injury caused by local governmental unit, 1 year./*Wrongful death,* 3 years. Exception: death caused by local governmental unit, 1 year.

NEW YORK—*Personal injury,* 3 years. Exceptions: intentional, 1 year; libel, 1 year; med. mal., 2½ years./*Wrongful death,* 2 years.

NORTH CAROLINA—*Personal injury,* 3 years. Exceptions: intentional, 1 year; libel, 1 year./*Wrongful death,* 2 years.

NORTH DAKOTA—*Personal injury,* 6 years. Exceptions: intentional, 2 years; libel, 2 years; med. mal., 2 years./*Wrongful death,* 2 years. (Claims against municipal governments for injuries caused by street defects must be filed within 90 days.)

APPENDIX I

OHIO—*Personal injury*, 2 years. Exceptions: intentional, 1 year; libel, 1 year./*Wrongful death*, 2 years.

OKLAHOMA—*Personal injury*, 2 years. Exceptions: intentional, 1 year; libel, 1 year./*Wrongful death*, 2 years. (Claims against a municipal government must be filed within 120 days.)

OREGON—*Personal injury*, 3 years. Exceptions: intentional, 2 years; libel, 2 years./*Wrongful death*, 3 years. (Claim against a municipal government must be filed within 120 days.)

PENNSYLVANIA—*Personal injury*, 2 years. Exceptions: libel, 1 year; actions against government, 6 months./*Wrongful death*, 2 years. (However, 1979 appeals-court decisions indicate, though not completely clearly, that a 2-year limit will now apply to all cases.)

RHODE ISLAND—*Personal injury*, 3 years. Exceptions: slander, 2 years (statement of law ambiguous on whether slander limit includes libel and invasion of privacy, but probably does); med. mal., 2 years./*Wrongful death*, 2 years.

SOUTH CAROLINA—*Personal injury*, 6 years. Exceptions: intentional, 2 years; libel, 2 years./*Wrongful death*, 6 years. Exception: certain highway deaths, 1 year.

SOUTH DAKOTA—*Personal injury*, 3 years. Exceptions: intentional, 2 years; libel, 2 years; med. mal., 2 years./*Wrongful death*, 3 years.

TENNESSEE—*Personal injury*, 1 year. Exception: slander only, 6 months./*Wrongful death*, 1 year. (Claims against a municipal government must be filed within 120 days.)

TEXAS—*Personal injury*, 2 years. Exception: libel, 1 year./*Wrongful death*, 2 years.

UTAH—*Personal injury*, 4 years. Exceptions: intentional, 1 year; libel, 1 year; med. mal., 2 years./*Wrongful death*, 2 years.

VERMONT—*Personal injury*, 3 years. Exception: injuries sustained while skiing downhill, 1 year./*Wrongful death*, 2 years.

VIRGINIA—*Personal injury*, 2 years./*Wrongful death*, 2 years.

WASHINGTON—*Personal injury*, 3 years. Exceptions: intentional, 2 years; libel, 2 years./*Wrongful death*, 3 years.

WEST VIRGINIA—*Personal injury*, 2 years./*Wrongful death*, 2 years.

WISCONSIN—*Personal injury*, 3 years. Exceptions: intentional, 2 years; libel, 2 years./*Wrongful death*, 3 years. (Claim against a municipal government must be filed within 120 days.)

WYOMING—*Personal injury*, 4 years. Exceptions: intentional, 1 year; libel, 1 year; med. mal., 2 years./*Wrongful death*, 2 years.

FEDERAL TORT CLAIMS ACT—*Personal injury*, 2 years to file for required administrative hearing; once agency has made ruling, plaintiff who rejects ruling then has six months to file suit./*Wrongful death*, same as for *personal injury*.

SOVEREIGN IMMUNITY

Under the Federal Tort Claims Act, suit is permitted against the United States Government only for injuries inflicted as a result of employee negligence. All such claims must first go through an administrative hearing by the agency involved, with suit permitted only if the plaintiff rejects the hearing board's findings.

The conditions, if any, under which a personal-injury suit may be brought against governments other than federal vary widely. In some states, the right to sue is unrestricted; in others, suit may be brought, but only under specific and narrow circumstances; in still others, the government must give permission before suit is allowed; in others, the right to sue does not exist. In some places the state government may be sued but local government units may not; vice versa in others. However, even where sovereign immunity exists, governmental units—including those of most cities—will, even so, defend and pay for suits brought against employees when that is guaranteed as part of their employment contract.

Based on 1979 studies, if you live in one of the following states, you have a generally unrestricted right to bring suit against your *state* government whenever you believe it or one of its employees was responsible for your injury. In states not listed, studies indicate the right to sue is either limited—often in very complex ways—or is nonexistent.

ALASKA
ARIZONA
CALIFORNIA
COLORADO
FLORIDA
HAWAII
IDAHO ($100,000 maximum damages payable)
ILLINOIS
INDIANA
KANSAS
KENTUCKY
LOUISIANA
MAINE
MISSOURI
MONTANA
NEBRASKA
NEVADA
NEW JERSEY
NEW MEXICO
NEW YORK
NORTH CAROLINA
NORTH DAKOTA
OKLAHOMA ($50,000 maximum damages payable)
OREGON ($100,000 maximum damages payable)
RHODE ISLAND
UTAH
VERMONT
WASHINGTON
WISCONSIN
WYOMING (but, as of 1979, law abolishing immunity was still under challenge in state appeals courts)

Based on 1977 and 1978 studies, the highlights of the laws governing personal-injury suits against *municipal* governments are as follows:

ALABAMA—Suit permitted; maximum payment of $100,000 per claim.

ALASKA—Suit permitted.

ARIZONA—Complex law in which the right to sue seems to be decided on a case-by-case basis.

ARKANSAS—Suit generally limited to cases involving injury caused by municipally owned vehicles.

CALIFORNIA—Municipality liability generally limited to actions brought against employees while carrying out duties of office.

COLORADO—Suit generally permitted; claims must be brought in 90 days; maximum of $100,000 when one person injured; maximum of $300,000 in multiperson injuries.

CONNECTICUT—Suit apparently permitted only against employees while carrying out duties of office.

DELAWARE—Suit appears generally permitted, but right to sue is decided on a case-by-case basis.

FLORIDA—Suit permitted; maximum payment of $50,000 when one person is injured and $100,000 in multiperson accidents or the amount of insurance carried by the municipality if that is larger.

GEORGIA—Suit generally not permitted, but some municipalities carry insurance to cover personal-injury cases, and in that event suit may be brought with maximum payment dictated by the amount of insurance available.

HAWAII—Suit generally permitted, although substantial restrictions against bringing suit against police officers who cause injuries.

IDAHO—Suit permitted; claims must be filed within 120 days; maximum payment of $100,000 when one person injured, and $300,000 in multiperson accidents.

ILLINOIS—Suit permitted except for accidents caused by government that occur in public parks and playgrounds; maximum payment of $100,000 per claim.

INDIANA—Suit permitted; maximum of $300,000 payment per claimant.

IOWA—Suit permitted.

KANSAS—Suit permitted.

KENTUCKY—Suit permitted, although on accidents caused by municipally owned vehicles, maximum of $10,000 when one person injured, $20,000 when two or more are injured.

LOUISIANA—Suit permitted.

MAINE—Suit not permitted, except for injuries caused by municipally owned motor vehicles.

MARYLAND—Suit generally not permitted; this law has been under court challenge and may be changed.

MASSACHUSETTS—Suit generally not permitted, although suits brought against public employees ordinarily will be paid by the local government or to the extent of insurance coverage.

MICHIGAN—Complex law, but suit apparently is only permitted for accidents caused by municipally owned motor vehicles and on government property; but the latter only when plaintiff can show the municipality had knowledge of the defect leading to the accident.

MINNESOTA—The employee who caused the accident must be named as the defendant, but the municipal employer is required to defend and pay. Suit not permitted for injuries caused by ice and snow on streets. Claims must be brought within sixty days. Maximum of $25,000 on a wrongful death suit; $50,000 when one person injured, maximum of $300,000 on multiperson injuries. Maximum of $30,000 on injuries caused by municipally owned vehicles.

MISSISSIPPI—Suit generally not permitted, but municipalities may purchase insurance for payment to citizens for governmentally caused injury, in which event maximum payment is limited by face amount of policy.

MISSOURI—Suit permitted.

MONTANA—Suit permitted, but amount of payment generally limited by face value of municipality insurance policy. Claim must be brought in 120 days. Law appears to prohibit recovery for pain and suffering.

NEBRASKA—Suit generally permitted; some complex but minor exceptions.

NEVADA—Suit permitted, but maximum recovery is $25,000.

NEW HAMPSHIRE—Suit permitted; maximum liability is $50,000 but municipalities apparently may purchase insurance permitting larger recoveries.

NEW JERSEY—Suit permitted when caused by an employee carrying out duties of job.

NEW MEXICO—Complex law, but apparently personal-injury

suits generally permitted against municipalities; maximum recovery of $300,000 per claim.

NEW YORK—Suit permitted.

NORTH CAROLINA—Suit generally not permitted, but municipalities may purchase liability insurance to pay for accidents caused to their citizens, in which event payment is limited to face value of policy.

NORTH DAKOTA—Suit permitted; maximum recovery of $20,000 per plaintiff up to maximum of $100,000 in multiperson accidents.

OHIO—Suit generally not permitted, but municipalities may purchase liability insurance to pay for accidents caused to their citizens, in which event payment is limited to face value of policy.

OKLAHOMA—Suit permitted; claim must be filed within 120 days.

OREGON—Suit permitted; maximum of $50,000 recovery when one person injured, $100,000 in multiperson injuries; claims generally must be brought within 180 days.

PENNSYLVANIA—Suit permitted.

RHODE ISLAND—Suit permitted; maximum of $50,000 recovery per claim.

SOUTH CAROLINA—Complex law, but suit appears to be limited to accidents caused by street defects and by motor vehicles owned by the municipality. Maximum recovery of $15,000 when one person is injured; $30,000 maximum in multiperson injuries. This law may be in the process of liberalization.

SOUTH DAKOTA—Suit not permitted, but municipalities may purchase insurance to pay for injuries caused their citizens, in which event payment limited to face value of policy.

TENNESSEE—Suit is permitted for motor-vehicle accidents, injuries caused by unsafe streets and unsafe public buildings. On former, maximum payment is $50,000 when one person injured, $300,000 in multiperson injuries; on latter, $20,000 per individual and $40,000 on multiperson injuries. Law appears to make it very difficult to bring suit against an employee for a wrongful action, such as police brutality. Claims must be filed within 120 days.

TEXAS—Suit generally permitted but with complex restrictions on when government is required to defend when an employee is

named as defendant. Maximum recovery of $100,000 when one person injured; maximum of $300,000 in multiperson injuries.
UTAH—Suit permitted.
VERMONT—Suit permitted. Maximum recovery of $75,000 when one person is injured; $300,000 on multiperson accidents.
VIRGINIA—Suit is not permitted.
WASHINGTON—Suit permitted.
WEST VIRGINIA—Suit permitted, but only up to the maximum amount of insurance the municipality has purchased for that person.
WISCONSIN—Suit permitted, but maximum recovery is $25,000 per claim. Claim must be filed within 120 days.
WYOMING—Questionable. Suit apparently is permitted against municipalities, but as of 1979, law abolishing municipal immunity was still on appeal in state courts.

In using this summary of state laws governing suits against municipalities, note that, because of the complexity of many of the statutes, the interpretations given here cannot be considered completely authoritative.

CHARITABLE IMMUNITY

The right to bring suit against a charitable body (such as a church or a charity-operated institution, including a hospital) is regulated by state law. The following table, intended to be accurate as of 1979, describes charitable-immunity laws by state. When a charitable institution or body is immune from suit, action may be brought directly against the employee or employees who allegedly caused the injury.

In the table, *Permitted* means that a personal-injury suit may be brought against any charitable institution or body without restrictions;

Limited means suit is generally permitted but with certain noted restrictions and exceptions;

Forbidden means suit may not be brought against any charitable institution or body.

ALABAMA—*Permitted*.
ALASKA—*Permitted*.

ARIZONA—*Permitted*.

ARKANSAS—*Limited*. Charity may not be sued directly, but suit may be brought against its insurer.

CALIFORNIA—*Permitted*.

COLORADO—*Limited*. Generally permitted, but a few exceptional situations in which forbidden.

CONNECTICUT—*Permitted*.

DELAWARE—*Permitted*.

DISTRICT OF COLUMBIA—*Permitted*.

FLORIDA—*Permitted*.

GEORGIA—*Forbidden*.

HAWAII—*Limited*. Many exceptions; law is complex and ambiguous.

IDAHO—*Permitted*.

ILLINOIS—*Permitted*.

INDIANA—*Permitted*.

IOWA—*Limited*. Generally permitted, except that a hospital "charity" patient may not sue the hospital for injuries inflicted.

KANSAS—*Permitted*.

KENTUCKY—*Permitted*.

MAINE—*Limited*. Charity may not be sued, but its insurer may be.

MARYLAND—*Limited*. Charity may not be sued, but its insurer may be.

MASSACHUSETTS—*Permitted*, except that hospital "charity" patients are limited to a $20,000 recovery.

MICHIGAN—*Permitted*.

MINNESOTA—*Permitted*.

MISSISSIPPI—*Forbidden*.

MISSOURI—*Permitted*.

MONTANA—*Forbidden*.

NEBRASKA—*Permitted*.

NEVADA—*Limited*. Exceptions are many and complex.

NEW HAMPSHIRE—*Permitted*.

NEW JERSEY—*Limited*. Generally permitted, but there are a few complex exceptions.

NEW MEXICO—Unknown. As of 1979, there had been no final determination by the courts as to whether or not charitable immunity was permitted, and if so under what circumstances.

NEW YORK—*Permitted.*
NORTH CAROLINA—*Permitted.*
NORTH DAKOTA—*Permitted.*
OHIO—*Permitted.*
OKLAHOMA—*Permitted.*
OREGON—*Permitted.*
PENNSYLVANIA—*Permitted.*
RHODE ISLAND—*Permitted.*
SOUTH CAROLINA—*Limited.* A charity may be sued for injuries allegedly caused by "reckless" or "intentional" wrongdoing.
SOUTH DAKOTA—No governing law. However, an insurer cannot refuse to defend a suit on the grounds that a customer is immune.
TENNESSEE—*Permitted.*
TEXAS—*Permitted.*
UTAH—*Permitted.*
VERMONT—*Permitted.*
VIRGINIA—*Limited.* Suit is permitted against charity-operated hospitals, but otherwise charities appear immune from suit.
WASHINGTON—*Permitted.*
WEST VIRGINIA—*Permitted.*
WISCONSIN—*Permitted.*
WYOMING—*Permitted.*

CONTRIBUTORY AND COMPARATIVE NEGLIGENCE

If your state, as shown in the table below, has a *contributory*-negligence law, you are not permitted to win in a negligence case if the defense can prove you were responsible to any degree whatsoever for your own injury.

If you live in a *comparative*-negligence state, your award will be reduced by the degree to which a jury decides you were at fault, and in some places if the jurors decide you were 50% or more at fault, you don't win anything.

Comparative laws are shown in the table as follows:
Comparative means the law applies only to negligence suits.
Comparative plus means the law also applies to suits brought on intentional and strict-liability grounds. Since negligence is not an issue in these cases, the award is reduced by the plaintiff's proven degree of assumption of risk for the injury.

APPENDIX I

Less than 50% means the plaintiff can win the comparative award only if found to be less than half at fault.

Equal means the plaintiff can win the comparative award only if found to be 50% at fault or less.

Slight means the plaintiff can win the comparative award as long as the jury decides the plaintiff's fault was slight. What "slight" means will vary from jury to jury.

1% base means the plaintiff can win a comparative award whenever the defendant can be shown to be at least 1% responsible. Thus, if the jury determines the injury is worth $10,000 but that the plaintiff was 90% at fault, the plaintiff receives $1,000, and so on.

For further information on contributory and comparative negligence, see pp. 215–18.

ALABAMA—*Contributory*.
ALASKA—*Contributory*.
ARIZONA—*Contributory*.
ARKANSAS—*Comparative plus; less than 50%*.
CALIFORNIA—*Contributory*.
COLORADO—*Comparative; less than 50%*.
CONNECTICUT—*Comparative; equal*.
DELAWARE—*Contributory*.
FLORIDA—*Contributory*.
GEORGIA—*Contributory*.
HAWAII—*Comparative; less than 50%*.
IDAHO—*Comparative; less than 50%*.
ILLINOIS—*Contributory*.
INDIANA—*Contributory*.
IOWA—*Contributory*.
KANSAS—*Comparative; less than 50%*.
KENTUCKY—*Contributory*.
LOUISIANA—*Contributory*.
MAINE—*Comparative plus; less than 50%*.
MARYLAND—*Contributory*.
MASSACHUSETTS—*Comparative; equal*.
MICHIGAN—*Contributory*.
MINNESOTA—*Comparative; less than 50%*.

MISSISSIPPI—*Comparative plus; 1% base.*
MISSOURI—*Contributory.*
MONTANA—*Comparative; equal.*
NEBRASKA—*Comparative; slight.*
NEVADA—*Comparative; equal.*
NEW HAMPSHIRE—*Comparative; equal.*
NEW JERSEY—*Comparative; equal.*
NEW MEXICO—*Contributory.*
NEW YORK—*Comparative plus; slight.*
NORTH CAROLINA—*Contributory.*
NORTH DAKOTA—*Comparative; less than 50%.*
OHIO—*Contributory.*
OKLAHOMA—*Comparative; less than 50%.*
OREGON—*Comparative plus; equal.*
PENNSYLVANIA—*Comparative; equal.*
RHODE ISLAND—*Comparative plus; 1% base.*
SOUTH CAROLINA—*Contributory.*
SOUTH DAKOTA—*Comparative; slight.*
TENNESSEE—*Contributory.*
TEXAS—*Comparative; equal.*
UTAH—*Comparative; less than 50%.*
VERMONT—*Comparative; equal.*
VIRGINIA—*Contributory.*
WASHINGTON—*Comparative; 1% base.*
WEST VIRGINIA—*Contributory.*
WISCONSIN—*Comparative; equal.*
WYOMING—*Comparative; less than 50%.*
UNITED STATES GOVERNMENT (under Federal Tort Claims Act)—Applies the law of the state in which the injury occurred.

APPENDIX II

Glossary of Legal Terms in Everyday English

AD DAMNUM. A Latin phrase meaning "to the damage." It refers to the clause in a lawsuit that states in specific dollars or in general terms the amount of money the plaintiff is demanding from the defendant.

ALLEGATION. Any charge of misconduct, made by a plaintiff against a defendant, that becomes a basis for a suit; also, a countercharge of the defendant against the plaintiff.

AMBULANCE CHASING. Solicitation of personal-injury cases by a lawyer or by someone in his employ. The practice is considered unethical by the American Bar Association, and a lawyer who engages in it is subject to censure or disbarment. Advertising by a lawyer for clients in the media, however, is not considered unethical. (See also RAINMAKER, this Glossary.)

APPELLANT. The party in a suit who asks for a higher-court review of the verdict in the case.

APPELLEE. The party in a suit who opposes an appeal from a verdict.

ARBITRATION. A system used in most jurisdictions to settle minor personal-injury claims through submission of the evidence for a decision to a panel that ordinarily consists of three attorneys. (See pp. 80–82.)

ASSAULT. See ASSAULT AND BATTERY.

ASSAULT AND BATTERY. Grounds for a personal-injury suit. An *assault* is any act, physical or verbal, carried out by one party with the deliberate or malicious intent of doing harm to another. A *battery* is any physical blow or unpermitted touching of the victim that results from the assault.

ASSUMPTION OF RISK. A ground for defense in a personal-injury case that prevails when it can be shown that the plaintiff, by his own acts or negligence, took over (assumed) the responsibility (risk) for the accident that occurred. (See pp. 212, 233; see also STRICT LIABILITY, this Glossary.)

BATTERY. See ASSAULT AND BATTERY.

BILL OF PARTICULARS. The part of a suit that details the circumstances and the effects of the injury that is the cause of the litigation.

BRIEF. A formal document, submitted to the court by a lawyer, in which the facts of the case and the applicable law are cited as the lawyer sees them.

BURDEN OF PROOF. The plaintiff's duty to establish, by the majority of the evidence, that the injury that is the subject of the suit was wrongfully inflicted by the defendant. This proof standard is less than in criminal cases, in which the defendant must be found guilty beyond reasonable doubt. (However, see CONTRIBUTORY NEGLIGENCE, this Glossary.)

CAUSE FOR ACTION. The legal basis for a suit.

CAVEAT EMPTOR. "Let the buyer beware." Under this doctrine, purchasers of goods have a positive duty to assure themselves of the quality of their purchases and have no legal recourse when the goods prove shoddy, dangerous, or inferior. Over the past fifty years, the doctrine has undergone considerable successful legal challenge in the courts, opening the way for persons injured by defective products to bring suit on strict-liability and/or negligence grounds. (See also PRODUCT LIABILITY, this Glossary.)

CERTIORARI. A writ issued by an appeals court directing that the trial court send it all the documents in a case so it can review them in deciding the appeal. *Certiorari denied* means that the verdict of the trial stands.

CLAIM. A demand by a person for money to compensate for an injury suffered, made against the party—or that party's insurer—that allegedly caused the injury. A *claim* becomes a *suit* when a formal demand for payment is filed in court.

CLAIMANT. One who demands compensation for an injury; a plaintiff. Although, technically, a claimant doesn't become a plaintiff until suit is filed, the terms are ordinarily used synonymously.

CO-COUNSEL. An attorney who sends a client to another attorney and receives a referral fee for so doing—almost always one third—from that attorney's share of the winnings. (See pp. 25–27.)

COLLATERAL SOURCE. Any person or entity, other than the defendant, that pays money to an injured person, due to the injury. Loosely used also to mean insurers, such as Blue Cross/Blue Shield, that pay toward the injured person's medical bills. Generally speaking, income derived by the injured person from accident- and income-insurance protection plans does not have to be repaid from the personal-injury-suit award, but that received from a workmen's-compensation insurer, Medicare and Medicaid, and private medical insurance plans ordinarily must be. (See also SUBROGATION CLAIM, this Glossary.)

COMMON LAW. From the Latin *communis*. The accumulation, over the centuries, of judicial decisions generally governing people's conduct including their right to sue one another. (See pp. 187, 204–6; see also STATUTORY LAW, this Glossary.)

COMPARATIVE NEGLIGENCE. A statute applied in some states and in cases brought under federal law whereby a victorious plaintiff's award is reduced by the degree of his fault in causing the accident. (See pp. 216–17; 263–65; see also CONTRIBUTORY NEGLIGENCE, this Glossary.)

COMPENSATORY DAMAGES. Any costs of an injury, for which payment is permitted in a suit, other than punitive damages. (See also DAMAGES, this Glossary.)

CONSORTIUM. See LOSS OF CONSORTIUM, this Glossary.

CONTINGENCY FEE. The percentage that the plaintiff pays his or her lawyer from the money that is won in a suit or claim. (See also Chapter Four.)

CONTRIBUTORY NEGLIGENCE. A finding by a judge or a jury, or an accusation by a defendant, that the plaintiff was partly at fault or entirely at fault in causing the injury that is the subject of the suit. In some jurisdictions, when any degree of negligence on the part of the plaintiff can be shown, the plaintiff loses; in others, the plaintiff's award is reduced by the judicially determined percentage of his fault. (See pp. 2–3; 215–18; 263–65; see also COMPARATIVE NEGLIGENCE, this Glossary.)

DAMAGES. One's injuries; also the total dollar value of an injury as expressed in a settlement award or a jury verdict. It is based on many factors but predominantly the plaintiff's injury-related loss of earnings, medical expenses, and pain and suffering. (See Chapters Seven through Ten; see also, in this Glossary, the following: EARNING CAPACITY, LOSS OF; GENERAL DAMAGES; MENTAL ANGUISH; NOMINAL DAMAGES; PAIN AND SUFFERING; PUNITIVE DAMAGES.)

DANGEROUS ANIMAL ACTS. Laws that make the owners of certain animals legally responsible for the injuries they cause, even when the injury occurs absent any negligence on the owner's part. (See also pp. 232–36.)

"DEEP-POCKET" DEFENDANT. A term used by lawyers to refer to a defendant—such as an insurance company, a large corporation, or a unit of government—that is financially capable of paying a judgment and is also perceived by the public (viz., by jurors) as having that capacity.

DEFAULT. Failure of a party to a lawsuit to take a required legal step the absence of which leads to the loss of the case.

DEFAULT JUDGMENT. An award granted to a plaintiff when

the defendant fails to take required legal steps to protect his interest, or when the defendant fails to offer a defense.

DEMURRER. A pleading, made orally or in writing, by one side or the other, about the legal weight of the evidence. Often used to describe a motion by the defendant alleging that, even if everything that the plaintiff says is true, is true, there are still not sufficient grounds for suit. When the judge agrees with a demurrer, the victorious party need not respond to the issue raised, and if the issue that can no longer be argued is one that is substantive to the suit, the practical effect can be a loss of the case by the party defeated by the demurrer.

DE NOVO or TRIAL DE NOVO. *Novo* is Latin for "new." As a legal term, it refers to a new hearing of a case, in which the finding in any previous hearing of it is not admissible. Often also used to describe a new trial ordered by an appeals court. More commonly, to describe the trial that occurs after either side has rejected the recommendation of an arbitration panel.

DEPOSITION. Oral questioning, taken under oath, of witnesses in a personal-injury case, admissible as evidence at trial. (See pp. 76–78.)

DETRIMENTAL RELIANCE. A party may not deny responsibility for an injury due to a permitted misrepresentation of the facts. For instance, an oil company may allow an independently owned station to use its advertising insignia; but if a customer uses the services of that station because he believes it is owned by the oil company, and is injured, he then has relied, to his detriment, on the belief that the oil company owned the station, and the oil company may then be named as a defendant.

DISCOVERY. This word has two meanings in personal-injury law: (a) the accumulation of evidence by both sides through questioning of one another's witnesses prior to trial; and (b) the date a person first became aware or should have been aware that he was injured, with the statute of limitations for filing suit beginning on that date. (See also STATUTE OF LIMITATIONS, this Glossary.)

DIVERSITY OF CITIZENSHIP. Refers to cases in which the plaintiff lives in one state and the defendant in another; suit then may be filed either in state or federal court.

DOUBLE DAMAGES, PROHIBITION OF. The legal doctrine holding that a defendant cannot be required to pay twice for the same injury. For instance, if both a child and its parents bring suit for injury to the child, the defendant cannot be required to pay the same items of cost to each plaintiff; neither can a person who was injured by one party and then had the injury worsened by medical malpractice in the treatment of it require both the doctor and the party that caused the injury to pay for the cost of the malpractice; the plaintiff must choose one or the other. However, if an injury indirectly caused harm to a second party, the defendant can then be required to pay that second party, as well as the first, for the item of damage. (See LOSS OF CONSORTIUM, this Glossary.)

"DOUBLE DIPPING." A practice by which attorneys collect excess fees by taking commissions from both the client and a subrogation claimant. (See pp. 153–57.)

DUTY. The degree of legal responsibility that a person has to exercise care to prevent an accident. (See pp. 203–4; 207–9.)

EARNING CAPACITY, LOSS OF. Grounds for a damage payment, consisting of existent and reasonably probable future loss of earnings as a result of a wrongful injury. An injury-related loss of ability to perform in an occupation for which the plaintiff has training is compensable, even though the plaintiff was not earning a living in that occupation at the time of the injury. (See Chapter Eight; see also DAMAGES, this Glossary.)

ESTOPPEL. A legal rule prohibiting a party in a suit from asserting that certain facts are true at one stage of the proceedings and then introducing contradictory evidence at a later stage, when that now appears to be to his interest.

EX CURIA. A Latin phrase meaning "without the benefit of a court," it refers to any action taken by a lawyer that is not part of a judicial proceeding, such as a privately negotiated settlement with the other side.

EX DELICTO. Any suit that arises from a wrongful injury or tort. It is contrasted with *ex contractu,* referring to a suit that arises from an alleged failure of one party to adhere to the terms of a contract.

EXEMPLARY DAMAGES. See PUNITIVE DAMAGES, this Glossary.

EXPERT. A witness who tells the truth for one's own side; a witness who lies for the other side.

FAILURE TO WARN. Violation of the duty to advise others of hazardous conditions on one's property or in the use of the products one sells. (See pp. 239–40.)

FORESEEABILITY. In negligence law, evidence that indicates that either the plaintiff or the defendant could reasonably have predicted the probability of the injury and taken steps to prevent it. In strict liability, the rule that requires a manufacturer to warn users of a product of dangers arising not only from its proper use but from reasonably predictable misuses. (See pp. 239–40.)

GENERAL DAMAGES. Compensation that is permitted for injuries that are the natural or inevitable consequences of an injury, such as pain and suffering. (See pp. 105, also Chapter Ten; see also MENTAL ANGUISH and PAIN AND SUFFERING, this Glossary.)

"HIGH-VOLUME" LAWYER. An attorney who handles large numbers of personal-injury cases at one time for plaintiffs. Often used to refer to lawyers who accept only relatively small cases on which victory is all but certain. Opprobriously, to describe lawyers who generate a lot of income by settling many cases quickly for less than they are worth. (See pp. 27–30.)

IMMUNITY. Protection from suit by statute. (See pp. 195–96; 256–63.)

IMPACT RULE. In negligence cases, the requirement that a plaintiff, to have grounds for suit, must have been touched by the defendant or by some instrument, such as an automobile, in the defendant's control. The impact rule does not apply to intentional torts. (See also INTENTIONAL TORT and NEGLIGENCE, this Glossary.)

INFORMED CONSENT. The right of a person to receive understandable information about the risks inherent in a service proposed for that person. Commonly used to refer to a doctor's duty to inform a patient of predictable dangers in a course of treatment for an illness; also, the form signed by the patient stating that the risks are understood and allowing the procedure to take place.

INJURY. Legally, any wrongfully inflicted harm, physical or emotional, by one party upon another. (See also TORT and TRESPASS, this Glossary.)

INTENTIONAL TORT. A ground for a personal-injury suit that occurs when the perpetrator deliberately seeks to harm or does harm to the victim, either by a physical blow, by verbal harassment, by threat, or through any other malicious form of action. (See Chapter Sixteen.)

INTERLOCUTORY JUDGMENT. A decision by a judge on a legal point raised during the course of litigation, but one that does not decide the merits of the case. An interlocutory judgment, however, will often substantially adversely affect one side or the other and can have the practical effect of making it impossible for the harmed side to win. (See also DEMURRER, this Glossary.)

INTERROGATORIES. Questions posed in writing by one side to the other side's witnesses. Sometimes also used to refer to a sheet of questions given to a jury in a complex case to help its members decide the issues.

INTERVENING INJURY. An injury that occurs after the injury that led to the suit, usually, although not necessarily, at the same site as the original injury. The defense will try to prove that the second injury is the reason for all or part of the damages the plaintiff is claiming.

INVASION OF PRIVACY. Grounds for a personal-injury suit that occurs when a party, usually a publication, without permission disseminates information about a person that, even though true, is not of public interest. (See pp. 227–28.)

JOINDER. The naming, by a defendant, of an additional defendant or defendants to a suit.

JUDGMENT. The verdict in a case. Also, often used to describe the amount of money a defendant is directed to pay.

LIABILITY. Legal responsibility for an act. A losing defendant is liable (must pay) the plaintiff for the injury that was caused. Liability is to the personal-injury suit what guilt is to the criminal prosecution.

LIBEL. The negligent or malicious publication of a false statement that harms the reputation of the person who is its subject. The term "publication" includes, but is not limited to, books, newspapers, magazines, television or radio broadcasts, letters, and memos. (See pp. 224–26; see also INVASION OF PRIVACY and SLANDER, this Glossary.)

LITIGATION. The name given to the entire legal process under which one party sues another. Litigation is to civil law what prosecution is to criminal law.

LOSS OF CONSORTIUM. The inability of spouses to enjoy sexual relations as a result of an injury to one of them. Both spouses have grounds for compensation.

MALPRACTICE. The misuse of a skill. Technically, there is no such offense as "malpractice" in the law, but the term is commonly employed by judges and lawyers and the general public to describe a wrongful injury inflicted, usually as a result of negligence, by a member of a licensed occupation, such as a doctor, while carrying out the duties of that occupation. (See pp. 213–15.)

MEDIATION. A system for resolving personal-injury suits in which an outside person, a lawyer or a judge, gets the two sides together to help resolve the differences between them. Mediation differs from *arbitration* in that the mediator makes no formal declaration on the merits of the case. (See also ARBITRATION, this Glossary.)

MENTAL ANGUISH. A ground for financial recovery in a personal-injury suit; the fear, worry, depression, or loss of life's pleasures arising from the circumstances of an accident or its aftermath. (See also PAIN AND SUFFERING, this Glossary.)

MERCHANTABILITY. The legal assumption that when a product is sold for public use, it should be safe to use for its advertised purpose. An implied warranty. (See also WARRANTY, this Glossary.)

MITIGATION. Evidence presented by the defendant to show that the amount of dollar damages claimed by the plaintiff is excessive.

NEGLIGENCE. An act, by one party, arising out of incompetence or carelessness or any failure to perform a known duty properly, that accidentally causes injury to another party. (See Chapter Fifteen; see also COMPARATIVE NEGLIGENCE and CONTRIBUTORY NEGLIGENCE, this Glossary.)

NOMINAL DAMAGES. An award, usually no more than one dollar, made to a plaintiff who has shown that a defendant caused a compensable injury, but for which there is no proof of the infliction of substantive harm or monetary loss.

NONSUIT. A declaration by a judge ending a suit in the defendant's favor, following a motion to dismiss it by the defense. Can occur prior to trial or during trial. Commonly, the dismissal is based on a determination that the plaintiff failed to substantiate an allegation of wrongdoing with admissible evidence, or that the plaintiff, through failure to respond to the defense motion, has abandoned the suit. (See pp. 160, 165; see also DEMURRER, this Glossary.)

NUISANCE SETTLEMENT. A term used mostly by insurance companies to describe a small amount of money paid to a plaintiff to end a claim or suit that is minor in nature and usually of little or doubtful legal merit.

PAIN AND SUFFERING. A ground for financial recovery in a personal-injury suit; essentially, the physical agony caused the plaintiff by the injury. It is to be distinguished from *mental anguish,* which relates to the fear caused by the injury. (See Chapter Ten; see also DAMAGES, this Glossary.)

PERSON. A "person," legally, may be not only a human being but any business firm, institution, or other organized private entity that is subject to the law.

PLEADINGS. In personal-injury cases, usually refers to that part of the suit that states the losses suffered by the plaintiff and the defendant's response to those allegations. Also used to refer to those items of loss that the plaintiff must state in specific dollar terms. (See also DAMAGES and SPECIAL DAMAGES, this Glossary.)

PRECEDENT. A ruling in an earlier case that is applied to determine the law in a current case.

PREEXISTENT CONDITION. A physical or emotional problem that a plaintiff had prior to the injury that is the basis of the suit. (See pp. 131–32.)

PREPONDERANCE OF THE EVIDENCE. The greater portion of the evidence. Plaintiffs who can show that the preponderance of the evidence favors them will prevail in a personal-injury suit *unless* contributory negligence on their part rules out a victory. (See also CONTRIBUTORY NEGLIGENCE, this Glossary.)

PRIMA FACIE EVIDENCE. The facts alleged by the plaintiff have sufficient legal weight to provide grounds for suit; once this is established, the suit cannot be dismissed as lacking in merit.

PRIVITY. A contractual obligation to perform a service limited to the parties involved in the agreement. Until courts admitted *strict liability* as a ground for bringing suit against sellers of defective products, the privity rule often defeated product injury cases. For instance, a man buys a new car from a dealer; a wheel falls off, causing injury to the buyer; the wheel rolls down the street, striking and injuring a pedestrian. Under privity, the buyer of the car has grounds for suit only against the dealer who sold it to him, not against the manufacturer; the pedestrian has no grounds for suit against anyone, because he was not party (privy) to the sale of the car. Under strict liability, the buyer of the car can sue the dealer and the manufacturer, and so can the pedestrian. (See also STRICT LIABILITY, this Glossary.)

PRODUCT LIABILITY. A term used to describe suits brought against manufacturers and distributors of goods that cause injury because of their defective or unreasonably dangerous nature when used in some reasonably foreseeable way. (See Chapter Seventeen; see also STRICT LIABILITY, this Glossary.)

PROXIMATE CAUSE. The direct or precipitating cause of an injury.

PUBLIC PERSONS. Elected officials, those who seek election, those otherwise holding public office, as well as entertainers and other individuals, who directly or indirectly receive benefits, usually financial, from the public's awareness of them. Ordinarily, a public person cannot be defamed unless the party accused of the libel has shown a reckless and malicious disregard for the truth. (See also LIBEL, this Glossary.)

PUNITIVE DAMAGES. An award made in a personal-injury case, in addition to any other award, when the perpetrator of the injury has been shown to have acted in gross disregard for the safety of the victim, either through malice or negligence. Sometimes also called *exemplary* ("to make an example of") *damages* or *"smart"* (in the sense of "pain") *money*. (See pp. 106–7.)

RAINMAKER. A lawyer who solicits new clients for his firm. The *rainmaker* is to be distinguished from the *ambulance chaser* in that the former sells his services to corporate clients, including insurance companies, while the latter sells his to the average citizen. The American Bar Association considers rainmaking ethical and ambulance chasing unethical. (See also AMBULANCE CHASING, this Glossary.)

REASONABLE-MAN DOCTRINE. A test applied to determine negligence in many personal-injury trials, by which the jury is asked to decide what a normally prudent person would have done to avoid the injury. Thus, if the jury decides that a "reasonable-man" plaintiff would have acted differently from this plaintiff, the defendant may be found innocent; if a "reasonable-man" defendant would have taken steps to prevent the injury that this defendant didn't take, then the defendant may be found liable.

REDUCTION TO PRESENT VALUE. The legal requirement that the gross amount awarded for a plaintiff's loss of future earnings be lessened to include the amount of interest the plaintiff could earn on the award over the years it is supposed to cover. (See pp. 109.)

REFERRAL FEE. See CO-COUNSEL, this Glossary.

REMITTITUR. The return of the record in a case by a court of appeals to the court that tried the case, accompanied by the upper court's order, such as: a new trial must be held, or the judgment of the lower court is confirmed, or the judgment of the lower court is confirmed as to the verdict but the damages awarded were excessive or insufficient and the case must be retried solely on damages, etc. (See also DAMAGES this Glossary.)

REPLEVIN. A court order requiring someone who has illegally taken possession of property to return it to its proper owner. A replevin action will sometimes be part of a suit brought on both property and personal-injury grounds. It is possible to win the replevin demand while losing the personal-injury suit, and vice versa.

RES GESTAE. A spontaneous utterance, by a plaintiff or defendant at or near the time of the injury, that is harmful to his case and which is admissible as evidence, under the theory that people are likely to speak the truth when they don't have time to reflect on the possible consequences the comment might have on any suit that is brought. Not all *res gestae* comments, however, necessarily state the truth about what happened, only what the speaker comprehended to be the truth, and they can be challenged on that grounds. For instance, if a person cries out, "It's all my fault," when injured, but did so because of a misunderstanding of the circumstances, the *res gestae* comment can be used by the defense but the plaintiff will be allowed to explain the circumstances.

RES IPSA LOQUITUR. Literally, "the thing speaks for itself." Some accidents, according to this doctrine, cannot occur unless there is negligence. For example, a man walking down the street is hit on the head by a bag of cement that falls from a second-floor window ledge; leaving cement in that dangerous position would be considered negligence *per se*. When *res ipsa loquitur* is invoked by the plaintiff and the judge agrees that the circumstances warrant it, the defense can no longer argue the act wasn't negligent, only that it wasn't responsible for it.

RES JUDICATA. A matter that has been acted upon or decided by a judicial proceeding, as contrasted to a legislative enactment.

Generally, any matter that has been determined in civil law through court decisions.

RESPONDEAT SUPERIOR. Literally, "the master is responsible" (for the acts of his servants). As applied to personal-injury cases, it means that employers generally are required to pay for wrongful injuries inflicted, during the course of their duties, by their employees upon nonemployees. (See pp. 182–83.)

RESPONDENT. One who is required to answer charges brought in a suit.

SETTLEMENT. The resolution of a claim or suit with payment to the plaintiff that is arrived at other than through a trial verdict. Normally, it is the result of private negotiations between the lawyers for the opposing sides, but it can also result from arbitration or the intervention of the judge who has been assigned to hear the case. (For when to settle or not settle, see especially pp. 83–90.) (See ARBITRATION and NUISANCE SETTLEMENT, this Glossary.)

SLANDER. A false oral statement (other than one broadcast by television, radio, or motion pictures) that negligently or maliciously harms the reputation of its subject. (See pp. 224–25; see also LIBEL, this Glossary.)

"SMART" MONEY. See PUNITIVE DAMAGES, this Glossary.

SPECIAL DAMAGES, or "SPECIALS." Injury-related costs of an injury for which a plaintiff may be compensated and which must be proved in specific dollar terms. Specials include both existent costs and those that are reasonably likely to occur in the future. Medical expenses and income losses are the most common form of special damages that result from an injury. (See Chapters Seven to Nine; see also DAMAGES and GENERAL DAMAGES, this Glossary.)

STANDARD OF CARE. The degree of responsibility to which a person is legally held for acts that cause harm to others; often used in conjunction with the duty of licensed people to provide competent services in their field of expertise. (See pp. 212–15; see also MALPRACTICE, this Glossary.)

STATUTE OF LIMITATIONS. The period of time a person has to file suit after an injury has occurred. (See pp. 197–98; 251–56.)

STATUTORY LAW. Any regulation enacted by a legislative body at the local, state, or federal level of government. Some laws controlling personal-injury litigation are statutory, others based on the common law. (See pp. 204–6; see also COMMON LAW, this Glossary.)

STIPULATION. An agreement between opposing sides in a suit that a certain allegation or statement is true.

STRICT LIABILITY. A legal doctrine holding that some situations, activities, animals, and products are by their nature unreasonably dangerous and that those who are in control of them can be held responsible for the injuries they cause even though the controller neither intended the harm nor caused it by a negligent act. (See Chapter Seventeen.)

SUBROGATION CLAIM. A demand for repayment made against a successful plaintiff by a party that has paid money on the plaintiff's behalf or directly to the plaintiff as a result of the injury that caused the suit. (See pp. 5–8; 89.)

SUIT. A legal document, filed in court and delivered to the defendant, in which the plaintiff sets forth the circumstances of an injury the defendant allegedly caused, and makes a demand for money to rectify the harm done.

SURVIVAL STATUTES. Laws, varying from state to state, permitting survivors of a person wrongfully killed to be paid for the decedent's pain and suffering, medical bills, funeral bills, and the like. Usually brought in conjunction with a wrongful-death suit. (See also WRONGFUL-DEATH STATUTES, this Glossary.)

"SYMPATHETIC" PLAINTIFF. A term used by lawyers to describe a plaintiff who, because of what he or she is—such as an injured child—is likely to evoke a favorable verdict and usually a large one from a jury even when the evidence in the case doesn't warrant such a result.

"TARGET" DEFENDANT. A term used by lawyers to describe a defendant that has a poor public reputation and is therefore likely to be found liable by a jury regardless of the merits of the case.

TORT. An action by which one party wrongfully takes or attempts to take another person's property, infringes on that person's privacy or civil rights, or harms or attempts to harm that person's body. (See also TRESPASS, this Glossary.)

TORTFEASOR. One who commits a tort, or wrongful injury. A defendant in a personal-injury suit is accused of being a tortfeasor.

TRANSCRIPT. A document reproducing the testimony given at a trial or deposition, as recorded by a court stenographer. (See also DEPOSITION, this Glossary.)

TRAUMA. An injury, physical or emotional.

TRESPASS. To violate another's rights; to commit a tort against that person. All personal-injury suits are technically known as *actions in trespass*. (See also TORT, this Glossary.)

TRIAL DE NOVO. See DE NOVO, this Glossary.

TRIAL MEMORANDUM. See BRIEF, this Glossary.

VICARIOUS RESPONSIBILITY. See RESPONDEAT SUPERIOR, this Glossary.

WAIVER. An agreement to give up a legal right.

WANTON CONDUCT. An injurious action of such recklessness or malice that it becomes grounds for a punitive-damage award; also, an action of such magnitude of misdoing that contributory negligence by the plaintiff need not be considered. (See also PUNITIVE DAMAGES and CONTRIBUTORY NEGLIGENCE, this Glossary.)

WARRANTY. A guarantee by a manufacturer or seller of a product that it is workable and safe to use for the purpose for which it was sold. Some warranties are in writing, with limitations on the guarantee period. Legally, however, warranty is assumed to exist by the fact that the product was offered for sale. A manufacturer or seller of a product, therefore, cannot be excused from an injury suit when the product proves unsafe or harmful, solely on the basis that no written guarantee of its usability was offered. (See also MERCHANTABILITY, this Glossary.)

WHIPLASH. A spinal injury to the neck of the victim, often caused by the impact of a rear-end automobile collision. Because the existence of whiplash is difficult either to prove or disprove medically, it is an injury that can sometimes be faked, and judges and juries often tend, as a result, to be skeptical of it as an injury allegation.

WRONGFUL-DEATH STATUTES. Laws, varying from state to state, that spell out the conditions on which survivors may bring suit. Compensation is based, usually exclusively, on the economic loss the death caused the survivors. (See pp. 198–99; see also SURVIVAL STATUTES, this Glossary.)

ZONE OF DANGER, or ZONE OF PERIL. In negligence law, the concept that a defendant cannot be held responsible for secondary injuries caused by his actions when they occur other than on the site at which the principal accident occurred. (See pp. 143, 211.

Index

Abortion, 191
Air, injuries occurring in the, 202
Ambulance chasing, 17, 24
American Bar Association, 25, 38, 156
American Civil Liberties Union, 39
Appeal, 100–1
  costs, 58–59
Arbitration, winning through, 80–82
Arbitration panel, 80–81
Armed forces, 196
Arrest, false, 223
Assault, 219, 223
  by police or company private detectives, 222–23
  intentional medical injuries, 230
  verbal, 220
Assets
  jointly owned, 184
  transferring, 184
Association of Trial Lawyers of America, 38

Attorney/attorneys. *See* Lawyer/lawyers
Automobile accidents, 167
Auto body shops, 10
Automobile insurance. *See* No-fault insurance
Automobile manufacturers, 10
Award
  deductible insurance, 179
  deduction of lawyer's expenses, 64–66
  distribution-sheet check, 148–49, 151–52, 154–55
  double dipping, 153–57
  getting what's due you, 148–57
  greater than insurance coverage, 179–82
  income loss, 109
  interest earnings, 66, 79–80
  and jury, 109, 110–11
  special-damage multiplier, 110–11, 113
  See also Judgment; Settlement

Bar associations, 22–23
Battery, 219, 223

Book of Leviticus, 185, 186
Blue Cross, 5, 6, 89, 153
Blue Cross/Blue Shield, 195

California, product-defect legislation, 241
Charitable immunity from suit, 196, 261–63
Child/children
  future-earnings predictions, 123
  and negligence, 204
  suing, 2
  suit against parent, 190–91
  suit on behalf of, 48, 123
  sympathetic plaintiff, 12
Civil cases
  against police force, 223
  assault, 219–20
  and perjury, 218
Civil-fraud suit, 164
Civil law, 187
Civil Litigation Division, U.S. attorney's office, 149
Claim, nonnotification of, 172–74
Co-counsel system, 25–27, 151, 152, 160–61
College of Trial Lawyers, 38, 44
Commissions, loss of, 118–19
Common law, 187, 204, 205, 206
Community Legal Services, 37
Comparative negligence, 216, 217, 263–65
Confidential relationship, lawyer/client, 53
Contingency-fee system, 5, 18, 53
  contract, 57–59, 66, 153
  deduction from total award, 64–66
  double dipping, 153–57
  flat basis, 58, 59–60, 61
  illegally high, 149–51
  sliding-scale basis, 58–59, 60–61
Contract violation, 156
Contract-violation suit, 164
Contributory negligence, 11, 215–18, 263–65
Cosmetic (plastic) surgery, 130–31
County courts, 199, 200
Court of Appeals, 100
Credit, effect on of unsatisfied judgment, 184, 220–21
Criminal cases, 187
  assault, 219–20
  and perjury, 218
Cross-examination, 94, 96

Damages, 104–13
  exemplary, 106
  general, 105, 107, 109–13
  income, 108–9, 125–27
  medical, 107–8, 135–37
  punitive, 106–7
  "reduction to present value" rule, 109
  special, 105, 107–9, 110–11, 113
Dangerous Animal Acts, 233–34, 237
Dangerous conditions, 236–37
Deductible insurance clause, 179
Deep-pocket defendant, 7, 8–9
Defendant/defense, 1
  deep-pocket, 7, 8–9
  how to tell if he or she is worth suing, 4
  insurance company as, 67–71
  investigation of plaintiff by, 67–71
  medical examination by,

INDEX

71–74
perjury by, 217, 218
quid pro quo, 84–85
reasonable-man doctrine, 206
recompense settlement offers, 13–16, 67, 73, 85–90, 98
right to question plaintiff, 75, 91
shallow-pocket, 7–8
standard of care, 212–13
strict-liability doctrine, 232
surveillance of plaintiff, 68–71
target, 9–12
uninsured, 4
U. S. Government. *See* Federal Tort Claims Act
Deposition, 76–78, 172
Detectives, company-employed, *See* Private detectives
Direct examination, 94
Distribution-sheet check, 148–49, 151–52, 154–55
Diversity-of-citizenship cases, 201
Divorce, 190
Doctors employed by insurance companies, 72
Documentation
  income damage, 125–27
  medical expenses, 128–35
Double dipping, 153–57

Earnings, 115
Employee
  outrageous conduct by, 228–30
  suit against, 182–83
  suit by, 191
  unionized, 192
Employer
  exceptionally dangerous conditions, 236–37
  hiring lawyer recommended by, 19
  outrageous conduct by employees, 228–30
Escape clauses in insurance policies, 175
Ethelbert (Anglo-Saxon king), 186
Exemplary damages, 106
Expenses
  deduction from total award, 64–65
  falsification of, 151–52
  paying your lawyer's, 62–63
  paying your own, 63–64
  See also Medical expenses
Experts, suing the, 213–15

False arrest, 223
Falsus in uno, falsus in omnibus doctrine, 218
Federal district courts, 199–200
Federal Employees Liability Act, 193
Federal Judicial Panel on Multi-District Disputes, 202
Federal Tort Claims Act, 59, 149, 150, 151, 156, 196, 200, 237, 256
Fee splitting, 25
Financial status, 68
Ford, Gerald, 227
Fraud, 184
Free press, 226–27
Free-speech guarantee, 224–25
Fringe benefits, loss of, 116–17

Glossary of legal terms, 266–82
Government
  right to punish, 185
  wrongful-death actions against, 223–24

See also U. S. Government
Government units, 10
Grounds
  for appeal of verdict, 100
  mental-anguish allegations, 144–47
  personal-injury suit, 1, 3–4

Hammurabi's Code, 186
Harassment, 221–22
Health-care provider, costs of, 135
Homeowner insurance, 171
Hospital care, costs of, 135
Hospitals, 10

Illegal-act injuries, 191
Immunity from suit, 195–96
  charitable, 196, 261–63
  sovereign, 196, 256–61
Income loss
  award, 109
  documentation, 125–27
  future, 114
  making the most of, 114–25
  owner-operated business, 119–20
  past, 114
Injury/injuries
  caused by illegal act, 191
  and delayed entry into job market, 120, 123
  intentional. *See* Intentional injuries
  side effects, 137
  skills rendered unusable by, 121–23
  workplace, 193–94
Insurance
  deductible clause, 179
  escape clauses, 175
  homeowner, 171
  no-fault (automobile), 167, 194–95, 201, 244–51
  personal injury, 171, 172
  personal liability, 167–68, 171
  product liability, 171
  professional liability, 167–68, 171
  umbrella policy, 174–75
  when jury award exceeds coverage, 179–82
  workmen's compensation, 191–93, 193–94
Insurance company
  as defendant, 67–71
  denial of coverage, 174–77
  doctors employed by, 72
  investigation of plaintiff by, 68–71
  reservation-of-rights letter, 175–76
  as target defendant, 11–12
  what to do when coverage is denied, 177–79
Intentional injuries, 219–20
  assault by police or company private detectives, 222–23
  battery, 219, 223
  harassment, 221–22
  invasion of privacy, 224, 227–28
  libel, 224, 225–26
  medical, 230
  outrageous conduct, 228–30
  problems in bringing suit, 220–22
  slander, 224–25
  when suit works, 222–30
  wrongful death actions against government, 223–24
Interest earnings, 66, 79–80

Interest payment, 101
Interrogatories, 75–76, 172
  for jury, 99, 102–3
Invasion of privacy, 224,
  227–28

Job, loss of, 116, 126
Job market, delayed entry into,
  120, 123
Jones Act, 193
Judge, 82–83, 99
Judgment, unsatisfied, 184,
  220–21
  See also Award; Settlement
Jury
  awards, 109, 110–11
  bifurcated trial, 100
  interrogatories for, 99, 102–3
  and perjury in testimony, 218
  selection of, 90–91
  and target defendants, 9–12
Justice system, 186, 187
  personal injury, 186

Law, 185–202
  charitable immunity from
    suit, 196, 261–63
  civil, 187
  common, 187, 204, 205, 206
  criminal, 187
  right to sue, 186–88
  sovereign immunity from suit,
    196, 256–61
  statutory, 204, 206
  waiving right to sue, 13
  where suit can be filed,
    199–202
  who can sue and who cannot
    be sued, 189–99
Law-school professors, 22
Lawyer/lawyers
  advertising by, 24
  advice on settlement vs.
    trial, 86–87
  age, 42
  basic qualifications, 35–37
  co-counsel, 25–27, 151, 152,
    160–61
  confidential relationship with
    client, 53
  contingency fee. *See*
    Contingency-fee system
  contract violation, 156
  deduction of expenses, 64–66
  double dipping, 153–57
  fee splitting, 25
  general practitioners, 33–34
  high volume, 27–30, 34
  how to find a lawyer, 17,
    18–25
  how to hire a good lawyer,
    35–44
  interview with prospective
    lawyer, 45–57
  malpractice suits, 163–70
  outside activities, 39
  paying expenses, 62–63
  personal injury, 17–18
  personality, 40–41
  protecting yourself from
    defense investigators,
    67–71
  quid pro quo arrangement,
    84–85
  race, 43
  replacing, 158–63
  sex, 43
  specialists, 30–33
  suing a lawyer, 167–68
  value of certificates on his
    office walls, 38–39
  when to sue for malpractice,
    163–67

your money and your lawyer, 57–66
Lawyer Reference Service, 23
Legal-malpractice suits,
  how to win, 168–70
  when to sue, 163–67
Legal terms, glossary of, 266–82
Leviticus, Book of, 185, 186
Lex talionis doctrine, 185, 186
Liability. *See* Strict liability
Liability insurance
  personal, 167–68, 171
  product, 171
Libel, 224, 225–26
Life's pleasures, loss of, 146–47

Malpractice, 213, 214, 215
Malpractice suits
  legal. *See* Legal-malpractice suits
  medical, 25, 137, 167, 168, 242
Martindale-Hubbell Directory, 38
Medicaid, 6
Medical damages, 107–8
Medical examination by defense doctors, 71–74
Medical expenses, 107–8, 109
  checklist, 135–37
  documentation, 128–34
  future electives, 130
Medical injuries, intentional, 230
Medical-malpractice suits, 25, 137, 167, 168, 242
Medical procedure, correction of unsuccessful, 137
Medicare, 6
Medication costs, 136
Media
  invasion-of-privacy suits, 227
  libel laws, 226–27

Mental anguish
  getting compensated for, 138, 142–47
  grounds for allegation, 144–47
Multi-District Disputes, Federal Judicial Panel on, 202

National Lawyers Guild, 38, 39
Negligence, 203–18
  and ability, 209
  comparative, 216, 217, 263–65
  contributory, 11, 215–18, 263–65
  and duty, 209
  and opportunity, 209
  precedents, 206
  product-liability suits, 238
  proximate cause, 207
  reasonable-man doctrine, 206–7, 208
Negligence quiz, 209–12
New Jersey, sliding-scale contingency fee, 59
New York
  courts, 100
  sliding-scale contingency fee, 59
No-fault insurance, 167, 194–95, 201, 244–51
Nonnotification of a claim, 172–74
Nonsuit, 160, 165
  pretrial, 165
Nursing care, costs of, 135–36

Oil companies, 10
Order of the Coif, 38
Overtime earnings, 115
Outrageous-conduct suits, 228–30

INDEX

Owner-operated business, 119–20

Pain, getting compensated for, 138–42
   your doctor's corroborative testimony, 141
Pain diary, 139
Parent, suits against, 190–91
Part-time earnings, 115
Peace bond, 222
Pennsylvania, product-defect legislation, 241
Perjury, 217
   risks in committing, 218
Personal injury, 188–89
   justice system, 186
Personal-injury insurance, 171, 172
Personal-injury suit, 1
   arbitration panel, 80–81
   based on negligence, 204–206
   continuation by survivors, 199
   family members against one another, 190
   grounds for, 1, 3–4, 104–7
   how to help prepare your case, 74–75
   how to tell if it is worthy, 3–4
   how to tell if it is worth pursuing, 4–9
   intentional injuries. *See* Intentional injuries
   legal advice. *See* Lawyer/lawyers
   liability. *See* Strict liability
   nonsuit, 160
   recompense without suing, 13–16, 67, 73, 85–90, 98
   right to question, 75–78, 91
   standard-of-care occupations, 212–13
   trial delay, 79–80
   what to do when coverage is denied, 177–79
   when award is greater than insurance coverage, 179–82
   where suit can be filed, 199–202
   who can and who cannot be sued, 189–99
Pets, as dangerous animals, 234–36
Philadelphia bar association, 23
Physical activities, 69
Plaintiff, 3
   appearance and deportment at trial, 90–98
   defense settlement offers, 13–16, 67, 73, 85–90, 98
   medical examination by defense doctors, 71–74
   perjury by, 217, 218
   quid pro quo arrangement, 84–85
   right to question defense, 75, 91
   selection of jurors, 91
   surveillance by insurance company, investigators, 68–71
   sympathetic, 12–13
   on the witness stand, 93–98, 99
Plastic surgery. *See* Cosmetic surgery
Police, assault by, 222–23
Police-brutality suits, 223
Precedents, 206, 213
Pregnancy diagnosis, 191
Pretrial questioning, 75–78
   deposition, 76–78
   oral, 75, 76

written (interrogatories),
75–76
Pretrial settlement conference,
82
Privacy. *See* Invasion of privacy
Private detectives, assault by,
222–23
Product liability insurance, 171
Product-liability suits, 30,
237–42
  foreseeability of misuse,
239–40
  proper-use warning, 238, 240
  public-interest gains, 242–43
  unreasonably dangerous
product, 240–42
Professional liability insurance,
167–68, 171
Promotion, loss of, 117–18
Proper-use warning, 238, 240
Property injury, 188
Prosthetic devices, cost of, 136
Proximate cause, 207
Psychosomatic pain,
injury-produced, 137
Public interest, 242
Public-interest activities, 227
Public transportation
companies, 10
Punishment, government right,
185
Punitive damages, 106–7

Questions and answers
  acceptance or rejection of
defense offer, 85–90
  denial of insurance coverage,
174–79
  how to find a lawyer, 17,
18–25
  how to hire a good lawyer,
35–44
  interview with prospective
lawyer, 45–47
  loss of income, 114–27
  nonnotification of claim,
172–74
  protecting yourself from
defense investigators,
67–74
  protecting yourself from suit
when you are uninsured,
183–84
  when jury award is greater
than insurance coverage,
179–82
  when you are sued as
employee, 182–83
Quid pro quo arrangement,
84–85

Railroad workers, 193
Reasonable-man doctrine,
206–7, 208, 213
Recompense settlement offer,
13–16, 67, 73, 85–90, 98
"Reduction to present value"
rule, 109
Reservation-of-rights letter,
175–76
Respondeat superior doctrine,
182, 183

St. Louis bar association, 23
Sea, injuries occurring on the,
202
Seamen, 193
Security clearance queries, 68
Settlement
  by arbitration, 80–82
  defense offers, 13–16, 67, 73,
85–90, 98
  distribution-sheet check,
148–49

to plaintiff's best advantage, 83–90
and probable trial award, 88–89
questions and answers before accepting or rejecting defense offers, 85–90
quid pro quo arrangement, 84–85
vs. trial, 86–87
See also Award; Judgment
Shallow-pocket defendant, 7–8
Side effects, of injury, 137
Skills, unusuable because of injury, 121–23
Slander, 224–25
Sovereign immunity, from suit, 196, 256–61
Special damages, 105, 107–8
  3× multiplier, 110, 111, 113
  5× multiplier, 110, 111, 113
Special diets, cost of, 136
Spouse(s)
  at interview with prospective lawyer, 47–48
  legally separated, 190
  suing, 2, 189
  suits by, 146
Standard-of-care occupations, 212–13
Standard-of-care quiz, 213–15
State courts, 199, 200
Statute of limitations, 2, 56, 150, 164–65, 197–98, 251–56
Statutory law, 204, 206
Sterilization, 191
Strict liability, 231–44
  Dangerous Animal Acts, 233–34, 237
  exceptionally dangerous conditions, 236–37
  faulty products, 237–42
  pets as dangerous animals, 234–36
Subrogation claim, 5–6, 89, 153, 156
Suffering, getting compensated for, 138
Superior Court, 100
Supreme Court, 100
Surveillance, 68–71
Survival action, 199
Sympathetic plaintiff, 12–13

Target defendant, 9–12
Threat, 220
Tips, earnings from, 115
Torts, 3, 188
Transportation costs, 136–37
Trial
  bifurcated, 100
  cross-examination, 94, 96
  delay of, 79–80, 82–83
  direct examination, 94
  helping yourself win at, 90–98
  jury selection, 90–91
  new defense offer during, 98
  settlement vs., 86–87

Umbrella insurance policies, 174–75
U.S. attorney's office, 149–51
  Civil Litigation Division, 149
U. S. Constitution, 187
U. S. Government, suits against. *See* Federal Tort Claims Act
U. S. Supreme Court, 100
  libel by media, 226
Utah, atomic-testing injury claims, 237
Utilities, 10

Verdict
  appeal of, 58–59, 100–1

reversal of, 100
See also Award; Judgment; Settlement
Veterans, 196
Veterans Administration hospitals, 196

Whiplash clinics, 129
Workmen's compensation, 154, 191–94

Workmen's Compensation Bureau, 194
Workplace injuries, 193–94
Wrongful-birth suits, 191
Wrongful-death suits, 123–25, 198–99, 201, 202
    against government, 223–24
    economic effects on surviving family, 123
    and survival action, 199